THE ANGELIC MOTHER
AND THE PREDATORY SEDUCTRESS

SOUTHERN LITERARY STUDIES

Fred Hobson, Series Editor

THE ANGELIC MOTHER AND THE PREDATORY SEDUCTRESS

Poor White Women in Southern Literature of the Great Depression

ASHLEY CRAIG LANCASTER

LOUISIANA STATE UNIVERSITY PRESS BATON ROUGE

Published by Louisiana State University Press

Manufactured in the United States of America
First printing

DESIGNER: Michelle A. Neustrom
TYPEFACE: Adobe Caslon Pro
PRINTER: McNaughton & Gunn, Inc.
BINDER: Acme Bookbinding

LIBRARY OF CONGRESS CATALOGING-IN-PUBLICATION DATA

Lancaster, Ashley Craig, 1979–
The angelic mother and the predatory seductress : poor white women in Southern literature of the Great Depression / Ashley Craig Lancaster.
p. cm. — (Southern literary studies)
"Eugenics and Politics: Unlikely Unions and the Stereotyping of the Southern Poor White Woman — Questioning the Eugenic Agenda: Faulkner, Caldwell, and Steinbeck: Three Responses to America's "Social Responsibility" — Making the Eugenic "Myth" a Reality: The Fictionalizing of Depression-Era Documentary Work — Up from Eugenics: The Gastonia Novels and the Redefining of the Southern Poor White Woman."
Includes bibliographical references and index.
ISBN 978-0-8071-4445-9 (cloth : alk. paper) — ISBN 978-0-8071-4446-6 (pdf) — ISBN 978-0-8071-4447-3 (epub) — ISBN 978-0-8071-4448-0 (mobi)
1. American literature—Southern States—History and criticism. 2. Women, White, in literature. 3. Rural poor in literature. 4. Literature and society—Southern States—History—20th century. 5. Southern States—In literature. I. Title.
PS228.W65L36 2012
810.9'352042—dc23

2011043187

Versions of the material on *Tobacco Road* and *God's Little Acre* in chapter 2 first appeared in "Weeding Out the Recessive Gene: Representations of the Evolving Eugenics Movement in Erskine Caldwell's *God's Little Acre*," *The Southern Literary Journal* 39. 2 (2007): 78–99. Copyright © 2007 by the Department of English and Comparative Literature of the University of North Carolina at Chapel Hill. Published by the University of North Carolina Press. Used by permission. A version of the material on *The Grapes of Wrath* in chapter 2 was published as "Subverting Eugenic Discourse: Making the Weak Strong in John Steinbeck's *Their Blood Is Strong* and *The Grapes of Wrath*," in *The Grapes of Wrath: A Re-Consideration.*, vol. 2, ed. Michael J. Meyer (New York: Rodopi, 2009), 421–28. © 2009 Editions Rodopi. V. Reprinted with permission.

The paper in this book meets the guidelines for permanence and durability of the Committee on Production Guidelines for Book Longevity of the Council on Library Resources. ♾

TO MY MOM AND DAD

whose lives are testimonies against
the myth of eugenic "science"

Contents

Acknowledgments . . . ix

INTRODUCTION . . . 1

1. EUGENICS AND POLITICS
Unlikely Unions and the Stereotyping of the Southern Poor White Woman . . . 13

2. QUESTIONING THE EUGENIC AGENDA
Faulkner, Caldwell, and Steinbeck—Three Responses to America's "Social Responsibility" . . . 45

3. MAKING THE EUGENIC "MYTH" A REALITY
The Fictionalizing of Depression-Era Documentary Work . . . 98

4. UP FROM EUGENICS
The Gastonia Novels and the Redefining of the Southern Poor White Woman . . . 134

CONCLUSION . . . 184

Notes . . . 189

Bibliography . . . 203

Index . . . 217

Acknowledgments

THIS WORK HAS BEEN INFLUENCED by a great number of people who have supported me and my research. I would like to offer a sincere thank you to my doctoral committee at the University of Mississippi—Jay Watson, Kathryn McKee, Benjamin Fisher, and Nancy Bercaw—who all encouraged me to pursue publishing my dissertation. Joseph Urgo, Natalie Schroeder, and Jamie Harker were also instrumental in helping me complete this book. I would also like to thank my classmates and friends, Taylor Hagood, Christopher Bundrick, and Kacy Tillman, for challenging me as I wrote and pursued publication. Taylor Hagood especially played an essential part. Several of my students have also encouraged me during this process: Kristen Stephens, Madison McLeod, and Devisha Hairston. I appreciate Kristen's help as I was finalizing the book, and I am thankful for Madison's and Devisha's encouraging messages and prayers.

I am also grateful to Louisiana State University Press. I have been honored to work with Fred Hobson, John Easterly, and Margaret Lovecraft. Not only have they been supportive of my work, but they have also been patient with me during this process. I am also thankful for the helpful comments provided to me by the anonymous reader. All of the comments I received from each reader and editor helped me to improve this book and to improve as a writer.

I have also had the privilege of being supported by several institutions and departments. The University of Mississippi English Department and library staff were instrumental in providing the necessary monetary and scholastic resources I needed to complete my research. I would also like to thank the English Department and library staff at Mississippi College and the library staff at Rhodes College for allowing me to use their resources. I am also especially thankful to the Itawamba Community College Communications Division, administration, and library staff for their outstanding encouragement and support.

Along with the academic support I have received, I am also blessed to have had emotional support from family and friends. My mom, dad, and sister have always encouraged me to reach for my dreams, and for that I can never thank them enough. I am also grateful for Cindy McRae and her suggestion that I write down all my dreams so that I would not allow my life to go by without fulfilling them. Publishing this book was at the top of that list. Most of all, I would like to thank my husband, Cory. He somehow knew when to encourage me, when to cry with me, when to rejoice with me, and when to force me to push ahead.

All of these people are truly my blessings from God. Thank you for helping me complete this journey and for celebrating with me in the completion of this book.

THE ANGELIC MOTHER
AND THE PREDATORY SEDUCTRESS

INTRODUCTION

IN *Playing in the Dark: Whiteness and the Literary Imagination,* Toni Morrison asserts that "white freedom" is based on a "parasitical nature" (57) which creates the power historically associated with whiteness because whites feed off of the "Other" in order to create their seemingly superior racial status. Morrison's focus in her text is how whites feed off of "American Africanism" (6). She describes how African Americans in American literature have helped to create an American identity, and she encourages readers to analyze what the "presence" of African American characters says not just about the content and meaning of the work but also about the life experiences and beliefs that the authors of that literature are bringing to their works (4–6). Morrison effectively argues that African Americans essentially have been used as catalysts in the creation of the definition of "American," a term that she says is generally associated with whiteness (72).

To explain how African American characters are used as objects of "parasitical" whites and by the authors who create them, Morrison identifies "common linguistic strategies" used to create African American literary identities. First and foremost, the use of "stereotypes" keeps the author from having to create an actual character with whom the reader can identify (67). Furthermore, an overemphasis is placed on "physical traits" and "animalism" in an effort to highlight the "differences" between the whites and the African American "Other" (68). The African American "presence" is also made to "evok[e] erotic fears or desires" (68). All of these separations between whites and the African American "Other" produce the belief that African Americans are incapable of meeting or living up to the high social and "civiliz[ed]" standards of white American society. She notes that what further separates the whites and African American characters is that often the African American characters seem to accept their subordinate positions willingly, making it seem as though they are content to maintain joyful servant status or as though this is the only role that they are capable of fulfilling (21–22). By creating African American characters who supposedly are the antithesis of their successful white counterparts, the African Americans are definitively excluded from "American" identity, and whites, in contrast, become the epitome of Americanness.

Although Morrison focuses her theory on uncovering the role of "American Africanism" in American literature, her study raises another question outside of this racial boundary: how is this definition of whiteness affected by those "whites," at least in racial status, who fail to meet the "civiliz[ed]" standards that have been used to form the superior white American identity? This question became imperative in the late 1920s and the 1930s as the Great Depression had begun to change the American economic landscape and as the separation of economic classes became increasingly wide. Morrison argues that the need for a solid definition of American strength came from a "fear of being outcast, of failing, of powerlessness; [a] fear of boundarylessness, of Nature unbridled and crouched for attack; [a] fear of absence of so-called civilization; [a] fear of loneliness, of aggression both external and internal" (37). Although Morrison's reasons for the creation of the definition are derived from America's early days as an occupied territory where settlers were searching for ways to break free from their "European" ancestry (36–37), these same reasons became a focal point again during the Great Depression. The American way of life was teetering on the brink of failure, and since the country had not previously faced such a financial crisis, a feeling of "powerlessness" overwhelmed most Americans. Moreover, the economic changes had brought about familial changes that had annihilated the social boundaries that America had created for itself since its inception. As a result of this disjointed identity, African Americans were not the only "Other" used to recreate the national identity.

Because of the economic trouble befalling America, poor whites, specifically southern poor whites, became the new "Other" that the "parasitical" whites used to reassert the power of American whiteness, and the southern poor white woman emerged as the focal point of this "parasitical" campaign. Interestingly, Morrison's theory about the creation of white

American identity can be transferred to the southern poor white woman, a seemingly unlikely companion to the African American "Other." Although this similarity may seem unlikely at first, the southern poor white woman has elicited such an overwhelming amount of scorn and dread in American literature that the purpose for this disdain cannot be overlooked or marginalized. In the late 1920s and the 1930s, the southern poor white female character was marked by dualistic stereotyped roles: the altruistic mother and the destructive sexual degenerate. These roles, which have been historically common stereotypes used to define women, emerged not just as an easy way to label the women but as a way to define America's future after the Depression.[1] Although the application of Morrison's theory to the southern poor white female literary identity seems to depart from her racial application, this is not actually the case. While the dualistic stereotypes of the southern poor white woman may be based in class hierarchy, the social identities and descriptions assigned to these women strip them not just of their individualism but also of their whiteness, or at least the traits that supposedly made whites the superior race. As a result, the African American characters and the poor white female characters are linked because the way that southern poor white females were drawn mirrors the "linguistic strategies" that were used to create African American literary identities.

The "Other" characteristics of the southern poor white female characters were further accentuated because all of their traits, whether positive or negative, were shrouded in supposed scientific reasoning. The American eugenics movement, which had been gaining prominence since the nineteenth century, had become a powerful force in American life, both in social and political standing. Susan Currell has noted that one of the main reasons for the increased prominence of eugenics in America during this time was the fear that the Great Depression was a consequence of the human "degeneration" that eugenicists had been warning of since the nineteenth century.

> The decline and descent of humankind that had been predicted by eugenicists for so long appeared to have reached its apotheosis in the manifest degeneration of culture and society at the start of the Great Depression. During that time, the physical health and eugenics movements gained

> increased momentum due to intensified fears of racial decline, male passivity, low levels of intelligence, moral and physical degeneracy, and low fertility. [. . .] By 1932, concerns over the future recovery of U.S. society reflected widespread belief that the country was not just economically depressed but also "diseased" in some way. (3, 5)

Therefore, when the United States seemed to be losing its identity as a result of the Depression, eugenicists offered a remedy for this suspected "'diseased'" society, and that remedy was found in the body of the southern poor white woman. In fact, eugenicists led the way by employing the dualistic stereotypes of the altruistic mother and the sexual degenerate, and by doing this, eugenicists made southern poor white women's ability to procreate a topic of national debate. This debate emerged as a result of how economic instability had begun to affect familial stability. With America's failing economy, the social role of lower-class women changed; instead of working solely as home caretakers, they had to enter the labor force. This new social role, however, was not widely accepted, especially in a society facing numerous economic challenges that had already caused too many negative social changes with the increase in poverty. As a result, American citizens were focused not only on decreasing poverty but also on returning to what they considered "traditional" familial and social standards, which included women focusing solely on their maternal role.

Various scientific and political movements altered their focus to address this desire to return to "traditional" standards. The American eugenics movement, which had once focused its attention on eradicating genetic inferiority from the lower class and had even helped to perpetuate the shiftless and degenerate image of poor white men, became more focused in the late 1920s on studying how environment affected the social mobility of lower-class people. As a result, eugenics became more of a mainstream concept, supposedly aimed at helping poverty-stricken people uplift themselves. With this mainstream attention, the new socially conscious work of eugenicists also garnered the attention of American Communist Party leaders and New Deal Democrats who also hoped to draw support from upper- and middle-class Americans.[2] While this union of ideas may have been focused on helping lower-class people recover from poverty, it also focused attention on the dualistic roles of the altruistic mother and the sexual degenerate. Eugenicists had been focused on the mothering abilities and the sexual proclivities of poor white women in their eugenic family studies since the nineteenth century, and with the economic crisis threatening gender dynamics in the Depression, placing the focus on these female stereotypes helped various political parties establish a standard by which appropriate social roles for women could be defined. Therefore, the dualistic roles forced upon southern poor white women helped to define either the advance or the decline of American society during the Depression.

The creation of these stereotypes was accentuated because, prior to the late 1920s, southern poor white women occupied a positive position in American literature, even if it was somewhat marginal. Although presented as secondary figures in most nineteenth-century literature about poor whites, these female characters have generally been portrayed more favorably than their poor white male counterparts. In his *Histories of the Dividing Line betwixt Virginia and North Carolina* (1841), William Byrd II pointedly describes poor white men in North Carolina as afflicted with an "Aversion to Labor" and a "Disposition to Laziness" (92).[3] Their only redemption comes from their wives, who make up for their husbands' deficiencies because they have a "better Spirit of Industry in themselves" (306). In Old Southwest humor stories, southern poor white males are generally portrayed as "bawdy" and animalistic, caricatures of the "half-wild, half-civilized [southern] landscape" (Cohen and Dillingham xv, xx). This "male-oriented genre" is full of stories of "frontier fights, hunts, contests, swaps, lawsuits, tricks, and physical pranks" in which the men are characterized as rugged, shiftless, and deceitful (Lenz 36, 47).[4] Women of the backwoods in Old Southwest humor stories are generally spared these negative characterizations. Some female characters are characterized as "equal to or tougher than their male counterparts" (48). One such female character, Sal Fink, is a courageous and independent woman, riding alligators and escaping from Indians, without the help of a man (Cohen and Dillingham xviii–xix). Other female characters are characterized as rulers of the domestic sphere. William E. Lenz has argued that the rugged, "half-civilized" backwoodsmen of these stories "submitted themselves to women's authority" when they "entered a dance, a woman's home, or pursued a relationship with a woman" because they considered themselves "ignorant, isolated, and relatively helpless" in these types of domestic social environments.[5] In a sense, these backwoodsmen of Old Southwest stories are as dependent upon the "better Spirit of Industry" of their female counterparts as Byrd's poor white men of North Carolina.

By the late 1800s, however, poor white female characters were no longer primarily relegated to secondary roles in southern literature. In fact, these women's struggles increasingly became the main focus from the 1880s to the early twentieth century. Carol S. Manning has argued that southern female authors in the late nineteenth century became "dissatisfied with traditional values and assumptions regarding the female role and began to question the [patriarchal] culture they had inherited" (244). To voice their dissatisfaction, they developed their own form of "modern southern literature," placing women's problems at the forefront of their works (244). Despite being a part of the marginal lower class, southern poor white women were not forgotten in this female-driven "modern southern literature." Poor white females, with their lives of "monotony, toil, and deprivation," allowed southern female authors the opportunity to showcase an alternative version of southern life that "exposed the irrelevance of the southern belle/lady ideal" that often excluded representations of southern women's social and/or economic problems (249). By putting the desperate lives of poor white women on display, authors such as Edith Summers Kelley, Ellen Glasgow, and Elizabeth Madox Roberts were able to offer a more "realistic" portrayal of southern women's lives, a realism previously underplayed or ignored in southern literature.

As poor white females began to become more prominent characters, their positive characteristics, once highlighted yet marginalized, also became an important factor in creating this new "modern southern literature." With her widely popular collection of short stories about Appalachian life, *In the Tennessee Mountains* (1884), Mary Noailles Murfree seems to point towards this new female-oriented literature.[6] Cynthia Ware in "Driftin' Down Lost Creek" is reminiscent of Byrd's poor white women driven by a "Spirit of Industry"; however, her "Spirit" drives her to be outspoken and political, taking on roles that break the "traditional" standards associated with southern women. To get her wrongfully imprisoned lover, Evander, released from jail, she begins a crusade, even speaking directly to the governor of Tennessee (59). Instead of appreciating Cynthia's courageous efforts, her mountain neighbors consider her "grotesque," and Evander abandons her after his release (56, 68). Despite her strength, Cynthia relegates herself to the single life forever because she has lost Evander (78–79). Although this story ends tragically, with Cynthia seemingly losing her independent spirit, and although this story is the only one in the collection with a main female protagonist, the "grotesque[ly]" outspoken nature of Cynthia still dominates the story and helps her to become one of the most memorable characters in the collection.

Murfree's "Drifting Down Lost Creek" is a precursor to other southern women's works that showcase not only the independent, political spirit of poor white women but also their sexual spirits. By the 1920s, Manning notes, the push for a female-centered southern literature "caught fire" because, with the passing of the Nineteenth Amendment, women gained confidence "as citizens and as writers" (247). As a result, southern authors such as Kelley, Glasgow, and Roberts published novels that actually focused entirely on the multi-dimensional qualities of poor white women. Judith Pippinger in Kelley's *Weeds* (1923), Dorinda Oakley in Glasgow's *Barren Ground* (1925), and Ellen Chesser in Roberts's *The Time of Man* (1926) are as independent and courageous as Cynthia Ware; however, these women are allowed to explore their independence and courage. Each female character knows her self-worth beyond her gender and class status. As young children and teenagers, still unburdened by financial or social problems, Judith is described as "dynamic" (Kelley 14); Dorinda looks as if she is in "arrested flight, as if she were running toward life" (Glasgow 3); and Ellen repeats over and over to herself, "It's unknowen how lovely I am, unknowen" (Roberts 66). When they become adults, they still try to fend off society's expectations either through sexual relationships or through independent labor because none of them wants to be trapped in the "traditional" roles of wife and mother. Despite the characters' youthful vitality, each of the novels ends hopelessly for the women, Judith and Ellen trapped in unfulfilling marital relationships and Dorinda trapped in her desires for her lost love, Jason. Financial and social expectations keep the women from fulfilling their once "dynamic" futures and from benefiting from their independent spirits.

Despite the tragedies that these characters' lives become, though, these stories still reveal a progression in how southern poor white females were depicted. Not only were they shown as persevering women helping the hapless men in their lives as Byrd's, Old Southwest humorists,' and Murfree's poor white females do, but they were portrayed as more akin to actual southern poor white women. Kelley, Glasgow, and Roberts actually give their characters the opportunity to face controversial issues affecting women, issues not necessarily associated with their duties as mothers and wives. Judith, Dorinda, and Ellen struggle with their social identities, forbidden love, and unwanted pregnancies, and in the course of dealing with these issues, the women are placed in precarious situations. Judith has an illicit affair, and then after getting pregnant by her lover, she tries to abort her baby to hide the secret (Kelley 282). Dorinda has to flee her family home after getting pregnant by Jason (Glasgow 143). As a young teenager, Ellen has sexual liaisons with a young college boy while he is home for the summer (Roberts 60–61). These seemingly transgressive acts do not, however, define these women negatively. In fact, none of the authors uses these incidents to belittle her protagonist; instead, these events build the women into more "dynamic" characters. By creating characters who have affairs and who feel oppressed by social expectations, Kelley, Glasgow, and Roberts reveal a side of southern poor white women not explored in previous representations. They have created women who actively question the status quo of their paternalistic society and take steps to escape their social expectations, even if, in the end, they find no reprieve from those constraints.

American fiction of the late 1920s and 1930s, however, shifted dramatically away from these "dynamic" representations. With the increasing economic pressures caused by the Depression and the rise of the eugenics movement, literature about financially unstable southern poor whites became prevalent and popular, and southern poor white women became increasingly important because their bodies produced the large, poverty-stricken families that Americans feared were further depleting their nation's economic resources—and their own. As a result, authors began constructing white female characters who faced many of the same obstacles that Morrison argues have plagued the African American "Other," and these obstacles all relate back to the "parasitical nature" of the white American identity and to maintaining white superiority. The southern poor white female character became a representation either of the nation's destiny to persevere through difficult times or to collapse under the weight of economic and social pressures. As a symbol with such monumental influence, the southern poor white woman was no longer characterized as individualistic and self-aware because her abilities now represented the abilities of an entire nation.

As a result, poor white females were presented either as altruistic mother figures, helping to save America's downtrodden lower class, or as sexual degenerates, threatening to destroy American society, and these eugenically driven dualistic roles took the focus off of the positive characteristics that make Judith, Dorinda, and Ellen such "progressive" characters. Authors of Depression-era poor white literature focus almost completely on the maternal abilities of these women. In fact, the women are only portrayed positively if they completely sacrifice their own identities, immersing themselves in their roles as wives and mothers, keeping them from ever showcasing their independent spirits. The positive image of poor white womanhood had become so restrictive in the 1930s that "progressive" female characters of the 1920s such as Judith, Dorinda, and Ellen would have been labeled degenerates because of their premarital and extramarital sexual activities. In fact, when sexual desires are attributed to poor white female characters in Depression-era literature, those desires are generally used to condemn the women. Women who engage in sexual activity outside of marriage in fiction of the 1930s are viewed as deviant, and their sexuality is viewed as socially destructive. Because of this switch in characterization, Depression-era poor white females do not resemble either the secondary female figures of the mid-nineteenth century or the progressive poor white female characters of the late 1800s and 1920s. The dualistic roles make them stereotypes used to define social standards. Regardless of whether they were portrayed as the saviors or the destroyers of American society, they too became the "Other" outside the boundary of unquestioned "civiliz[ed]" superior whiteness.

Both the fiction and the nonfiction of the Depression era were also dominated by these images, and the South came to be seen as the breeding ground for these eugenically labeled poor white women. During the Great Depression, the South had become increasingly desperate economically, and as a result, since eugenics was "a class-based movement," eugenicists "challenged [. . .] the South's long history of white supremacy" (Nies

121). Therefore, authors in the 1930s began to use the dualistic stereotypes in an effort to help explain and to generate political activity that they hoped would alleviate southern poverty and help to retain that "long history of white supremacy." However, authors struggled to create characters who were not covered in the social anxieties created during the Depression. In fact, authors followed eugenic family study patterns as they created works which further defined their southern poor white female characters as either social saviors or social destroyers. Four novels of the 1930s, William Faulkner's *As I Lay Dying,* Erskine Caldwell's *Tobacco Road* and *God's Little Acre,* and John Steinbeck's *The Grapes of Wrath,* are centered on the roles of poor white women in the survival or destruction of their families. However, although these novels follow the structural pattern of eugenicists' family studies, which generally condemn poor white women, the authors present their works more as open questions about the true influential power of these women. As a result, Faulkner, Caldwell, and Steinbeck seem more like reflections of the American society that was being asked by its social, political, and scientific leaders to accept the "Other" status of these women and, therefore, to condemn the poor white class that they represent. Unlike eugenicists, though, who dismiss these women and their families as genetically unredeemable, these authors reveal how they, and quite possibly their readers, struggled with condemning poor whites even if this act meant saving America, as they were being told.

The nonfiction of the Depression era is as important as the fiction because it also reflects the public perception and hesitation as it relates to poor whites; however, the nonfiction had the potential to generate further negative repercussions for these women because these works supposedly presented real-life scenarios. These documentary authors were supporters of Roosevelt's New Deal, sociologists, and communist sympathizers, and although they generally wrote about poor white life as a way to draw attention to the South's excessive poverty, they also helped to promote eugenic ideology and to suppress the social and political activity of southern poor white women. In fact, their presentations of the women are often contradictory and seem more like fiction than nonfiction, suggesting that these authors too are struggling with how to reconcile how they have been encouraged to see these families with how these people actually present themselves in reality. Unlike the authors of fiction, though, the documentary authors often manipulate their southern poor white female subjects to fit them into the socially directed stereotypes of the altruistic mother and the sexual degenerate. Instead of creating realistic representations of poor white women, they often just highlight the "differences" between poor white women and upper- and middle-class whites and at times use those "differences" to "evok[e] erotic fears and desires" just as the African American "presence" was used. By focusing on the "differences," these authors mostly managed to draw attention to poor whites by labeling them as the new "Other" outside of the South's "long history of white supremacy."

Although most Depression-era authors portray their poor white female characters in these dualistic stereotypes, without considering the challenges that prevented most actual women from conforming to these roles, four female authors of "Gastonia novels," about the plight of working mill women in the early 1930s, do address how these stereotypes confine and suppress these women's political and social voices. Novelists Mary Heaton Vorse, Myra Page, Grace Lumpkin, and Olive Tilford Dargan actually challenge these dualistic images by placing their female characters in prominent positions in the labor movement and in the political activity of the 1930s. These four authors create female characters who must fight their way out of socially and eugenically prescribed roles in order to exist outside of their mothering capabilities and sexual activities. By focusing on lower-class females who try to break free from these stereotypes, the Gastonia novelists return to the 1920s trend of focusing on the "dynamic" lives of poor white women; however, by portraying women's entrance into the labor movement, these novelists are able to create female characters even more "progressive" than the poor white female characters of the 1920s: working women with a real possibility to have truly independent lives not confined by their dependence on men. With their focus on working mill women, the Gastonia novelists seem intent on returning to and advancing the positive representations of southern poor white females. Also embedded in these novelists' representations is the idea that they, unlike Faulkner, Caldwell, and Steinbeck, feel a special need and obligation to change the public perception that these women were the cause of American society's "decline and descent" and, therefore, deserved to be the new "Other" in American society. Although part of their decision to align themselves with these women may have been just feminine solidarity, these novelists also share a personal connection with their subjects since they all worked alongside these women, some even at the Gastonia strike. Moreover, the novelists, like their poor white subjects, are trying to assert their independence as well, but instead of doing it on the picket lines, they are asserting it through their writing.

With such an intense focus on southern poor white women in Depression-era literature, understanding why authors portrayed them in certain roles helps to explain the reason for the women's importance in American society. Inasmuch as poor white females were becoming increasingly important in literature from the eighteenth century to the early twentieth century, authors of Depression-era literature, focusing on the altruistic mother and the sexual degenerate stereotypes furthered by the eugenics movement, halted the positive progression of poor white females and made them into stock characters. Instead of highlighting their involvement in the labor movement and in political activities, most Depression authors forced these once "dynamic" figures into static characterizations, stripping poor white women of their agency in the turbulent economic environment. While authors who portrayed poor white females as either altruistic mothers or sexual degenerates did place the women in prominent social positions—because these stereotypes, either positively or negatively, represented the strength and the perseverance of American society in such a tumultuous time—they also stripped poor white females of their ability to exist outside of their spousal and maternal roles. Instead of women seeking their own individual identities, whether in their relationships or in their work, southern poor white women became seen as symbols reflecting America's hopes or fears about poverty and its effect on America's future. As a result, while the stereotypes may have helped to stabilize an ever-changing American society, they also hindered the social development of lower-class southern women whose social and economic realities were made even more unstable by these confining dualistic stereotypes that definitively made them an "Other" with the potential to strip the superiority from the white "American" identity.

1

EUGENICS AND POLITICS

Unlikely Unions and the Stereotyping of the Southern Poor White Woman

DURING THE LATE 1920S and the 1930s, representations of poor white women in literature became dominated by the issue of motherhood. In fact, because of the Great Depression and widespread anxiety about the economic hardships disrupting society, southern poor white mothers emerged as representatives of America's future possibilities. These mothers, however, did not simply represent America's desire to withstand difficult times and to emerge from the struggle rejuvenated; for many thinkers, they also represented America's possible failure if it did not remain entrenched in its conservative traditional values. These values centered on the country's determination to adhere to traditional family structure and to the traditional gender roles of the Progressive movement. The ideology of the early twentieth century that men should work while women stayed at home with the children, however, no longer worked in this desperate new situation. Men could no longer act as sole "breadwinners" while women worked at home as the primary caretakers (Odem 105–6). Women had to begin working outside the home just so their families could survive (Hall et al. 310–11). While women seemed willing to accept their new role as "breadwinners" alongside their husbands, the majority of the population was not ready to accept this new facet of female identity, which created too many questions about "female independence and sexuality" (Rafter, *Creating Born* 48).

As a result of this anxiety about the economy and changing familial roles, political parties once at odds began working together as they attempted to gain support for their causes and for their plans to revive America. Groups such as the Communist Party of the United States (CPUSA) and the Roosevelt administration found common ground by focusing on a return to family traditions and by focusing on the American mother figure. The CPUSA "promoted images of stable family values anchored by working-class women as sacrificing mother" as a way to become "an American party firmly within American political and cultural traditions" (Rabinowitz, *Labor* 55; Shaffer 76), and the Roosevelt administration used these same images to garner support for the New Deal as the Democratic Party hoped to reestablish American power (Rabinowitz, *Labor* 57). By concentrating on "American [. . .] traditions," the CPUSA and "New Deal Democrats" wanted to appeal to Americans' desire to normalize their now uncertain social and economic lives (57).

This focus on family values and motherhood did not just connect these two dominant political parties to each other; it also helped align the CPUSA and "New Deal Democrats" with the American eugenics movement. Since the late nineteenth century, eugenicists had stressed the importance of motherhood to the future of America. Using the study of genetics and America's conservative family values, eugenicists hoped to identify genetically "inferior" people, especially women, who would supposedly cause America's downfall because of their ability to reproduce generations of "inferior" people. Eugenicists shifted their genetic identification strategy by the 1920s and 1930s to become environmentally conscious so that Americans would not see them as class-stereotyping. Like the CPUSA and "New Deal Democrats," eugenicists wanted to address economic concerns; however, eugenicists saw this as a way to uncover genetic inferiority. Despite this shift in eugenic ideology, however, the focus on poor white women still persisted. From eugenic family studies of the nineteenth century to "socialist eugenics" works of the 1930s, the eugenics movement continually focused on these women as either America's saviors or America's destroyers (Joravsky, *Lysenko* 260).

As eugenics began to grow in popularity in the late nineteenth century and the early twentieth century, it became a dominant part of America's ideology, and both the CPUSA and the Roosevelt administration used the nation's focus on eugenic concerns to create their own images of motherhood. These groups concentrated on labeling poor white mothers as either sexual deviants set to breed generations of "delinquents" or as "altruistic" mothers set on saving their own families as well as other needy families from destitution (Rafter, *Creating Born* 159, 89).[1] These opposing images of poor white motherhood, however, did not allow for these women to emerge as anything more than symbols. Claire M. Roche has suggested that the identity of poor white women has been created in terms of their ability to procreate (274), and this focus on motherhood by these three converging groups in the early twentieth century—the CPUSA, the Roosevelt administration, and American eugenicists—helped to create this identity because poor white women, whether they worked as caretakers or laborers, were viewed only through their reproductive abilities and their ability to care for their children.

EUGENICS AND WOMEN

In the late nineteenth and early twentieth centuries, American eugenicists aimed much of their race betterment endeavors at African Americans and immigrants; however, they also focused a great deal on maintaining social class dynamics, regardless of race.[2] With the rise of industrialism and the growth of "slum-ridden cities," upper- and middle-class whites no longer felt as though they had a power position in American society (Rafter, *Creating Born* 57). The movement of lower-class individuals of various races and nationalities into industrialized working spheres disrupted class dynamics in American society and disrupted upper- and middle-class whites' expectations of privileges (57). While the privileged whites worried about members of the lower class moving into their cities, they also had reservations about rural poor whites who did not accept their role in the new industrial society driving the American economy (Rafter, Intro. to *White Trash* 17). Elizabeth Yukins notes that, because of these societal changes, eugenicists had to focus not only on the "inferiority" of "non-northern European" people but also on the inferiority of lower-class whites. In fact, the "increase[ed] visib[ility]" and the economic failure of poor whites spurred the eugenics movement because "[d]ominant whiteness was threatened by the spectre of inadequacy and fallibility within its own racial borders" (167). By focusing on "individual genetic weakness rather than racial superiority," eugenicists hoped to "maintain the ideology of white superiority" and to pinpoint "'degenerate' whites" who "threatened the purity of superior white 'germ plasm'" (167).[3] By identifying supposedly genetically "inferior" people, eugenicists wanted to define and distinguish characteristics of a normal person in contrast to those of an abnormal person. Therefore, eugenicists labeled poor whites and "non-northern European" races as the "Other" in American society by defining themselves as "altruistic, fit, and worthy," and to eugenicists, "[a]ltruistic behavior [. . .] confirm[ed] character, distinction, and middle-class standing" (Rafter, *Creating Born* 89). Eugenicists hoped that this separation among the white classes and among the other races would give upper- and middle-class whites a chance to retain the privileges they anticipated losing in the new American economy.

Using Gregor Mendel's "laws of heredity" and Francis Galton's "family study method" of determining the genetic makeup of individuals, American eugenicists began to conduct their own family studies, and many of the studies focused on rural poor whites (Black 26–27; Rafter, Intro. to *White Trash* 1).[4] With family studies such as Richard L. Dugdale's *"The Jukes": A Study in Crime, Pauperism, Disease, and Heredity* (1877) and Henry H. Goddard's *The Kallikak Family: A Study in the Heredity of Feeble-Mindedness* (1912), the image of "the degenerate hillbilly family, dwelling in filthy shacks and spawning endless generations of paupers, criminals, and imbeciles" became what Nicole Hahn Rafter calls the "central, confirmational image" of the eugenics movement (Intro. to *White Trash* 2), and the term "feeble-minded" became an all-inclusive phrase to describe those "degenerate[s]" whom eugenicists defined as socially or mentally unstable (Kline 25).[5] With poverty as their starting point for identifying "inferior" individuals, eugenicists looked for obvious physical disfigurements they referred to as "Mendelizing human characters" and for what eugenicists called defective "mental" and "moral" traits (Kellicott 142, 143).[6] Detecting inferiority based upon "Mendelizing human characters" gave eugenicists specific traits to look for such as "color blindness, [. . .] albinism, [. . .] certain forms of deaf mutism and cataract, [and] imbecility" (142). Proving that "mental" and "moral" traits were defective was more difficult because these traits left no physical evidence; therefore, eugenicists argued that, if "a trait did not skip a generation in a family[, then . . .] it was a Mendelian trait" (Ludmerer 60). Focusing on these methods of identification, eugenicists conducted family studies to reveal "tribes whose inferior heredity was considered the source of alcoholism, crime, feeble-mindedness, harlotry, hyperactivity, laziness, loquacity, poverty, and a host of other ills" (Rafter,

Intro. to *White Trash* 1). Eugenicists also argued that "inferior" women and men were usually plagued by specific problems according to their gender: "immorality and sexual degeneracy among women, shiftlessness and unemployment among men" (English 173). For eugenicists, poor whites represented the antithesis of the "altruistic, fit, and worthy" characteristics that "confirm[ed . . .] middle-class standing."

Despite identifying "inferior" characteristics both in female and male members of the lower-class community, eugenicists placed most of the responsibility for genetic inferiority on lower-class women. Steven Noll argues that all working women became targets during this period because industrialism gave them an opportunity to step out of their traditional roles as wives and mothers. Although lower-class rural women had generally worked on their family farms, not until industrialization increased did the work of these women become visible and financially viable for their families and for society. Grace Hutchins's 1934 leftist analysis of women's working lives, *Women Who Work,* notes that the Census Bureau referred to female farm workers as "'unpaid family workers' who work in cotton or tobacco or beet fields, or in other farming pursuits, with the rest of the family, without any separate wages for their individual labor" (28). Not only did these women not receive any profit from their work, but they also received no power. Even after the women fulfilled their multiple responsibilities of "farming the land, raising the children, and maintaining the home," they had no authority in their homes or their work because their husbands or their fathers ruled their homes (Byerly 75; Hall et al. 17–19). Industrialism offered these "'unpaid family workers'" a chance to escape from their subordinate positions and to become a part of the "cash labor" system (Byerly 75–76). Before World War I, usually only widows or young single women preparing for marriage worked in the mills; however, by 1920, when child labor was reduced, married women—whose husbands had previously prevented them from doing "public work" away from the farm and home—also began working in the mills (Hall et al. 69, 154).[7] Women's wages were needed to keep the family financially sustained, so although the men saw themselves as giving up their "dignity and self-respect" by letting their wives do "public work," they really had no other options (Hall et al. 154).

This opportunity for women forced changes in the traditional perceptions about proper female social roles, and those people who did not want to alter their social perceptions found it easier to identify nontraditional women as mentally and physically unstable (Noll, "'A Far Greater'" 31–33). With an income, young working girls showed off their financial freedom by wearing "sheathlike dresses [and . . .] sheer silk stockings," smoking, drinking, and cavorting with men from the upper- and middle-class mill towns, and as a result, these single women were generally thought of as sexual deviants (Hall et al. 223, 254, 219). Even though these women's choice of dress and their behavior may have compelled upper- and middle-class whites to focus on their sexuality, Rafter notes that the practice of condemning the sexuality of lower-class women was a common practice for eugenicists. According to eugenicists, lower-class women broke social standards because not only did they enjoy having sex but they also enjoyed having sex "with multiple and often highly unsuitable partners—very old, very young, or feebleminded men and sometimes other women" (Rafter, *Creating Born* 159). Even more disturbing was the fact that these women did not seem ashamed of their sexual activities (160). For eugenicists, this lack of shame, coupled with the supposed "feeble-minded" mental capacity of these "inferior" women, made them sexual predators. As such, "feeble-minded" women posed much more of a sexual threat than their "feeble-minded" male counterparts because not only could they have "inferior" children like themselves but they could also attract a wide variety of male sexual partners (159). According to eugenicists, "feeble-minded" men could only attract "feeble-minded" women, but "feeble-minded" women could attract both "feeble-minded" men and "normal" men (160). Noll further explains this overwhelming attractiveness of lower-class women by stating that "normal" men found "feeble-minded" women too mentally unstable "to protect themselves from untoward sexual offenses" (*Feeble-Minded* 115).[8] Despite the predatory qualities thus implicitly assigned to these "normal" men, eugenicists still insisted upon designating lower-class women as destructive sexual deviants.

For eugenicists, this discussion of feminine sexuality had begun at the very beginning of the twentieth century. Even eugenicists who were comfortable with feminine sexuality were making a designation between fit and unfit mothers. Havelock Ellis, a British psychologist and eugenicist, had as early as 1901 argued that "the sexual impulse between the two sexes [was] fairly balanced" (*Studies* [1: 256]). Although Ellis's view of feminine sexuality broke convention, his view of "appropriate" sexual impulses did not. In 1906, his definitions of family and of good parenting became a precursor for eugenicists' views of the next thirty years. Ellis wrote, "The family is a great social influence in so far as it is the best instrument for creating children who will make the future citizens" (*Studies* [4: 570]), and he also notes that "the mother [. . .] is the child's supreme parent" (2). Of course, he also designates the difference between "qualified" mothers and un-"qualified" mothers (611). According to Ellis, "qualified mothers" had an important and positive "claim on society" (611), but those who were not "qualified" needed to be stopped from spreading "social defects" (602). He noted that Americans had readily accepted "abortion" as a way "to correct what, rightly or wrongly, they regard[ed] as social defects" (602). However, he does add that eugenicists should find a way to stop abortion from being used as a tool to rid society of these "defects" and begin focusing on "natural and harmless methods for preventing contraception"; of course, at the time, his main alternative suggestion to stop abortions was "castration or other slighter operation" (611, 612).

By the next decade, the reproductive capabilities of these supposedly "inferior" women had become a national focus and had even led to a national reproductive campaign. Eugenicists spread the idea that America's future was endangered because, while the upper and middle class had begun to have fewer children, "inferior" women continued to have numerous children (Kline 97). The contrasting lack of procreation in the upper and middle class, according to eugenicists, would lead to "race suicide," a term that became a national catch phrase for the movement (62). Wendy Kline states that, in the 1910s, "two opposing models of womanhood" dominated American thought, the "mother of tomorrow" and the "moron" (3, 29). The "mother of tomorrow" represented the "progressive, forward-looking, socially responsible, moral, and civilized woman who would raise tomorrow's children" (29), and she also represented eugenicists' focus on "positive eugenics," a campaign to encourage upper- and middle-class women to have more children. This focus on "positive eugenics" even extended into the 1920s with eugenicist Albert Edward Wiggam's appeal to possible "mother[s] of tomorrow." To appeal to upper- and middle-class white women, he wrote, "She is the natural conservator of the race, the guardian of its blood. [. . .] And this improvement of life, the perfecting of the babe at her breast, is not only a woman's supreme duty, but is her one deathless passion" (280). On the other hand, the "moron" woman represented "a biological threat to the health and advancement of the race" because "her sexual behavior indicated her primitive savagery" (Kline 29). Not only would these women not have the ability to take care of their children, they would possibly have children who shared their mother's genetic inferiority. Yukins describes how eugenicists interpreted poor white "inferior" women's increased sexuality and reproductive capabilities as criminal activities. She says that, according to eugenicists, these women's sexual traits led to "a moral offense (bastardy) [. . . ,] a biological offense (degeneration) [. . . , and] a cultural offense (crime)" (173). Because of these conclusions about the genetic inferiority of lower-class women, eugenicists furthered Ellis's ideas that the "moron," or the un-"qualified" mother, did not have the moral capabilities to take on the female primary responsibility as caretaker.

Even though eugenicists hoped that their disturbing conclusions about "inferior" mothers would spur upper- and middle-class families to join in the "positive eugenics" campaign, this was not the case. Eugenicist William E. Kellicott, in his 1923 book *The Social Direction of Human Evolution*, described the failure of "positive eugenics" by writing, "Sitting quietly at home, a nation may degenerate and collapse, simply because it has given full play to selective reproduction and not bred from its best" (129). The "selective reproduction" Kellicott was referring to was occurring because upper- and middle-class women had begun to use birth control (Kline 62). Ironically, though, birth control was viewed by Margaret Sanger, the leader in the birth control movement and one of Ellis's lovers, to be a major factor in the "negative eugenics" campaign that focused on stopping the procreation of the "moron" women (Grosskurth 410).[9] In her writings, Sanger went back and forth "between images of the poor as exploited and as unfit" (Paul, *Controlling* 94); however, her motto for her journal *Birth Control Review* was actually "To Breed a Race of Thoroughbreds" (Grosskurth 410). The writings in *Birth Control Review* reflect Sanger's belief that birth control could stop the reproduction of feeblemindedness, therefore, acting as a "respectable" means of "social control," the type of "natural and harmless" method that Ellis hoped could take the place of the use of "abortion" as a eugenic tool (Paul, *Controlling* 95, 96). Kline notes that some eugenicists did not consider birth control a practical means of protecting society from "unfit" mothers because it required trust in "individual regulation" (65), and even if eugenicists did consider birth control a viable factor in the "negative eugenics" campaign, it did not become readily available until the 1960s because "[t]he birth-control movement at this time still bore the mark of radicalism" (63).

Because birth control was not a promising solution, eugenicists turned to different ways to control the birthrate of lower-class women (Larson 161). First, eugenicists segregated "inferior" women from the rest of the population by putting them in state-sponsored institutions (Kline 32). These institutions "for the care and treatment of feeble-minded individuals" first appeared in "northern and midwestern states" in the "nineteenth century," and early in the 1920s, they began to appear in states across the South (Noll, *Feeble-Minded* 4).[10] Sterilization, a cheaper alternative than segregation, became more popular after the *Carrie Buck v. Bell* case was decided by the U.S. Supreme Court in 1927 (Kline 32). The court upheld the constitutionality of state sterilization laws, and Justice Oliver Wendell Holmes wrote in his opinion for the landmark case, "We have seen more than once that the public welfare may call upon its best citizens for their lives. It would be strange if it could not call upon those who already sap the strength of the State for lesser sacrifices [. . .] in order to prevent our being swamped with incompetence. [. . .] Three generations of imbeciles are enough" (qtd. in Laughlin 52). Carrie Buck, a poor white woman, and other lower-class women became victims of "[t]herapeutic sterilization" supposedly aimed at helping them with their problems as well as saving the future of American society (Woodside 48).[11]

EUGENIC FAMILY STUDIES

To promote their findings about hereditary characteristics, sociologists and eugenicists used the family study method. In her research on family studies published between 1877 and 1919, Rafter "located fifteen family studies published in the United States" (Intro. to *White Trash* 3). Daylanne K. English, however, has found that the Eugenics Record Office conducted hundreds of "unpublished studies of 'defective' families [. . .] between 1910 and 1918" (145).[12] Even though a great number of the studies went unpublished, Rafter points out that "several of the family studies became enormously popular, reaching wide audiences" (Intro. to *White Trash* 2). In fact, she suggests that these "studies created a powerful myth about the somatic nature of social problems" (2).[13] Part of the "myth" emerges simply by giving the studied families pseudonyms "signifying devolution" (28). While the authors may have meant to protect these families by giving them fictional names, they certainly took liberties with the fictional names they used to represent the families. Names such as the "Kallikaks," the "Tribe of Ishmael," and the "Zeros" create a feeling of hopelessness.[14] These studies also created a "myth" about the female members of these families because the authors tended to place greater responsibility for families' failures on the females rather than on the males. Women often appear in these studies merely as oversexed, dangerous females who then become mothers of "defective" offspring. The authors also tend to blame the women for the men's failures, making the men seem like the women's pawns in their sexual deviancy. Of course, what Rafter calls a "myth" about these poor white families actually seems to have become part of the early twentieth-century ideology of the United States as a result of those studies that did become popular.

Despite the overwhelming acceptance of eugenic family studies by the American public, the investigating and reporting methods used by the authors make their conclusions about the families seem more like propaganda literature than scientific studies (Rafter, Intro. to *White Trash* 26). The authors of the studies, typically members of the lower middle class, usually began their research with a family or group that displayed traits that made them seem outside the norm of society (2). In order to study a family's history, the authors would examine information collected from "public records, memories of neighbors, and recollections of family members" (2). Authors used the term "family" loosely because, for their purposes, the term described "a number of family units *and* those who married (or mated) into them" (18). Rafter suggests that, for this reason, Dugdale put the family name "Jukes" in quotation marks. Other studies such as *The Hill Folk: Report on a Rural Community of Hereditary Defectives* include no indication that the "family" line is not direct (18).[15] Of course, this loose definition of a "family" made it less difficult to create a pattern, and if the authors found that a trait appeared at least one time in the "family" line that they created, then the authors could categorize it as a "Mendelian trait" and as "hereditary" (Rafter, Intro. to *White Trash* 2, 6). Also, while some family study authors recognized the environmental conditions affecting their subjects, most assumed that biological problems took precedence over environmental problems. As a result of this assumption, authors usually stressed that a class-based society was a natural process of life because they felt that people who fell in the lower class were in that position because of "unfortunate heredity" (6). Over time, family study authors did not even consider environmental effects on these families; instead, the studies reflected a growing disdain for supposedly "degenerate" families and a growing desire to use "negative eugenics."

One of the most popular and most influential family studies was Dugdale's *"The Jukes": A Study in Crime and Pauperism, Disease, and Heredity.* This particular study became a guide for many of the family studies to follow and, indeed, fits the formula that Rafter detected when researching family studies. Dugdale's study became so well known that the family's nickname, the "Jukes," "became part of the working vocabulary of social references in [America]" (Rafter, Preface to "Hereditary Pauperism" 34). After visiting thirteen New York state prisons in 1874, Dugdale decided to focus his study on the "Jukes" because of their history of criminal activity (Dugdale 7). Upon further investigation, Dugdale found that "[t]hey had lived in the same locality for generations, and were so despised by the respectable community that their family name *had come to be used generically as a term of reproach*" (8). Although Rafter cites Gertrude C. Davenport's 1902 study of a Swiss family, the Zeros, as the first family study to place a strong focus on the danger of "inferior" females, Dugdale too places the majority of the blame for the "Juke" family's failures on its women (Rafter, Preface to Davenport, "Hereditary Crime" 66).[16] He spends much of his time discussing the "harlotry" of the "Juke" women and how it is a "hereditary characteristic" that needs no special "environment" in which to flourish (Dugdale 19, 26). Then, he states that a "Juke" man would have a better chance at changing his criminal ways if the women in his family would become "reputable" (26). This indictment of the women even comes directly after Dugdale equates the "prostitution" of "Juke" women with the "crime and pauperism" of "Juke" men. Although their crimes appear equal, obviously Dugdale sees the women as much more important than the men to the family's future progress in society.

In later family studies, women take the forefront again as the authors explore the dueling roles of "mother of tomorrow" and "moron." Davenport's account of the Zero family, "Hereditary Crime," follows the line of a degenerative family living in "an isolated village in a Swiss valley" (68).[17] Jörger, who originally documented this family, noticed that a large number of the family members inhabited the asylum where he was a director and that they shared their family name with "the most sturdy, sane, and respected families" in the village (Davenport "Hereditary Crime" 68). While conducting the study, Jörger found that this family broke into three branches, two "good" and one "bad" (68–69). Of course, Jörger's study makes the matriarch into the sole damaging gene source of the family. The three branches descended from an upstanding "miller" in the community and his wife, who "was a blood relative" of her husband and whose "blood was tainted with insanity" (69). They had two sons, and while one son married a "healthy, moral, and sturdy" woman, the other son had two wives, a "good" woman and a "bad" woman. The "bad" wife was related to his mother, making her blood just as "tainted" as his mother's (69). From this union, "the vagabond and criminal branch" of the Zero family emerged (69). Oddly enough, Jörger does not attribute this degenerative line to any of the men in the family, despite the fact that the two sons must also have been "tainted" by their mother's blood. The blame for this family that has caused "one hundred years [. . . of] burden" to its village falls solely on the Zero women (72). While Jörger's study follows Dugdale's decision to blame women for genetic consequences, Jörger takes the focus a step further by creating two versions of motherhood, with "moral[ity]" as the distinction between the women.

Goddard's *The Kallikak Family: A Study in the Heredity of Feeble-Mindedness,* "the all-time best seller among family studies," also promoted this dualistic image of "good" mother / "bad" mother (Rafter, Preface to Kite, "Two Brothers" 74).[18] For Rafter, Goddard's study is the first one "fully to realize the potential of the bad-mother theme" (74). Goddard begins his study with a young woman named Deborah Kallikak who, although she looks like a normal woman, has actually been diagnosed as feebleminded (Goddard 2). Her family line has been traced back to her "great-great-grandfather" Martin Kallikak, an illegitimate son of a respectable soldier named Martin Kallikak Sr. and "a feeble-minded girl" he met at a tavern (17–18).[19] Martin Kallikak Jr.'s line is filled with harlotry, drunkenness, crime, incest, and feeblemindedness (29). In Elizabeth S. Kite's version of *The Kallikak Family,* titled "Two Brothers," she emphasizes that Martin Jr. had three daughters who caused "scandals" because they seduced "sons of prominent citizens" (77).[20] Just as in the Zero family line, no blame is placed on Martin Sr. because he eventually married another woman, "a respectable girl of good family" and had a family free of "defectives" (Goddard 29). Once again, the father of the clan seems completely independent of his wife's hereditary problems and actually seems more like the seduced "sons of prominent citizens" focused on in Kite's versions of the family study. He was a victim of seduction by a "feeble-minded" woman, supporting the conclusion that "feeble-minded" women are inherently sexual deviants ready to fill society with "inferior" children.

The genetic abilities of the southern lower class also faced the scrutiny of eugenic family studies, and in Arthur H. Estabrook and Ivan E. McDougle's *Mongrel Virginians: The Win Tribe,* poor white women seem even more dangerous than they do in other studies because their sexuality is supposedly the cause of the downfall of the white race. In 1926, Estabrook and McDougle published *Mongrel Virginians* in an attempt to answer questions concerning the "growing interest in the subject of racial mixtures particularly in the South" (7). While they did focus most of their study on "a small group of Indian-negro-white crosses," Estabrook and McDougle also focused on how poor whites contributed to the creation of this "group" (7). They found that the Win tribe had been able to expand because poor white women were so sexually promiscuous that they did not mind "mat[ing] into this group" (150). The miscegenation between poor white women and the racially mixed Win tribe resulted in the creation of light-skinned children who could pass as white. Since the racially mixed children are difficult to identify, Estabrook and McDougle argue that the only way to find them is to consider all families "very poor, living on the land as tenant farmers" as possible racially mixed families (195). With this description of how to locate people passing as white, Estabrook and McDougle implicate most poor whites in their search. Then, after the authors imply that poor whites may actually be racially mixed individuals, they emphasize how serious this concern should be taken by noting that racial mixing is now affecting "counties all over Virginia, Delaware, Maryland,

North Carolina, South Carolina, and Tennessee" (176). With this ominous conclusion about how miscegenation is spreading across the nation, Estabrook and McDougle have effectively made sexually deviant poor white women seem like the destroyers not only of their own class of people but also of the entire white race.[21]

While these family studies agree on the sexually dangerous nature of the supposedly "inferior" women in the families, they do not always agree on the cause of these families' failures. Rafter has commented that Dugdale's study of the "Jukes" "was widely read as proof of heredity's dominance over environment" (*Creating Born* 38); however, Dugdale clearly establishes a concern for both the biological and the environmental conditions of the "Juke" family. In his conclusion, Dugdale states, "[C]apacity, physical and mental, is limited and determined mainly by heredity," but he also says, "[I]t is [. . .] capable of marked modification for better or worse by the character of the environment" (65).[22] Even if the environment only "superficially correct[s]" the problem in an individual, Dugdale sees the effort to help the "inferior" person as necessary to help society (65). For Goddard, however, no hope exists for these "inferior" families. In fact, he condemns supposedly "defective" people to a life of degeneracy regardless of their circumstances: "If all of the slum districts of our cities were removed to-morrow and model tenements built in their places, we would still have slums in a week's time, because we have these mentally defective people who can never be taught to live otherwise than as they have been living" (70–71). Goddard uses his study as a call to arms to stop "pity[ing]" the rapidly increasing group of "inferior" people (104). These two influential studies reflect an ongoing discussion about the effects that biological and environmental influences have on the lower class, and this debate would change the way eugenicists determined the genetic inferiority of a person in the 1920s and 1930s.

EUGENICISTS SHIFT FOCUS

Despite the popularity of Dugdale's and Goddard's family studies, "the work of sociologists and anthropologists" concerning the nature and origins of human behavior" began to gain recognition in the 1920s; as a result, eugenicists had to reconsider how they identified supposedly "inferior" people (Kline 97). "[S]ociologists and anthropologists" began to question the total control of heredity over a person's capabilities since they focused their studies on the effects that "nurture or environment" had on an individual, making identifying supposed inferiority based on class status seem socially irresponsible (97–98). The effects of environment also came to the forefront because environmentalists and some eugenicists rejected the practice of segregating and sterilizing lower-class people simply because of their class status. This concern over class-based stereotyping emerged as geneticists and eugenicists began to believe that Mendelian traits used to identify "defective" people were carried as "recessive" genes, thereby allowing some "defective" people to "pass for normal" because they did not have "inferior" physical traits (Jennings 10; English 168). Diane B. Paul and Hamish G. Spencer argue in "Did Eugenics Rest on an Elementary Mistake?" that eugenicists, with their knowledge of the Hardy-Weinberg theorem, would have recognized that this "recessive" gene theory problematized their attempts to rid society of defectives through segregation and sterilization (117–18). According to the Hardy-Weinberg theorem, "[w]hen genes are both recessive and rare, the number of carriers will vastly exceed those actually affected" (Paul, Intro. to Shaner 3). Even though they are "recessive," these Mendelian "defective" traits could still be passed from one person to another, and without any method of identifying individuals with these unstable "recessive" genes, eugenicists could no longer expect that simply exterminating physically "inferior" members of the lower class with birth control, abortion, segregation, and sterilization "would rapidly eradicate various undesirable traits" in the population (Paul, "Genes and Contagious" 159). These "recessive" genes did not take into consideration class boundaries as they were passed from generation to generation. Because eugenicists now had to take into account environmental influences and because of the "recessive" gene theory, getting rid of "defective" genes now became a slow process that might take multiple generations to achieve (159).

In order to accelerate this process, eugenicists needed a new way to uncover "hidden" defectives. H. S. Jennings in his 1930 work *The Biological Basis of Human Nature* argued that, because of "recessive" genes, "most of the difficulties of society come from individuals that do not show single sharply defined pathological traits, such as insanity or feeblemindedness"

(10, 243). This recessive gene theory provided support for the idea that two types of people with "defective" genes existed: those who could be identified by their physical traits and those who continued to thrive physically unrecognizable as defectives (234).[23] Eugenicist Edward M. East had already written about this theory in a 1917 article, "Hidden Feeblemindedness," and in his 1927 book, *Heredity and Human Affairs,* he created a timeline for the discovery of the recessive genes. He argued that, if a person considered "normal" procreated with a person who had a defective gene, the baby would have "normal mentality" but would never be a "pure" normal (East, *Heredity* 44), and later in life, if this child and another "cross bred" individual procreated, their baby would, more than likely, have physically recognizable feebleminded traits (44). These conclusions led to the belief that feeblemindedness possibly could not appear for at least three generations, and they explain Justice Holmes's comment about "[t]hree generations of imbeciles" in his opinion in the Carrie Buck case. Although Carrie and her mother, Emma, were considered sexual deviants by eugenicists, they were not officially declared "inferior" until after the birth of Carrie's child. Social workers could not conclusively detect genetic inferiority in Carrie and Emma because they showed no physical traits of inferiority; however, when a nurse declared Carrie's baby Vivian "not quite normal" because of her appearance, the social workers now had evidence against the two older Buck women (Black 115).[24] The "mental" and "moral" traits had previously just been part of the evidence against a supposed "defective," but now, eugenicists began to put more focus on them since the Hardy-Weinberg theorem helped them to conclude that they would have to wait three generations to identify "defectives" physically.

With more focus being put on "mental" and "moral" traits and on the recessive gene theory, eugenicists had to reevaluate their plan to create a strong future for America. By the late 1920s and the 1930s, eugenicists decided to incorporate environmental concerns into their plan. A group of socially conscious geneticists, referred to by Paul as "socialist geneticists," such as H. J. Muller, Jennings, East, and Raymond Pearl, began working with the leftist movement in America "to develop a socially responsible eugenics" that worked to eliminate "social classes" as a way to differentiate between genetic effects and environmental effects on a person (Paul, "Eugenics" 14, 15, 16). These eugenicists and leftists maintained that "[t]here could be no valid comparison of intrinsic worth of different individuals [. . .] in a class-stratified society" (14). Muller, a leading American eugenicist, had directed this new push for a "socially responsible eugenics" since he first finished his book *Out of the Night: A Biologist's View of the Future* in 1925.[25] Muller argued that "in our present society, with its gross inequalities, it would be obviously unfair to measure his [man's] original genetic aptitudes by his finally formed faculties" (85). Jennings echoed these sentiments in his own writing, emphasizing how improving the environment could only make the process of race betterment more successful than the previous efforts of eugenicists.

> Measures of public health must be carried out, [. . .] economic ills conquered, grinding poverty abolished. When these things are done, when the human plant is given conditions under which it can unfold its capabilities without stunting, poisoning, and mutilation by the environment, then it will be possible to discover what ills are primarily due to defective genes, and to plan such measures as are possible for their eradication. (250)

Harry Hamilton Laughlin, the author of the model sterilization law, even added an environmental stipulation; a person could only be declared "socially inadequate" if he or she lived in a "normal environment" (66). This dual focus on nature and nurture by eugenicists "saved the movement from extinction, and it also widened eugenicists' sphere of influence and further popularized their goal to improve civilization" (Kline 106).

Of course, because eugenicists focused on helping members of the lower class improve their living conditions, they identified genetic inferiority by pinpointing lower-class people who did not respond to the opportunities given to them. Although "socialist geneticists" put forth a national effort to be environmentally conscious, they specifically highlighted their findings in the southern United States. Tenant farming and sharecropping had increased in the 1920s; however, mill work supposedly offered a reprieve from the poverty that tenant and sharecropping families faced if they stayed on the farm (Flynt 66). Not all of the suffering farmers chose to move to the mill towns, and some who did move chose to return because of the lack of jobs and the bad conditions of the jobs that were offered (Flynt 70–71; Hirsch and Terrill xiv). This lack of movement for economic reasons proved to be enough for some eugenicists to condemn these farmers, even despite the criticisms of the mill jobs. In 1929, *Eugenics: A Journal of Race Betterment* focused on why this lack of movement condemned members of the lower class. Thomas Nixon Carver in his article, "The Economic Test of Fitness," argued that those who cannot raise themselves "after a few generations" from "the lowest and most unskilled occupations" prove themselves to be "of poor stock" (6). In that same issue of the journal, Estabrook, co-author of *Mongrel Virginians,* emphasizes how Carver's theory can be applied to the lower class of the South when he cites the "Southern Appalachians" as a place with many "inferior sections" of people (10, 11). Since the "energetic" and "ambitious" lower-class people have moved away, he deduces that those mountaineers who have stayed "are of a lower intellectual level" (12). He had suggested this same point in *Mongrel Virginians* because he encouraged his readers to study "tenant farmers" to learn how genetically "inferior" people live (195). Estabrook sums up his and Carver's "socialist geneticist" methods of pinpointing genetically "inferior" people in places such as the South where opportunities in mill towns supposedly offer economic relief: "[S]lum conditions in the country are due mainly to definite factors of biological selection—namely that the more capable and energetic have migrated, leaving the less capable behind" (Estabrook 12).

In 1929, Ira Caldwell, father of the soon-to-be-popular author Erskine Caldwell, wrote a five-part series of articles for *Eugenics: A Journal of Race Betterment* that reflects the principles of "socialist geneticists" and the ideas about the southern lower class held by Estabrook. His series of articles, titled "The Bunglers," chronicles the life of a family he studied in his hometown of Wrens, Georgia (Miller 129). Writing about this group of poor whites, he describes members of the Bungler family who have "Mendelizing human [physical] characters" (251), and he describes the family's lack of intelligence that has resulted, for some, from not attending school regularly and, for others, from not having the mental capabilities to learn (209, 293, 299). He also documents their break from the traditional nuclear family unit and how they seem to adhere to their own brand of familial and sexual morality.[26] At the end of the series, Caldwell calls for the sterilization of this family and families like it (383). Even though he seems to condemn the Bunglers just as authors of previous family studies had done, Dan Miller has found that Caldwell, before writing the articles, followed the principles of the "socialist geneticists" and tried to improve the living conditions of this family.[27] Caldwell moved the Bunglers from the outskirts of Burke County to his hometown of Wrens, where he put the children in school, gave the father a job, and gave the family healthy meals and nice clothes (Miller 124). Within months of coming to Wrens, the Bunglers moved back to their farm (125). Because of this experience, Caldwell furthers the argument that Estabrook and McDougle highlight at the conclusion of *Mongrel Virginians.* According to Caldwell, since only a percentage of suspected "inferior" poor whites can be "rehabilitated," the others may create a "great army of delinquents" who could become the dominant population in America (383).

COMMUNISM AND EUGENICS

Since eugenics is often associated with right-wing conservatism, linking Communist class-conscious ideals with eugenics and genetic work seems contradictory; however, "socialist geneticists" fervently argued that their eugenic "policy could only be successfully pursued in a society that provided approximately equal opportunities to all its members" (Paul, "Eugenics" 14). Their model for this "equal" society was the Soviet Union because it offered "the first socially responsible opportunity" to "apply" their theories (14). Paul notes that American scientists looked to the Soviet Union for "scientific development" (14), and the Soviet Union provided just this type of "development" in the field of genetics in the 1920s and early 1930s. In *The Lysenko Affair,* David Joravsky recounts how, during this time, Soviet "Marxist geneticists" believed that "*self-development*" needed to be studied as a correlation of "nature" and "environment" (Winn 521, 523).[28] Soviet Marxist geneticists tended to focus on environment as a hindrance for genes that could flourish, if given the opportunity, in another environment. As a result, according to these geneticists, members of the lower class have always had good genes; they just need a suitable environment that corresponds with their specific genes (264).

Soviet Marxist geneticists followed some of the main principles of the early eugenics movement in America; however, these geneticists did not want to use class as a way to identify genetically "inferior" people. Some geneticist leaders even desired "a socialist eugenics" to take the place of what they saw as a "'bourgeois'" dominated eugenics movement, which Soviet Marxist geneticists felt put too much emphasis on the lower class and its supposed inferiority (Joravsky, *Lysenko* 260, 262).[29] Karl Kautsky, a eugenicist and a Soviet Marxist once thought of as just as great a thinker as Friedrich Engels, did not want just to control the population of the lower class, as most eugenicists did. He wanted to improve "the quality of the population" because he felt that "a uniformly high level of health and education would heighten the importance of hereditary differences, making it necessary to plan for the reduction of poor and the increase of good hereditary types" (Joravsky, *Lysenko* 256). During the Bolshevik Revolution, Kautsky's desire to improve "[p]ublic health" became part of the government's plan to improve society (258).[30]

In 1927, Commissar of Health N. A. Semashko argued that the focus of the movement should, first, be on changing social improprieties and, then, on improving "maternal health and child care" (262). This focus on women's function in "socialist eugenics" became increasingly prominent in A. S. Serebrovskii's contribution to the 1929 first "Five Year Plan" (266). Serebrovskii, a prominent Communist geneticist, wanted to improve the biology of human beings, and he aimed to do this by focusing completely on female reproduction (266). Part of his plan was to educate women to have babies only through "artificial insemination" so that pre-selected genetically "superior" sperm could be used to impregnate the women (Joravsky, *Soviet* 306). By implication, this "Plan" involves reducing women to mere reproductive machines for the Communist movement and the eugenics movement.[31] Bolshevik leaders saw this plan as a rebuke to women; however, Joravsky notes that the leaders were "especially" angered because they had "overlooked" this "method of social improvement" (266). By 1936, however, the Soviet geneticists' attempts to create "a socialist eugenics" could not continue not only because the world was beginning to learn of the atrocities committed by Germany in the name of eugenics but also because, despite all efforts to the contrary, the lower class was still being targeted by certain geneticists who still adhered to the "'bourgeois'" eugenics theories (Joravsky, *Lysenko* 266).

Although the threat of arrest and terror led many Soviet geneticists to stop or, at least, to cover up their studies (Joravsky, *Lysenko* 118), the effects of "socialist eugenics" still continued to be felt in the American movement. Paul notes that American eugenicists were attracted to Soviet eugenics and that Muller had actually moved to the Soviet Union in 1934 to continue his research ("Eugenics" 20). Muller's book *Out of the Night* stands as an example of how, even though "socialist eugenics" became taboo in the Soviet Union, it still flourished in other parts of the world, particularly in the United States. When Muller finally published his book in 1935, he sent a copy of it, along with a personal letter condemning the use of eugenics for "'bourgeois'" purposes, to Stalin (Paul, "Eugenics" 21). Hoping to convince Stalin of the worthiness of his project, Muller thought this gesture would help revive the study of eugenics in the Soviet Union, but Stalin did not appreciate Muller's attempts to win his favor and actually stopped all reviews of *Out of the Night* from being published in the country (Carlson 233). Despite this rejection, *Out of the Night* was accepted "enthusiast[ically]" in other countries (Paul, "Eugenics" 21). Reviews of the book suggested that Muller's ideas "were scientifically unproblematic" (21). Even such different publications as the *Journal of the American Medical Association* and the *New York Times* gave positive reviews to *Out of the Night* (23, 34). Reviewers accepted Muller's class-conscious view of eugenics. In his book, Muller argues, "[W]e cannot hope, except in special cases, to gain much knowledge as to what rôle in determining any given individual's distinctive moral make-up [. . .] was played by genetic differences in intelligence and emotional trends, and what rôle by the differences in our highly unequal environment" (88). Even though Muller's statements echo those made by other Soviet and American eugenicists, the excitement generated by *Out of the Night,* presumably, garnered a wider audience for the ideas.

While Muller voiced standard principles of "socialist eugenics," he also offered his own approach to "positive eugenics" by building on previous "socialist eugenics" theories on this topic. In fact, the final chapter of *Out of the Night* is almost completely dedicated to "positive eugenics" and to the role of women in his plan. Muller begins his call to women by advocating their right to birth control so that they will not feel like pawns to men's will (104–5); then, he advocates increased efforts to change childbirth procedures (105). He also supports creating "public utility organizations" to assist women with childcare duties, making mothering a public instead of a private role (105–6). While these views seem moderate and distinctly helpful for mothers, he also echoes as well as adds to part of Serebrovskii's "Five Year Plan." He advocates the use of "artificial insemination" just as Serebrovskii did in 1929; Muller argues that, through this process, "[f]ifty thousand" genetically "superior" children can be born in one generation (111). In this part of his plan, he insists that men and women have "almost" the same amount of influence on the genetic ability of their children (110–11); however, his personal addition to the Serebrovskii plan suggests that women play the most important role. He argues that the future of eugenics rests on "[w]hether or not human eggs could be caused to develop without fertilization—without a father" (109–10). According to Muller, this process of reproduction would not "interfer[e] with [women's] personal lives—or even [. . .] their theologies" (110). Obviously, if Muller envisions a eugenic solution without the help of fathers, women and men cannot possibly hold "almost" the same amount of genetic influence. *Out of the Night,* just as other eugenic works do, puts women at the forefront of the argument.

Muller not only emphasizes the importance of women to the eugenics movement but also represents how eugenicists hoped to reach the general American public in order to widen their popularity. By using "positive eugenics," Muller argues that in "a paltry century or two [. . .] it would be possible for the majority of men to become of the innate quality" (113). In presenting this argument, he uses examples of genetically "superior" men that would appeal not only to the academic community but also to ordinary Americans. First, he says that men can be created in the likeness of "Lenin, Newton, Leonardo, Pasteur, Beethoven, Omar Khayyám, Pushkin, Sun Yat Sen, [and] Marx," (113), and later, he says the world can be full of "Billy Sundays, Valentinos, Jack Dempseys, Babe Ruths, [and] even Al Capones" (114). Listing academic and creative intellectuals alongside American pop culture figures is an attempt to appeal both to the upper-class elites and to middle- and lower-class Americans influenced by iconic symbols of American culture. This attempt to appeal to the mass American population reflects efforts made by the American eugenics movement of the late 1920s and the 1930s to try to capitalize on its new "socially responsible" approach to eugenics. According to Christina Cogdell, in *Eugenic Design: Streamlining America in the 1930s,* by 1928, "over 375" colleges taught classes "with eugenic or genetic content" (104). Not only did schools across America teach eugenics, but it was also becoming a part of popular culture. According to Cogdell, "museums across the nation featured exhibits related to race betterment" (94). Radio programs were used to spread eugenic ideals (100–101). "Better Babies and Fitter Family Contests" promoted the idea of "positive eugenics" in America (101). Both "the YMCA and YWCA" showed their support for the movement's ideals. As a result of this abounding focus on eugenics, English argues "that it became nearly invisible as an ideology" (33).

As an "invisible [. . .] ideology," eugenics became a prevalent part of American political policies and even American political parties. Herbert Hoover addressed the issue of children and their future in his 1928 acceptance speech for the Republican presidential nomination by saying, "Racial progress marches upon the feet of healthy and instructed children. There should be no child in America that is not born and does not live under sound conditions of health" (37). After becoming president, Hoover pursued this agenda by inviting eugenicists to run the White House Conference on Child Health and Protection in 1930 (Kline 101). Because of this national focus and because of the 1927 Supreme Court decision in the *Buck v. Bell* case to support sterilization, "[s]eventeen states enacted or raised sterilization laws" (107). This focus on the welfare of children coincided with America's struggle during the Great Depression to understand changing familial roles as women were forced to leave their place as primary caretakers and engage in "public work" (Odem 105–6; Hall et al. 310–11). A 1936 Gallup poll actually stated that "82 percent of Americans believed that employers should not hire married women" (Hall et al. 312). With America's economic situation and family values so unstable, the eugenics movement, the Communist Party of the United States (CPUSA), and Roosevelt's administration profited by focusing on normalizing these issues once again, and in the CPUSA's and Roosevelt's attempts to gain America's support, both used eugenic ideology and, therefore, further spread the movement in America.

POLITICAL MOVEMENTS CONVERGING

This desire for the eugenics movement to appeal to the American general public—a focal point of Muller's work—also became the desire of the

CPUSA. At the 1935 American Writers' Congress, Kenneth Burke gave an influential speech that helped lead the CPUSA into the Popular Front, a time during which the Communist Party also put its focus on appealing to a wider range of Americans (Hapke 75). Burke encouraged his fellow Communists to focus on "the symbol of the 'people'" rather than on "the symbol of the 'worker'" (Denning 443). Although CPUSA leaders such as Mike Gold chastised Burke for his statement, those who spoke out against Burke later recognized the speech as a way to take the party in a new, more populist direction (443). Burke's new direction for the CPUSA came at a time when the party's membership, although slightly increasing each year, still remained at a relatively low number. The Great Depression helped the party grow because disillusioned, unemployed workers saw hope in its policies and in how these policies had supposedly worked in the Soviet Union (Dixler 33). According to Elsa Dixler, between 1930 and 1932, the party's membership rose from "7500" to "12–14,000" members (33). Although this growth seems promising, the party also faced in the early 1930s "external repression and internal functional disputes" (Shaffer 75). As a result, the party closed itself off to outside influences, therefore closing itself off to the majority of the American people. Burke's call to focus on the "'people'" in his speech was his attempt to urge the party to open itself to ideas and movements from which it would have normally separated itself.

By opening up to different influences, the CPUSA "strove to present itself as an American party firmly within American political and cultural traditions" (Shaffer 76). To connect with "American [. . .] traditions," the CPUSA employed Muller's strategy in *Out of the Night;* it used "icons of pop culture" such as "Hollywood, Mom, the Dodgers, [and] Abe Lincoln" in order to appear "comfortably American" (Rabinowitz, *Labor* 58). Party leaders also thought it necessary to work with anyone who wanted to help the working class, and they thought it necessary to make "anti-fascism, rather than agitation for socialism the core of its strategy" (76).[32] This more inviting "strategy" attracted membership that no longer included just the unemployed and the proletariat worker since "employed intellectuals" also began to see the CPUSA as the hope for America's future (Dixler 33). As a result of these new memberships, the dynamics of the party changed drastically, and "by the mid-thirties, at least half [of the membership was] middle class" (33–34). Because of these shifts in rhetoric and in membership, the CPUSA also allowed itself to become involved with New Deal leaders and union organizers (Dixler 34; Shaffer 76). In fact, the CPUSA gave "support to Franklin Roosevelt, his party, and his program" after CPUSA leaders had previously referred to the New Deal as "proto-fascist" (Dixler 34). Along with these political affiliations, the CPUSA became more actively and openly involved in the eugenics movement. In fact, eugenics became an increasingly visible part of the CPUSA's policies and in the CPUSA's associations with new political allies during the Popular Front.

In 1936, the American Marxist journal *Science and Society* appeared, acting as a voice for the party's scientific concerns and clearly indicating a connection between the party's principles and "socialist eugenics." According to the editors, the journal's purpose was "to publish articles, communications, and reviews illustrating the manner in which Marxism integrates the various scientific disciplines and illuminates the interdependence of science and society" ("Title Page" i). Denning's study of American communism referred to *Science and Society* as "a leading journal of Marxist thought" and cites Burke as a "contributing editor" to the journal (442, 443). This "leading journal" between 1936 and 1942 included at least fourteen articles specifically about the study of genetics and its relation to eugenics.[33] J. B. S. Haldane, a geneticist and communist supporter known for his work as one of Engels's editors, contributed several articles to *Science and Society* (Joravsky, *Soviet* 11), and rebuttals or additions to his arguments continued to spur discussions in multiple issues during its first six years of publication. The editors even included reviews of eugenic scientific books. While *Science and Society* did not completely focus on genetic and eugenic discussions, a favorable approach to these topics did dominate the content. Even rebuttal arguments did not deny the importance of genetic theory; the authors of the rebuttals usually just stated their own versions of genetic theories or genetic understanding.

As a leading contributor to the journal, Haldane promotes many of the theories focused on during the "socialist eugenics" movement by Soviet Marxist geneticists and by American eugenicists and geneticists. Haldane's first eugenics article in a 1937 issue of *Science and Society* actually seems like his outlet for expressing the concerns of the "socialist eugenics" movement and for establishing the movement's distinct connection to Communism. In "A Dialectical Account of Evolution," Haldane argues the importance of environment in recognizing an individual's full potential by stating that a "living organism [. . .] reacts to changes in the environment so as to bring itself back to normal. [. . .] A sufficiently gross interference kills it, but if it is not killed it struggles back towards the normal structure and function" (474). After showing how a change in environment may reveal better qualities of an individual's genetic makeup than previously seen, Haldane also argues that both "survival" and "fertility" may "affect the fitness" of an individual (479). At the end of his article, he indicates his knowledge of Soviet Marxist geneticists and attempts to solidify his genetic claims by stating that "the intellectual technique of Marx, Engels and Lenin makes for clear thinking" (486). Despite Haldane's desire to validate his theory, he does follow the pattern of the eugenic family studies, Serebrovskii's "Five Year Plan," and Muller's *Out of the Night* when he shifts his focus to women without providing evidence for his claim. He gives women the most genetic influence in a family when he remarks, with seemingly no connection to the rest of the article, that "the great bulk" of a person's "group of characters [genes]" is "inherited through females only" (476). This article marks the first in a series of discussions and reviews focusing on the principles of "socialist eugenics," and it also, once again, emphasizes the importance of women in eugenics and accounts of heredity.

Even though the continued focus on women by "socialist geneticists" does not seem out of character for this particular group within the party, the CPUSA, not known for its attention to women and their issues, also began to focus on women and their social roles. Before the Popular Front, the party traditionally emphasized a dominant male rhetoric in which the words "'proletarian' and 'manly' were nearly synonymous" (Coiner 164). Leftists journals such as *New Masses* played up the role of males in the proletarian movement (Foley 221). According to Deborah Rosenfelt, "proletarian prose and criticism tended to flex their muscles with a particularly masculinist pride," and she cites Gold as one of the principal party leaders supporting this rhetoric (395–96). Gold, in a 1928 editorial article for *New Masses* titled "Go Left, Young Writers," described his version of a proletariat writer in explicit masculine terminology: "His writing is no conscious straining after proletarian art, but the natural flower of the environment. He writes that way because it is the only way for him. His 'spiritual' attitudes are all mixed up with tenements, factories, lumber camps and steel mills, because that is his life" (188–89). Coiner suggests that, in its focus on the "workplace" and on the male as the only "'worker,'" the party endorsed "the traditional sexual division of labor" (164), and since women, at least in the party's viewpoint, did not represent the "'worker,'" then women had no place in the party's rhetoric. During the Popular Front, however, women not only had to enter the workforce in order to help support their families but also made up "over 40 percent of [the party's] membership," so a shift away from the masculine agenda became necessary (Rabinowitz, *Labor* 58).

The CPUSA needed to focus attention on female workers because their wages and gender expectations left them vulnerable to employers who increasingly took advantage of them. In the southern United States, women's work in the mills revealed both that men were definitely not the only "'worker'" as Gold suggested and that women had fewer rights as "'workers'" than their male counterparts. Although lower-class women thought moving to the mills would bring "economic independence" and help them escape their subordinate social roles, once in the mills poor white women still found themselves in subordinate positions. Women made far less money than male workers. In fact, female mill workers only made "60 percent" of what the men made (Hall et al. 67). Because of these lower wages, mills preferred to hire women instead of men. *Women Who Work* author Hutchins noted that, in 1934, in North Carolina, South Carolina, Georgia, and Alabama "over 100,000 women" worked in textile mills (28). Before World War I, women not only made less money, but they were also confined to lesser jobs that offered no chance for upward mobility (Hall et al. 67–69). Women only had opportunities to work as "weavers" and "spinners" because the mill employers considered them to be "patient, neat, careful" (67–68). When the male workers left to fight in World War I, women took over their jobs and subsequently "every branch of machine shop manufacture" (Hutchins 34). At the end of the war, though, women lost their privileges as the closing of northern mills caused an oversupply of willing laborers (Hall et al. 198–200). The young, unmarried women suffered because of a lack of education and because of the social constraints placed upon them. Second-generation workers never gained the education their parents expected them to get when they moved from either their farms or the mountains (Byerly 76; Hall et al. 36). Although the children went to work early in life, as they became older these young adults, especially the girls, usually felt trapped because they saw no options for their lives other than marriage, children, and mill work (Hall et al. 158–59). Without complete financial, employment, and extracurricular freedom, these mill women really did not have the "independence" they desired.

Due to this lack of freedom, Hutchins stressed that working women could become a great force for the Communist Party. She actually urged union leaders to focus their attention on the "young girls" in the mills and on the mothers who faced "the double burden" of working at the mills and caring for their children (38, 41). The young female workers expected more from their lives than their parents did when the latter first moved to the mills in the 1880s and 1890s, and the mill mothers, whether working as sole supporters as widows or as co-supporters with their husbands, felt they had gained some power because their families did depend upon their financial support (Hall et al. 231, 310). As a result of these new personal expectations and new financial obligations, female workers wanted to increase their roles as political activists (310). Because of their desire for increased wages and shorter work days and because the women made up such a large percentage of the employees, women actually led many of the strikes that took place in the textile mill towns (213, 219). Their efforts, however, were often curbed because of their gender, with claims of "sexual misbehavior" especially being heaped upon the young, unmarried women who, as previously discussed, used their wages to enjoy themselves materially and socially (219). Despite the female workers' valid complaints, upper- and middle-class whites still labeled them as troublemakers, seemingly linking them to the sexually deviant eugenic "moron" girls whose personal actions were dangerous to society.

While the young, unmarried female workers faced opposition in their activist efforts, working mill mothers gained support. Hutchins's presentation of these lower-class female workers in her communist critique of women's work reflects this distinction. Although she urges the union to find new ways to recruit young, unmarried female workers, she never offers a way to get them effectively involved (Hutchins 38–39). On the other hand, she provides ample reasons for mill mothers to get involved, and their reasons for involvement focus not upon themselves but upon the desperation of their children. Noting that working mill mothers are "forced" to "neglect" their children in order to work and that women workers in the South are in worse conditions because of the excessively bad working conditions, Hutchins suggests that mill mothers be "organized to demand maternity insurance; day nurseries to take care of young children in connection with each industrial plant; lunches served at school for the other children; community kitchens; working hours limited to 7 a day; and above all, higher wages both for themselves and for their husbands" (56). Although Hutchins's suggestions to garner more female union support are important, only one of the suggestions, the seven-hour work day, applies to a woman who does not have a husband or children. These suggestions connect the female mill workers' activist notions to their familial obligations rather than to their personal rights. Just as Gold diminishes women's role in the workforce, so too do these suggestions by Hutchins, along with the accusations of "sexual misbehavior" against the striking mill women because the working women are still not seen as "independen[t]" laborers. Whether working on the farm, in the mills, or for the CPUSA, the women still had to defer to their family positions.

Despite women's increased membership in the CPUSA, their importance as familial supporters, and their struggle for "independence" as laborers, the party's views on women's appropriate social roles did not change, and "the traditional sexual division of labor" endorsed by the party continued.[34] Barbara Foley argues that, for the party, women's desires to break free "from the restrictions of childbearing, nuclear-family parenting, and economic independence" were not part of the "class struggle or, for that matter, Communism" (224), and just as Hutchins's suggestions for female mill workers center upon motherhood, only "as mothers" could women "find expression as historical subjects" during the Popular Front (Rabinowitz, *Labor* 58). Rabinowitz notes that, as a result of the increased female membership, the continued growth of the party during the Popular Front "depended upon a corresponding protonatalist rhetoric"; hence the party's decision to use the iconic "Mom" figure to appeal to traditional Americans (58). The CPUSA used the image of "[t]he starving child and its desperate mother" to emphasize how capitalism caused the destruction of the American family (Dixler 158). This emphasis on motherhood had become part of national politics just as much as it became a focal point for the CPUSA. Women such as Eleanor Roosevelt and Secretary of Labor Frances Perkins gave a voice through "New Deal programs" to "women's 'domestic' concerns" during the Great Depression (Rabinowitz, *Labor* 46). As a result of this mutual focus on women, the CPUSA and leaders of the New Deal even joined forces in 1937 in an effort to make Mother's Day into a day for peaceful action rather than a traditional day of recognition. Popular Front groups, Secretary Perkins, and National Labor Relations Board member Elimore M. Herrick worked together to sponsor "Mother's Day for Peace" (57). Communist and "New Deal Democrats" found common ground with "maternal values" as their core as they both emphasized the "responsibilities [of mothers] as mobilizers of family resources and nurturers of human life" (*Labor* 57; Hall et al. 310).

Their common ground, however, rested on the "maternal values" that had been focal points of the eugenics movement since Goddard's *The Kallikak Family* first appeared in 1912. Like eugenicists, leaders in the CPUSA and the Roosevelt administration did not just recognize the importance of the "mother of tomorrow" without acknowledging the problem of the reproductive capabilities of the "moron." Since mothers represented the future progress of America, the "social responsibility" of parenting rose to the forefront of these groups' focus on motherhood and family values (Kline 106). The CPUSA emphasized its commitment to family values by adopting a sexual policy that advocated "monogamous marriage" rather than "sexual promiscuity and sexual irresponsibility" (Dixler 43, 27).[35] This sexual policy, pointedly issued at women by leading party members such as Granville Hicks, allowed the party to adhere to the bourgeois standards of their new middle-class members and allowed it to set a standard by which "conventional" families were created so that mothers could enact their "social responsibility" (42–43, 48). Along with affecting the CPUSA sexual policy, the idea of "social responsibility" also affected eugenicists and the Roosevelt administration as well as the ways in which they used each other's policies to further their agendas. Since "Roosevelt's New Deal policy" called for "social responsibility" and direct governmental intervention into the "lives and welfare of the American family," eugenicists used this New Deal rhetoric of family stability and social "welfare" over individual choice to garner support for their push for sterilization laws in America (Kline 106–7). Kline also argues that Roosevelt's administration capitalized on eugenic ideas of "strengthening the race and preserving the family" because the ideas "held great public appeal and paved the way for New Deal social liberalism" and its commitment to public welfare (98–99). Americans responded to the call for "social responsibility" for both of these movements by advocating the passing of sterilization laws between 1931 and 1939 and by their acceptance of "New Deal policies" that would save the American family (107, 99).[36] As evidenced by these policies, "social responsibility" depended not just on the "nurtur[ing]" mothers but also on those women who did not have the capabilities to uphold this iconic "Mom" image.

Not only did the identities and futures of southern poor white women suffer because the scientific, social, and political campaigns of the Great Depression and the Popular Front put such a focus on motherhood, but the women also suffered because their lives and families became the main focus of proletarian novels and nonfiction documentaries of the late 1920s and the 1930s. Like the eugenicists and the political leaders of the period, the authors of these works portrayed poor white mothers as the foundation of American values and of America's regenerative ability. These saving images of the "mother of tomorrow," however, are often coupled with images of the "moron" who is set to destroy the future of America. Fiction and nonfiction works of this period are inundated with images of "ideal and failed mother figures" (Hapke 66), and usually, poor white women are only allowed to exist within these roles, even when the women in the works have gained prominence as laborers or as political activists. Because of this dominating dualistic imagery appearing in the literature, the eugenic agenda continued to find a place in American culture as well as in American politics. As a result, the "myth" of poor white motherhood, formerly only associated with eugenic family studies, became part of American ideology. Poor white mothers emerged as the symbolic holders of America's future possibilities.

Although the authors seemed to embrace the dualistic images of poor white women that eugenicists had touted, their presentations of these women emerge not as condemnations of the lower class but, instead, as documents of social questioning. Unlike eugenicists who were intent on eradicating any person who bore either physical or mental evidence of what they considered genetic inferiority, the authors of these works seem more interested in trying to understand the poor white population that eugenicists had said would prove fatal to America's future. Their works actually show a reluctance to complete the eugenicists' plan to rid America of the supposed lower-class problem in America. Instead of presenting poor whites as dangerous people intent upon creating havoc, these authors wrote their own eugenic family studies. Their studies add what the "scientific" studies leave out. Along with highlighting the eugenically damning traits, the authors also focus on the unwavering family ties, the helplessness of the family members, and even at times the strength of the family members. As a result, the families presented are not just test subjects; they seem more like real people who are not as disconnected from "normal" people as eugenicists wanted the American public to believe.

This difference in portrayals of poor white families and poor white mothers is not surprising because the American public was used to being inundated with the "positive eugenics" message. They had been told to be "the natural conservator[s] of the race" (Wiggam 280), but this literature also presents them with the question of whether Americans really want to be part of the "negative eugenics" campaign. With each family study presented, the readers and the authors are asked whether they want to take part in the abortions, segregations, and sterilizations used by eugenicists to eradicate the supposed inferiority destroying America. By focusing these works not just on the description of the families and their "supreme parent" mother but also on the future and seemingly final judgments cast on these families, the authors challenge themselves and their readers to become part of the eugenic process, thereby making it virtually impossible to focus only on the "positive" aspects of the eugenic movement in America.

2

QUESTIONING THE EUGENIC AGENDA

Faulkner, Caldwell, and Steinbeck—Three Responses to America's "Social Responsibility"

DURING THE 1930S, as the nation seemingly banded together, even reconciling opposing political viewpoints, a desire to rebuild America's economy emerged as a top priority. Although the entire nation was suffering as a result of the Depression, the plight of the South became a significant problem in efforts to bring America back to prosperity. While most of the nation considered the 1920s a "prosperous" time, the South had already begun an economic decline that only worsened with the Depression (Flynt 66). With agriculture as its main source of income, the South suffered during the 1920s due to the increasing numbers of tenant and sharecropping farmers (66). In *Dixie's Forgotten People: The South's Poor Whites,* J. Wayne Flynt has noted that, "[b]y 1930, 55.5 percent of all Southern farms were operated by tenants" (66). Of the farmers who lived as tenants, a large number actually worked as sharecroppers (67), and most of these tenant farmers and sharecroppers were white because African American families had begun moving to the cities (67). Poor white tenant families only increased their poverty by having large families. Flynt explains that the "South's birth rate was significantly higher than any other region's, producing population growth at twice the national rate" (66). Another contributing factor to the failure of the agriculture system in the South was the return to farm life by southerners who had previously moved to the mill towns only to find poor working conditions and few job opportunities. These returning families, like those that never left their farms, found that the farming system not only kept them from getting out of poverty but also put them increasingly in debt with each passing year (Flynt 70–71; Hirsch and Terrill xiv).

National interest in the plight of southern poor whites was pushed by 1930s literature, which explicitly set out to uncover poverty in the South that had seemingly gone unnoticed by politicians during the 1920s (Flynt 74–75). While southern writers such as Edith Summers Kelley, Ellen Glasgow, and Elizabeth Madox Roberts had written in the 1920s about the economic distress of rural southern poor whites, some authors of southern poor white literature in the 1930s lived outside the South, thereby indicating the increased national focus on this problem, and the 1930s novels also generated a wider audience than those of the 1920s (75). In fact, three of the most popular novelists during the 1930s made the plight of southern poor whites the focus of their novels. William Faulkner, Erskine Caldwell, and John Steinbeck emphasized the economic and moral degradation of poor whites during the Depression. Faulkner's *As I Lay Dying,* Caldwell's *Tobacco Road* and *God's Little Acre,* and Steinbeck's *The Grapes of Wrath* reached a variety of audiences as best-selling novels, television shows, Broadway plays, and Hollywood blockbuster movies.

In a period when profit seemed scarce in American society, these four novels generated a great deal of attention both from the public and from politics. Because Americans across the nation were either reading about or viewing productions based upon these novels by Faulkner, Caldwell, and Steinbeck, the literary focus helped to spur political involvement. The CPUSA, which supported proletarian literature from all regions, appreciated this literature because leftists thought of "the farmer as the virtual embodiment of the American way" (Casey 96). By connecting communist principles with this symbol of "the American way," just as they did with the iconic "Mom" image, leftists hoped to increase their credibility (96).[1] New Deal Democrats also became active in their attempts to resolve the South's economic issues. Agencies such as the Rural Rehabilitation Division and the Farm Security Administration (FSA) were formed by the Roosevelt administration in an attempt to help alleviate the Depression-increased poverty of southern poor whites (Flynt 80, 83). The FSA was actually instrumental in helping "tens of thousands of tenant families" (84–85). Although southern white poverty was not totally alleviated even with the help of New Deal policies, at least the economic destitution of poor whites had finally become a part of the national discussion with the help of popular literary appeal (92).[2]

Along with the national focus on the economic concerns of southern poor whites, eugenic concerns about this group also began to gain national attention. The economic decline of the South in the 1920s had largely gone unnoticed by the rest of the nation, but eugenicists were actively concerned during this decade with how the South was affecting the nation. As evidenced by the works of Arthur H. Estabrook, Ivan E. McDougle, and Ira Caldwell, the economic failures, the familial growth, and the sexual propagation of southern poor whites had become a concern for eugenicists hoping to create a stronger nation. In the 1920s, eugenicists addressed these concerns by supporting state-sponsored institutions that began to appear across the South and were set up to house supposedly "inferior" lower-class women (Noll, *Feeble-Minded* 4). In addition to segregating lower-class southern women, eugenicists also sterilized them along with their white male counterparts. In fact, so many sterilizations were performed on lower-class southerners that the procedures became known as "'Mississippi appendectomies'" (Smith B1).[3] For those women who did become pregnant, eugenicists supported the use of abortions (Ellis, *Studies* 4: 602).

Faulkner, Caldwell, and Steinbeck all incorporate the ideas of "socialist geneticists"; however, they do so in varied ways (Paul, "Eugenics" 14). In *As I Lay Dying,* Faulkner tackles the issue of environmental influence versus genetic influence by defining the Bundrens and, therefore, their ability to succeed by their proximity and interaction with Addie (Paul, "Eugenics" 14). *Tobacco Road* and *God's Little Acre* reflect Caldwell's adherence to the theories of "socialist geneticists"; however, Caldwell presents a much more foreboding view of his characters than did Faulkner and Steinbeck. Unlike Faulkner and Caldwell, Steinbeck reflects in *The Grapes of Wrath* more of an adherence to the theories of Bolshevik geneticists than to the traditional eugenic class-based ideology. Despite the authors' differences in how they apply the theories of "socialist geneticists," they all still use the eugenic family study method to present their ideas.

These authors also reinforce the dualistic roles forced upon southern poor white women. With the South's increasing poor white population as a national concern and a eugenic concern, Faulkner, Caldwell, and Steinbeck place their poor white female characters at the center of their own family studies, and just as they present eugenic ideology differently, they also present opposing representations of southern poor white women. While Caldwell focuses on the sexually deviant "moron" image of poor white women, Steinbeck focuses on the class-saving abilities of altruistic poor white mothers (Kline 29). Faulkner, like Caldwell, puts his main focus on the deviant image of poor white women; however, his characters garner more pity than Caldwell's because they ultimately do not want to be the burdens to their families and society that their nature makes them. By using these two distinct dualistic images of poor white women to create their characters, Faulkner, Caldwell, and Steinbeck are not only able to define their eugenic arguments with specific examples but they are also able to define their future expectations for southern poor whites hoping to escape poverty. Even Faulkner, despite his unwillingness to define the Bundren women as completely unredeemable characters, places the hopes of the family on the existence, or actually absence, of the female family members. As a result of the authors' eugenic ideologies and their use of the sexual deviant and altruistic mother images in their fictional portrayals, Faulkner, Caldwell, and Steinbeck called national attention to their poor white subjects' poverty; however, the novelists also helped to promulgate the poor white myth already attached to the culturally defined dualistic roles of poor white women perpetuated in the 1920s and the 1930s.

DESIRE WITHOUT ABILITY

In 1930, William Faulkner introduced his version of the poor white southern family in his novel *As I Lay Dying* (hereafter abbreviated *AILD*). A little over 2,500 copies were originally printed in 1930 (Karl 421), and in 1933, a "second printing" of the novel was released (Cox xxii).[4] Part of the draw of the story was Faulkner's tale about how he wrote the novel and how he characterized the Bundren family. Joseph Blotner notes that Faulkner first wrote the title "As I Lay Dying" the day after the Wall Street crash on October 25, 1929 (633), and Faulkner said he was so certain of what he wanted to put in his novel that he wrote the original draft in 47 days and that his final draft was not much different from his original draft (634, 641). Because of his timing in writing the novel, the notion that "Faulkner deliberately [...] emilinate[d ...] every vestige of moral and social significance" from the content of *AILD* seems highly unlikely (Swiggart 58).[5] In fact, *AILD* seems to have been a reaction and a response to the economic and social hazards driving America during that time. How he creates Bundren family members in the novel also suggests that he may have been acknowledging, and in some ways critiquing, the prevalent eugenic ideology of this period, especially since he centers this novel and the entire Bundren family upon a central female figure, Addie Bundren.

Faulkner's early works have been connected both to Darwinian and eugenic ideologies. In *Darwin and Faulkner's Novel: Evolution and Southern Fiction,* Michael Wainwright notes that the novelist first became aware of Darwinian ideas in 1925 at the Paris Exposition, and he further enhanced his knowledge of this topic by reading works influenced by Darwinian ideology.[6] Faulkner's connection to eugenic ideology can also be traced to his style and content. Frederick Hoffman and Robert Coughlan have argued that Faulkner was imitating the style of Aldous Huxley, a supporter of eugenics, in *Mosquitoes, The Sound and the Fury,* and *AILD* (Hoffman 42–43, Coughlan 61). Along with mimicking the style of a well-known eugenicist, Faulkner also mentions Havelock Ellis, a prominent psychologist and eugenicist, in his 1927 novel *Mosquitoes.*[7] Ellis broke convention when he openly acknowledged "that sexual desire was no less intense in women than in men" (Robinson 17). However, Ellis also argued that America's primary goal should be to "[mould] the human race" by methods such as sterilization, birth control, and—as long as they are not done by "qualified" mothers—abortions, putting into question his ultimate view of feminine sexuality.[8] Like most of his eugenic counterparts, Ellis also put the most emphasis on the mother's parenting role, arguing that the mother is directly responsible for a child's "physical needs," "intellectual development," and "sexual enlightenment" (Robinson 36). Ultimately, these duties, according to Ellis, made the mother the "supreme parent" (*Studies* 4: 2). Since eugenic ideology had become so prevalent in the late 1920s and the 1930s, Faulkner's exposure to it is not surprising.

Despite this exposure, Faulkner does not seem like a strict follower of eugenic principle because, instead of condemning those who seem genetically unfit, as eugenicists do, his characters, specifically in *AILD,* seem like an attempt to redefine eugenic ideology so that poor whites have some possibility at eugenic redemption. In this novel, Faulkner tackles issues that Ellis was also concerned with, such as feminine sexuality, abortion, and motherhood, and he uses the ever-popular eugenic prototype poor white family to present the economic woes of America, seemingly following in the pattern of eugenic family studies. However, each member of the Bundren family, including Addie, is too dynamic to fit the negative eugenic stereotype perfectly. In the *Portable Faulkner*, Malcolm Cowley has argued that Faulkner's characters are not dynamic because they have no choice in how they live and in their actions: "Even when they seem to be guided by a conscious purpose, [. . .] it is not something they have chosen by an act of will, but something that has taken possession of them" (xxiv). Cowley's definition of a Faulknerian character does not, however, fit any member of the Bundren clan. In fact, Faulkner actually negates this definition in his presentation of Addie and her relationship with her children. The Bundrens—although moved by the central figure Addie and how her life choices and her heritage have affected them mentally, morally, and economically—are not "possess[ed]" by her, and at times their individuality, unburdened by her, becomes clear. Even Addie, a seemingly failed "supreme" mother, has her redeemable moments. Taylor Hagood in his recent work *Faulkner's Imperialism: Space, Place, and the Materiality of Myth* has argued that Faulkner often writes in "the perspective of hybridity, whether in terms of race, gender, class, region, or any other formulation in which one can be 'in-between'" (18). This "hybridity" is a dominating force in *AILD* as the Bundren children struggle with how they allow their mother to influence their lives and as Faulkner struggles with how to reconcile his eugenic influences with his obvious sympathetic support of this family.

By making Addie his primary character, Faulkner centers his novel on eugenically dissecting the poor white woman and her family. David Minter has said that *AILD* is "the story of inadequate parents" who have "stunted" their children (118, 119). Although Minter assigns the blame to both Addie and Anse, eugenicists would have considered Addie the "supreme" parent as the mother; however, despite having the responsibility of being the "supreme" parent to her children, Addie does not fit the "[mould]" of the altruistic mother who has the ability to affect her children positively. Mattie Ann Burns has argued that "[w]hether she was an 'acceptable' mother is never clearly defined [. . .] nor is it a great matter" (95). This assumption by Burns, however, overlooks how important the parental mother figure had become during the late 1920s and 1930s.

For some Americans, Addie's mothering skills would have determined the course of her family. Addie bypasses the questioning, though, having to do with her family and her role therein because she openly states her disdain for motherhood. In the one central chapter she narrates, she recounts how this contempt for mothering actually started when she was a teacher, before meeting Anse. When disciplining her students, she says that she enjoyed "whip[ping]" them because beating her students became a way to make them "aware" of her pain (*AILD* 170). After finally becoming a mother to Cash, her first child, she seems to know definitively that motherhood does not suit her because his birth leads to her realization that "living was terrible" (171). Diane Roberts has argued that "Addie is not a 'true mother'" because "she is the antithesis of self-sacrifice" (201). Addie does not want to "sacrifice" for her children because that would be a "violat[ion]" of her individuality (*AILD* 172). Her desire to please herself even leads to her affair with Preacher Whitfield (174). This affair creates the only meaning that she is able to find in her life. Sally Page has read this affair positively by saying that Addie "desire[s . . .] an inner vision of perfect union and fulfillment," but Addie suffers because she never finds this perfection (112). Page does not recognize, however, that Addie's "desire[s]" during this time period would have been seen as unnatural, especially as a poor white southern mother. Her socially specified role is to fulfill her duties as a "supreme" parent and by failing, or not wanting to fill this role, Addie puts into question her genetic ability by eugenic standards and would have been seen as solely responsible for her "stunted" children.

This questioning becomes even more relevant when assessing Addie's parental influence because, although she is primarily absent from the text, she still remains its center. Deborah Clarke highlights Addie's importance by saying that "even killing the mother does not silence her" (36), and David Williams argues that Addie's role makes her "not only 'larger than life' [. . .] but larger than death as well" (103). Clarke and Williams seem to have built their arguments on the fact that Addie has managed to direct her family even after her passing. Anse confirms that this journey to Jefferson was Addie's idea (*AILD* 105), and this journey ultimately becomes like the "whip[pings]" she gave as a teacher: punishment. Not only are the family's actions still controlled by Addie, but their identities are also wrapped up in hers. After her death, Darl explains to Vardaman the separation he feels from his mother by making it seem as though they are the same person. When he tells Vardaman that he no longer has a mother, Darl says, "Because if I had one, it is was. And if it was, it cant be is. Can it? [. . .] Then am I not" (101). By declaring himself "not" real because Addie has died, Darl shows how interwoven his life is with Addie's. Donald M. Kartiganer has argued that Darl lacks a "substantial sense of himself" (25). Darl lacks this "sense of himself" because his life status relies upon her life status, which essentially takes away his individuality. Although Darl is the speaker in this situation, Darl also seems to be the representative speaker for the family since he has the ability to narrate events that do not even take place in his presence. Addie's complete control, both in life and in death, would have been disconcerting to eugenicists, who would have considered her an unfit mother. As the "supreme" parent, at least by the power she wields over her children, her violent and sexually elicit lifestyle would have made it seem as though she was infecting her children not just genetically but behaviorally as well.

Although Faulkner's dangerous presentation of Addie seems destined to lead to a negative portrayal of her children, Faulkner withdraws this complete eugenic condemnation from them by focusing on their "[hybrid]" nature. Faulkner's drawing of Addie's children does not dismiss her obviously strong influence in their lives; however, he does highlight their struggle with balancing their connection to their mother with their personal inclinations and their public personas. Michael Millgate has argued, "A major source of ironic [. . .] effects in *As I Lay Dying* is the frequency with which characters are completely mistaken in their judgments of each other, and of themselves" (106). These "mistaken [. . .] judgments" of others and self are the driving force creating the "hybridity" of the Bundren children, and these "mistaken [. . .] judgments" are generally the product of their relationship with their mother, Addie. In fact, their reactions to Addie, her death, and her burial often create contradictory images of the Bundren children that in no way seem to represent their actual natural inclinations. Irving Howe has argued that "Addie's sons, in their struggle toward self-definition, discover that to answer the question, *Who am I?,* they must first consider, *What was my mother and how did she shape me?*" (180). This connection to Addie, although necessary for their personal growth, is precisely what makes each son appear eugenically unstable.

Vardaman, Addie's youngest child, is the most obvious example of how this question and this natural connection have become a cancer upon Vardaman's emotional growth. After Addie's death, Vardaman disassociates himself from the horror of this event by declaring, "My mother is a fish" (*AILD* 84). This famous line from the novel hearkens back to the fish that Vardaman catches and cleans at the beginning of the novel. Interestingly, this fish that Vardaman believes is his mother is also the fish that "[he], and pa and Cash and Dewey Dell" dine on after Addie's death (67). By making Addie part of their diet, and therefore their nourishment, Vardaman draws the conclusion that she is, literally now, still a part of each of her family members who have partaken of her body. Although this fish association could be easily dismissed as a child's anxiety that will eventually pass, Tull, the Bundren's neighbor, is genuinely frightened by Vardaman's response to Addie's death because, when Vardaman shows up at his door mumbling about the fish and Cash and Addie's coffin, he says that Vardaman gives him the "creeps" and that the world is full of "sorrow and afflictions" (70–71). Tull's pondering about "sorrow and afflictions" is clearly related to Addie's death, but he also seems to reference the mental "[affliction]" that has fallen upon Vardaman. Unlike Tull, who credits his wife Cora with "guard[ing]" him from these problems, Vardaman not only does not have a "guard" in Addie, but Addie is the very reason for his "creep[y . . .] afflictions" (71). For Tull, Vardaman's age and familial tragedy do not overcome the awkward mental state that has taken over the child.

Like Vardaman, Cash responds to his mother's death in a way that creates a false impression of him that does not match his usual behavioral patterns. At the beginning of the novel, as Addie's life comes to a close, Cash is a dominant figure in her life, but only because he positions himself outside the window so that she can see him building her coffin (*AILD* 14). Even after Addie dies, his main focus remains on the coffin and its proper construction. In fact, Cash's mind has become so narrowly concentrated that his narrative is not a story or a collection of his thoughts but a list of his steps in building the coffin so that it will be suited for Addie's body (82–83). This list provides the structure and order that his life is lacking without his mother, but it also makes him appear cold and heartless. His obsession with the coffin problem also extends into their journey to Jefferson because he constantly worries about it being off "balance" (97).

The work to which Cash dedicates himself appears fruitless because the coffin actually becomes a complete disaster as holes are bored into her face and as it gets overturned in the river (88, 150). Ironically, though, Cash has a reputation of being a "good carpenter" (24), so his failure in building Addie's coffin seems inconsistent with his actual abilities. Cash explains this discrepancy. In the list he provides of his actions, Cash admits that he is making the coffin "on the bevel" because of Addie's "animal magnetism" (83). Since he repeatedly uses phrases such as "sideways" and "slant" in his list as well, Cash seems to be associating his mother's "animal magnetism" with an unbalanced force (82–83). Just as Vardaman becomes emotionally burdened by Addie's death, Cash becomes burdened with the desire to "fix" his mother's "sideways" behavior even in her death. However, despite his best effort, he cannot succeed in this personal challenge, and his failure becomes one of the focal points of the novel.

Just as Cash attempts to disconnect himself from Addie's "sideways" behavior by trying to "bevel" her coffin, though unsuccessfully, Darl also allows his mother's life to control his emotions and his personal choices. Like Vardaman, Darl is emotionally distraught by his mother and her death; however, unlike Vardaman, Darl feels extreme anger toward his mother and her ruling of the lives of their entire family. He wants to disassociate himself from their familial status so much that he constantly refers to his mother as "Addie" throughout the novel, stripping them of their intimate mother/son relationship. Not only does Darl act cruelly towards his mother, but he also reacts angrily to his siblings because, for him, they represent Addie. At one point, Darl actually taunts Jewel, Addie's favored son, by saying, "[D]o you know that Addie Bundren is going to die? Addie Bundren is going to die" (*AILD* 40). Darl desires to separate himself from his mother so much that he lashes out at anybody who elicits her attention or love. He seems unable to reconcile his need for a mother with the mother he has been allotted, who he feels has betrayed his family. This anger even leads him to burn down Gillespie's barn, which ultimately leads to his commitment to a mental institution. All of these actions—the disassociation, the anger, and the violence—make Darl seem like a perfect candidate for eugenic intervention; however, Darl does not act without provocation. He displays such anger and disrespect for Addie because she has participated in an adulterous relationship, and he ultimately burns the barn to burn her body and perhaps save his family from the burden of the journey. His efforts to save his family, though, only end in destruction, just as Cash's do, because the last time Darl is allowed to narrate the story, he has become emotionally detached completely, referring to himself in the third person and "laughing" uncontrollably (254).

Unlike the other children in the family, Jewel is the product of Addie's affair with Whitfield, which immediately would have made him a eugenic concern; however, he too possesses traits that make him a "[hybrid]" character. Jewel does not know that Anse is not his father, but Darl hints at Addie's indiscretion when he says, "Your mother was a horse, but who was your father, Jewel?" (*AILD* 212). This type of antagonism leads to a separation between Jewel and his siblings, which causes Jewel to react in fits of anger. For example, when Cash worries about keeping Addie's coffin on "balance" during the ride to Jefferson, Jewel screams, "Pick up, goddamn your thick-nosed soul to hell, pick up!" (96). Jewel's anger is reminiscent of his mother's reaction to her students during her time as a schoolteacher. Not only does Jewel's anger make him seem like a disturbed Bundren, but his seeming lack of interest in Addie's death also makes him appear emotionless. When Jewel is not cursing over Addie's dead body and throwing her coffin into the wagon, he generally spends his time taking care of his horse. Darl actually repeats the phrase "Jewel's mother is a horse" because Jewel nurtures the horse and worries about the horse, not his family, during the journey, especially when the Bundrens try to cross the river. Cora says that Jewel only cares about "doing something that [makes] him money or [gets] him talked about" (24). Although these violent and self-serving images of Cash do diminish his character, Jewel's own version of his love for his mother solidifies these traits as products of his despair. In fact, he imagines keeping her all to himself so that he can protect her before she dies: "It would just be me and her on a high hill and rolling the rocks down the hill at their faces and teeth and all by God until she was quiet" (15). Because this scene also exhibits his violence, he showcases how his mother's death and his need to save her makes him so desperate, and like Vardaman with his fish, Jewel needs something, anything, to help distract him from this pain, which for Jewel is his horse.

Although the children's seemingly negative traits are connected to Addie, she actually does realize the problems she has caused, and she desires to right these wrongs, which ultimately denotes her "[hybrid]" nature as well. Unlike the women of the eugenic studies who seem unconcerned by how they are affecting society, Addie is burdened by her transgressions. She tries to correct her affair and the child it produced by giving Anse two more children, Dewey Dell and Vardaman (*AILD* 175). Not only does she try to earn peace in her relationship with Anse, but she also tries to earn peace with Jewel, the son she feels as though she has scarred just by having him. When Jewel deceives his family by working Mr. Quick's land to buy his horse rather than doing his chores, Addie does not reprimand Jewel; instead, she weeps for him and the trouble and the lying that she believes she has passed onto him (135–36). Both of these attempts to make amends backfire on Addie. Warwick Waddlington has referred to Addie as "the center of a web of mutual betrayals and revenges running throughout the family" (35). This "web" actually begins because she divides her children. Addie shows the most affection to Cash and Jewel, the two who are specifically hers, and this favoritism causes anger, cruelty, and violence amongst the siblings. The favoritism that Addie shows toward Jewel also leads to her teaching her children the very trait for which she is trying to make amends: "deceit" (136). Watching Addie's reaction to Jewel's lies, Darl becomes aware that Addie is crying over her "deceit" just as much as she is crying for Jewel's, and because Darl is obsessed with understanding why his mother dotes on Jewel, he deduces that Addie's deception is connected to Jewel (136). Addie's "deceit," despite her "hat[red]" of it, is just as much the foundation for that "web of mutual betrayals and revenges" as her favoritism (136).

Dewey Dell's "hybridity" does not reveal, as her brothers' does, how Addie's absence redeems her; instead, her "hybridity" is closely akin to Addie's because Faulkner presents Dewey Dell who also wants to right her wrongs but cannot. David Williams describes Dewey Dell as "the mirror image of her mother" (110). This reflection is a product of the two women's extracurricular sexual activities. Although Dewey Dell does not cheat on a husband, she does engage in premarital sex with Lafe, a boy from town. Diane Roberts argues that Faulkner's sexual characterization of Dewey Dell showcases her as a positive figure because "she does not challenge the conventional definition of the feminine but fulfills it" (202); however, Roberts overlooks how many negative eugenic traits are highlighted through Dewey Dell. Not only does Dewey Dell appear like the poor white seductress about whom eugenicists warned "normal" men, but her description of why they had sex makes her urges seem uncontrollable. She says that she *had* to have sex, emphasizing four times that she "could not" stop her sexual desires (*AILD* 27). Although Mary Michele Bendel-Simso argues that Dewey Dell says this to "[legitimate] her sexual desire," this description actually resembles some of the stories of the poor white female women of eugenic studies (75). Faulkner may also have been following Ellis's theory that women had just as much sexual desire as men; however, because the product of this interclass relationship is a child, Faulkner also raises the question as to whether this sexuality is dangerous.

Dewey Dell tries to solve her pregnancy problem, but like Addie, she finds that her attempts are unsuccessful and actually cause more social disruption. After having an initial emotional reaction to Addie's death, Dewey Dell concentrates for the remainder of the novel on how to get an abortion. Even this focus seems sporadic, though. Dewey Dell describes how she feels about Addie's death and about her unborn child by saying, "I try to but cant think long enough to worry. [. . .] I dont know how to worry. I dont know how to cry. I tried, but I cant" (*AILD* 59, 60). This confusing statement makes her seem emotionally disturbed, like her brothers, but it also puts into question her mental capacity because of her inability to "think long enough" (59). Her plan to get an abortion would have been a plan that Ellis would have agreed with because she would not have fit his "qualified" standards; however, she even fails to abort her baby correctly. First, Moseley, a pharmacist in Mottson, denies her (203), and then, MacGowan tricks her into having sex with him for his fake abortion concoction (247). Her inability to complete this task is disturbing as seen from Ellis's perspective about how the mother is the "supreme" parent, and her final sexual encounter with MacGowan adds to the disturbing effect because Dewey Dell does not seem affected by his deceit. In fact, the only emotion she shows is anger because she knows he has not given her the remedy she so desires (251). As a result, Dewey Dell ends the novel by making herself seem like a potentially negative future social influence. Because of Dewey Dell's sexual openness with Lafe and MacGowan, eugenicists would have argued that she leaves little doubt that this first illegitimate child is *just* the first.

Despite the final disturbing prospect that Dewey Dell will, in fact, become the mother of a child, Faulkner does not end the novel with a sense of desperation. Actually, the novel ends with a sense of future hope for most of the Bundrens, and this hope seems like a product of the family's ability to move on mentally and emotionally from Addie's death. Anse, Addie's husband, is generally considered throughout the story to be lazy and worthless both by the townspeople and by his children; however, by the end, Cash describes him as "holding his head up" and "proud" (*AILD* 260). Addie's self-constructed burial journey has allowed him to get teeth and, as a result, to feel like a new man (260). Vardaman transitions from talking about his mother as a fish to sitting contentedly in the buggy, eating a banana, no longer acting as a "creep[y]" child (260). Cash has even grown as a person during the journey because, instead of citing lists, one of his last chapters to narrate reveals how he has moved beyond his desire for structure and has begun to empathize with his siblings, especially Darl (*AILD* 233; David Williams 117). Jewel, the son once defined by anger and self-interest, willingly gives up his horse for his family after the river debacle (*AILD* 193). Darl is the only son who does not change for the better, and Vardaman acknowledges this difference when he analyzes the changes that have happened to his family between Addie's death and the end of their journey: "[Darl] went to Jackson [. . .] lots of people didn't go crazy. Pa and Cash and Jewel and Dewey Dell and me didn't go crazy" (251). What separates Anse, Cash, and Jewel from Darl is that they all let go of Addie and stop letting her "guide" their lives. In fact, Faulkner highlights the importance of Addie's removal even further by giving Anse a new Mrs. Bundren, a town woman with a gramophone, who already seems to have been a positive influence on Anse (260). Patricia R. Schroeder argues that "the Bundrens end up triumphing over Addie's death and reintegrating themselves into the society of the living" (35). However, despite the initial impulse to think of the Bundrens as starting a fresh, positive life with their seemingly more "qualified" mother, Faulkner highlights what Vardaman, in his youth, does not understand when he makes his list of family members who have survived Addie: Dewey Dell's pregnancy. Because Dewey Dell, "the mirror of her mother," with her illegitimate child is still part of this family and still struggling, without success, to right the wrongs she has committed and possibly will commit, a shadow still follows this family that has only just become unburdened by Addie's negative influence.

Just as Faulkner creates a "[hybrid]" representation of the Bundren family that does not always fit eugenic convention, he also reveals conflicting attitudes among the townspeople who interact with the Bundrens. The most harsh attitude directed at the Bundrens, specifically Dewey Dell, comes from MacGowan. He justifies his sexual manipulation of Dewey Dell by calling her a "[c]ountry woman" (*AILD* 241), and rather than making him seem like a victim of Dewey Dell's sexual prowess, he seems more like a predator. Although this scene is disturbing, most of the people are kind towards the Bundrens. Sylvia Jenkins Cook notes that Faulkner emphasizes the townspeople's "charity[, . . .] compassion[,] and resilience" in dealing with the Bundrens (*From Tobacco* 46). Cora and Tull frequently visit Addie on her deathbed, and Tull even sacrifices his mule when they try unsuccessfully to cross the river (*AILD* 127). Samson allows the Bundrens to spend the night in his barn because the rain interrupts their journey (115). Their "charity" makes this family's poverty seem "accepted" rather than "horr[ific]" (Cook, *From Tobacco* 46). Faulkner even extends the "charity" given to the Bundrens to include hope. Moseley not only refuses to help Dewey Dell have an abortion, but he also tells her that "the Lord" gave her that baby (*AILD* 203). This completely contradicts Ellis's eugenic perspective that abortion is appropriate, at least for mothers who are not "qualified." Despite the overwhelmingly positive town reactions, though, the novel contains an ever present sense of anger from the townspeople because of the Bundrens' poor choices, and the townspeople are particularly angered by their decision to take the journey itself, which they consider "trouble" (89). Ironically, the townspeople blame Anse for this "trouble," instead of Addie. Because of all these conflicting responses to the Bundrens, Faulkner seems just as unwilling to define the Bundrens' public perceptions as he is to define their character descriptions.

Although Faulkner may not have been willing to characterize the Bundrens as unredeemable characters hampered by genetic inferiority, critics' reviews of *AILD* declared the Bundrens a model of the eugenically inferior family. In a review for *The Saturday Review of Literature,* Basil Davenport referred to *AILD* as a novel focused on "mental abnormality" with a "grim and unrelieved" tone (362). Kenneth White said that the novel is filled with "steadily increasing horror" that "[does] not offer a pleasant or inspiring view of humanity" ("Notes on Novels" 27). Clifton Fadiman's review, "Morbidity in Fiction," actually highlighted that Faulkner uncovers "the phosphorescent rottenness of the [Bundren] family" (501). These reviewers are not focused on the complex "hybridity" of the Bundrens and their chance at redemption after the death of their mother; instead, they seem to think that Faulkner's purpose is to expose the Bundrens as monsters who do not fit the "pleasant" image of "humanity." The reviewers further reveal the characters' eugenically deficient qualities, not just in the ways they describe the novel, but also in the ways they describe the Bundrens. Davenport calls them "shiftless poor whites" burdened by "a strain of insanity" (362). White refers to the Bundrens as "a poor and ignorant family" ("Notes on Novels" 27). Fadiman places all the Bundrens in the same category: characters with "distorted mentalities" ("Morbidity" 500).

The review in *The New York Times Book Review* titled "A Witch's Brew" offers the most blatant eugenic description of the Bundrens, labeling them "a witch's brew of a family" that "suggests inbreeding of the sort that undoubtedly weakens the stock in certain of our backwood districts" (6). Despite Faulkner's efforts to highlight how each Bundren child's negative attributes can be directly connected to his or her relationship to Addie and how each of their lives, except for Dewey Dell's, has been altered in a positive way by Addie's death, these reviewers, like most eugenicists, could not see beyond what is eugenically categorized as moral and mental failure. The reviewers' impressions could possibly have also been steered by Dewey Dell's unborn child, which seemingly represents a new generation of this "witch's brew." Ultimately, they did not share in any of Faulkner's sympathy for the Bundrens.

Despite the reviewers' interpretations, Faulkner's use of "hybridity" in his characters shows that he is not only unwilling to condemn this family, but he also reveals a compassion and understanding for the supposed "degenerate" people this family represents. Myra Jehlen argues that in *AILD* Faulkner "explores the limits of perception and language precisely because [. . .] he is driven to pierce false masks, the myths which he is coming more and more to realize have distorted Southern reality. In other words, Faulkner cares so much about perception in these novels because there is something he wants to see clearly but can't" (42). The "myth" Faulkner has focused his attention on dispelling is the eugenic one that poor whites have a natural tendency for genetic inferiority. In fact, Faulkner seems to highlight how most poor whites are not degenerate at all. His version of the southern poor white family is actually a "[hybrid]" in itself. In his presentation of Addie's sons, Faulkner blames environmental circumstances for their behavior, and just as environmentalists argued, once the sons were removed from their mother's behavior, their personalities changed in a positive way. For Addie and Dewey Dell, however, environmental influences do not alter their deficiencies. Addie is consistently driven by a desire to please herself, and Dewey Dell is driven by her sexual desires. Neither of the women ever emerges as a capable woman who is able to take on that role of "supreme parent" successfully. Moreover, because their attempts to become better women by social standards are continually thwarted, Faulkner does make their lives seem hopeless, especially since Dewey Dell seems destined to follow in her mother's footsteps.

In spite of these conflicting images of hope and hopelessness, Faulkner does create an overall sense of sympathy for each character. In fact, the Bundrens reflect Faulkner's definition of man that he offered years later in 1950 when he accepted his Nobel Prize for Literature. Each member of the Bundren family, even Addie and Dewey Dell, has "a soul" and is "capable of compassion and sacrifice and [. . .] endurance" (Faulkner, "Address" 724). His sympathy and hope for these characters are seemingly what keep Faulkner from ending Dewey Dell's story with a successful abortion. Just as Faulkner is unwilling to confine any of the Bundrens completely to the eugenically dangerous category, he also seems unwilling to let Dewey Dell's child be sacrificed to popular eugenic ideology. What he does seem willing to do, though, is shine a light on women like Addie because, although the town may have been fooled into thinking Anse was the family's burden, Faulkner makes it clear that Addie is the true source of the family's problems.

THE POWER OF SEX

At the beginning of the 1930s, Erskine Caldwell, son of eugenicist Ira Caldwell, authored two books that helped him become a best-selling author and that helped bring the plight of southern poor whites into national focus. *Tobacco Road* and *God's Little Acre* "sold millions of copies, tens of millions, and were translated into forty-three languages" (Nordan vi). Literary critics and Communist Party members such as Malcolm Cowley and Mike Gold considered Caldwell one of the top American authors of the early twentieth century (Miller 155, 156). Even William Faulkner placed Caldwell on his list of top five American authors of the 1930s (Miller xii). While both of the novels attained success as literary works, they also garnered attention because of their crossover appeal and lurid content. *Tobacco Road* was rewritten as a play by Jack Kirkland and made into a successful Broadway production (Nordan vi). *God's Little Acre* gained attention because it became the focus of an obscenity charge brought by the New York Society for the Suppression of Vice in 1933. Influential authors such as H. L. Mencken and Sinclair Lewis, along with many other writers, helped Caldwell challenge this case and defeat the charges (Miller 176). This negative publicity only helped to bolster the sales of the novel. *Tobacco Road* and *God's Little Acre* were also converted into successful Hollywood movies in 1941 and 1957, respectively (285, 365–66).[9] With their success and their controversy, both novels remained at the center of national attention and helped to keep the nation's focus on the degrading poverty of southern poor whites.

The attention was not exactly positive, however, and the first installment of Caldwell's successful portrayal of poor whites, *Tobacco Road,* sets the stage for the conflicting interpretations of his work. In 1932, when the novel was published, reviewers such as James Gray and Jack Conroy read it as Caldwell's call for social justice for southern poor whites. Gray argued that the novel forced Americans who assumed that all people shared a "high standard of life" to stop overlooking "the squalor that exists in hidden corners" (15), and although Conroy thought that Caldwell did not show enough sympathy for his characters, he called *Tobacco Road* "a social document of no small importance" (18). Even though Gray and Conroy focused on the "social [...] importance" of the novel, other critics could not disregard their criticisms of how Caldwell presented his poor white characters. Kenneth White referred to the novel as "comic" and to Caldwell's social commentary as "cheap sentimentality" ("American Humor" 19). J. Raiford Watkins, who actually praised the novel as "a great story," did not see the characters as sentimental or "comic"; instead, his review reads much like the reviews for *AILD.* He called the characters "the lowest element of the white race in the state," and representatives of a "pitiable small percentage of backwoods people reduced to miserable semi-savagery" (12). Although Caldwell said that he wrote *Tobacco Road* as a way to help the impoverished white community, his degenerate and animalistic portrayals of the characters overshadowed, for some critics, any positive intention he may have had, especially since his images reflected the negative social perception of poor whites in the early twentieth century.

In fact, with Caldwell's connection to the eugenics movement through his father, the conflicting perceptions of the novelist's work become increasingly pertinent. Caldwell's creation of the Lester family can even be traced to the eugenic family study, "The Bunglers," written by his father, Ira. Both works are set in Wrens, Georgia, the town that Ira Caldwell moved the Bunglers to in an effort to lift them from their poverty (Miller 124). Caldwell also models Sister Bessie and Dude on two members of the Bungler family highlighted in his father's articles ("The Bunglers" 334). Along with these specific connections between *Tobacco Road* and the Bungler articles, Caldwell, like his father, continually reiterates the degrading poverty that the Lesters must face and what seems to be their unwillingness to improve their situation. Jeeter Lester, the father of the family, refuses to move his wife, mother, and two remaining children to the cotton mill towns, so they have to live destitute in a rotted, wooden tenant shack (Caldwell, *Tobacco* 15, 16). Rather than move to the cotton mill town, Jeeter desires to maintain his rural way of life on the land that his grandfather and father once owned, but since his father's time as a farmer, the family's prosperity has steadily decreased until Jeeter's family has reached poverty (63–65). Eugenicists considered this unwillingness to move in pursuit of prosperity as an indication of a genetic weakness, as evidenced by the articles by Thomas Nixon Carver and Arthur H. Estabrook. Of course, even though Jeeter chooses to stay in a rural area, he has not actually done any farming in "seven or eight years," according to his wife, Ada (59). Like the Bunglers, who have become worse off with each generation and who choose poverty, the Lesters really do seem like the problematic poor whites about whom eugenicists such as Caldwell's father, Carver, and Estabrook worried.

Unlike the Bundrens of *AILD,* who are almost all redeemed after Addie's passing, the Lester family of *Tobacco Road* is overwhelmed by the negative characteristics eugenicists associated with "inferior" poor whites, making this family's fate seem hopeless. Jeeter and Ada Lester, despite their poverty, have "seventeen children," five of whom have died (Caldwell, *Tobacco* 6, 65). Of their twelve remaining children, only two of them, Ellie May and Dude, continue to live at home, and Jeeter and Ada do not know where nine of their children now live (66, 6). Ada even remarks that she cannot remember some of their children's names (75). Both of the children who remain at home have the "inferior" characteristics associated with poor whites. Dude is described as "not hav[ing] very much sense," and his daily activity generally consists of bouncing a ball off of the Lesters' rotted house (31, 6–7). Ellie May is afflicted with a physical disfigurement that eugenicists would have recognized as a "Mendelizing human character": a harelip (Kellicott 142). Even Sister Bessie, the woman Dude marries, has a physical disfigurement. Her nose has "failed to develop properly," and as a result, it "has no bone in it [. . . and] no top to it" (45). With this abundance of "inferior" traits, Caldwell's presentation of the Lester family seems categorically influenced by eugenic concerns.

Although the entire family displays "inferior" characteristics, the afflictions of the women in the Lester family make them seem like victims not only of physical disfigurement but also of "mental" and "moral" deficiencies (Kellicott 143), and as a result, they oftentimes appear even more deficient than the other Lesters and capable of pulling their family members even further into depravity. In fact, Ellie May and Sister Bessie both resemble the stereotypical "moron" girl afflicted with feeblemindedness and sexual deviancy. Although men usually do not take interest in Ellie May because of her harelip, her sexual appetite does not seem to have suffered. Caldwell actually introduces Ellie May by having her seduce Lov, the husband of her younger sister Pearl. During the seduction scene, Ellie May acts so perversely sexual that Dude compares her actions to those of the family's "old hound [. . .] when he got the itch" (Caldwell, *Tobacco* 18). Later, after she has forced herself onto Lov, she lies in the yard "twitch[ing] nervously" long after Lov leaves (39). Not only does Ellie May's seduction of Lov highlight her overwhelming and seemingly violent sexual desire, but it also highlights how "inferior" her family is in relation to other groups. During this entire episode with Lov, a group of black men stands across the road from the Lesters' home, watching and "laughing" as Ellie May and Lov struggle in the yard (33–35). Eugenicists Estabrook and Ivan E. McDougle in *Mongrel Virginians: The Win Tribe* noted that miscegenation had become a "growing" fear for southerners and eugenicists because southern poor whites and various other groups had begun to have racially mixed children who could pass for white (7). Although this scene in *Tobacco Road* seems to draw upon those fears because the black men have seemingly been given access to Ellie May's sexuality by the other Lesters who let them watch, the black men actually place themselves above Ellie May and her family because they have openly said previously that they would never "fool with Ellie May, unless it was the nighttime" (Caldwell, *Tobacco* 29). For these black men, sleeping with Ellie May would not be a chance to have sexual relations with a white woman and to have light-skinned children who could "pass" for white; instead, to them, Ellie May and her family are a sideshow for their entertainment. Even the black men's disdain for Ellie May, though, cannot keep her from having an orgasm openly in the yard and her family from helping Ellie May trap Lov for her pleasure.

Sister Bessie's obsessive sexuality not only affects the Lester family but also other lower-class and middle-class whites. Sister Bessie does not act like an evangelist who has just lost her husband; in fact, she perverts her supposed religious authority by seducing sixteen-year-old, feebleminded Dude in front of his family. While praying with Dude and the other Lesters, Sister Bessie and Dude fondle one another as the other Lesters watch (Caldwell, *Tobacco* 51, 55). After Dude and Sister Bessie get married, her sexuality reaches a new plateau one night in Augusta, Georgia, when she is used as a prostitute in a brothel (150). Instead of being upset the next day, she only says, "I had the best time last night. [. . .] They sure know how to treat women real nice," and she even desires to return to that hotel at a later date (152). The hotel manager seems to know when he sees Sister Bessie that he can use her as a prostitute and that she will not complain, and as he has suspected, Sister Bessie never questions him about the night's events and never collects any money for her services (145). Despite her disfigurement, Sister Bessie's proclivity for having sex made her a target for any man to use her who would have her. Just as eugenicists feared that sexually deviant women would cause the corruption not only of lower-class "inferior" men but also of supposedly "normal" men, Sister Bessie seems like the typical "moron" girl who is a danger to society (Rafter, *Creating Born* 160).

While Ellie May and Sister Bessie represent the type of women that eugenicists would have recognized as socially dangerous, Pearl, the youngest Lester child and the character Watkins calls the "outstanding personage" of the novel, does not share any of the detrimental qualities with these women or even with the rest of her family (12). Unlike Ellie May and Dude, Pearl is incredibly beautiful and intelligent. She is described as incapable of ever appearing "plain or ordinary-looking" because she becomes "more beautiful everyday," and she apparently has "more sense than any of the Lesters" (Caldwell, *Tobacco* 25, 31). Since so much emphasis is put on how different Pearl looks and acts compared to her family, the other Lesters' "inferior" characteristics actually seem heightened. How the other Lesters treat Pearl also shows the divide in this familial behavior. Pearl's marriage to Lov is the product of a business deal between Lov and Jeeter (25); however, Pearl refuses to talk to Lov or to sleep with him, further distancing her behavior from that of Ellie May and Sister Bessie.[10] Even though Lov keeps trying to beat Pearl, literally, into submission, Pearl refuses to return to the Lester home because she feels just as out of place in her family's home as she does in Lov's (2–3). This emotional distance between Pearl and the rest of her family becomes clear when the identity of Pearl's biological father is revealed. Pearl's father is not Jeeter, but a man with whom Ada had an extramarital affair (31). Although this information first suggests that Jeeter is the cause of the other children's inferiority, Caldwell specifically notes that Pearl "inherited" her "sense" and her beautiful physical appearance from her biological father (31). Instead of giving Ada some reprieve from her children's deficiencies, Caldwell suggests that this man's "superior" traits just overpowered her negative traits. In fact, just by making Pearl a product of an adulterous relationship, Caldwell indicts Ada for her sexuality just as he does Ellie May and Sister Bessie. Fortunately for Pearl and her biological father, they escape the degeneracy of the Lester family. Ada's lover left for Texas shortly after their sexual encounter, and Pearl does what the Lesters refuse to do when she "run[s] off" to Augusta hoping to find a better life for herself away from her "family" (166–67).

Although the Lesters, with the exception of Pearl, seem plagued by "inferior" physical, "mental," and "moral" characteristics, Caldwell refuses to blame them completely for their economic downfall. He also blames Captain John Harmon, the man who employed Jeeter as a sharecropper and whom Jeeter depended upon for economic support. When the captain left for the city, however, he took his store credit with him and abandoned the Lesters without the ability to farm (Caldwell, *Tobacco* 65). One of the reasons that Conroy called *Tobacco Road* a "social document" was because he considered the captain the villain (18). Just as the captain does not help the Lesters, neither do the townspeople. Unlike the townspeople in *AILD,* Caldwell's townspeople actually make the Lesters' lives worse. When Sister Bessie and Dude buy their car, the salesmen ridicule them and sell them an overpriced vehicle (Caldwell, *Tobacco* 88–93). With these statements about society's unwillingness to help the Lesters, Caldwell acknowledges that, although they may be "inferior" and may choose to stay in the rural area to their economic detriment, they have also been hindered by other environmental factors out of their control, similar to Ira Caldwell's conclusion in the Bungler articles. Caldwell actually makes the captain and the townspeople, the supposedly "normal" people, seem just as "morally bankrupt" as the Lesters (Keely 42).

Regardless of Caldwell's decision not to place complete responsibility on the Lesters for their downfall, the remaining Lesters seem content to continue Jeeter and Ada's legacy. After Jeeter and Ada burn in their home, Dude, Sister Bessie, Ellie May, and Lov decide to stay together in the desolate rural area. Since Pearl has run away, Ellie May has taken her place in Lov's home, and he has accepted her role as his new "wife" (Caldwell, *Tobacco* 183). Dude, with Sister Bessie by his side, destines himself to become an inert farmer "like [his] Pa" (184). Leigh Anne Duck has argued that Caldwell has the remaining Lesters stay in the rural South because, by keeping them in a "fixated temporality" away from the rest of society, upper- and middle-class whites do not have to "[fear]" that these type of people will invade their territory (99–101). With these two couples riding together in Dude and Sister Bessie's car heading towards Lov's house, which the four of them now refer to as "their house," Caldwell may be confirming that they will stay on the farm; however, he is also highlighting the beginning of two new families just at the beginning of growth.

While Sister Bessie's excessive sexual activity has never led to children before—making her relationship with Dude seem less dangerous—Ellie May's only sexual encounter so far, presumably, has been with Lov in the yard at the beginning of the novel. As a result, Caldwell opens the door for the "inferior" Ellie May and the brutal Lov to begin their own family and to create another generation of seemingly genetically "inferior" Lesters who also threaten the nation's future growth. In a 1932 review of *Tobacco Road,* Jonathan Daniels argued that this ending diminished his hope for Ellie May and Dude because their futures seem so bleak (25). Despite this tragic ending, though, Caldwell's unwillingness to blame the Lesters completely for their poverty makes him seem, like his father, reluctant to condemn a family that has been so negatively affected by its environment and that has not had all the advantages necessary for success.

Despite the novel's later success, *Tobacco Road* was not immediately accepted by the American public because of mixed critical reviews and its overtly sexual content (Miller 137–42, 147).[11] The CPUSA, however, not only saw potential in Caldwell's work, but its leaders also wanted Caldwell to write specifically for their cause (155–56), and after the release of *Tobacco Road,* Caldwell became increasingly involved with members of the CPUSA. Along with associating with leftist critics during the 1930s such as Cowley and Matthew Josephson, Caldwell also became a client of Maxim Lieber, a "tough, ruthless" literary agent "committed to leftist causes" (143, 155). Gold, editor of *New Masses,* also became a frequent companion of Caldwell. Even though Gold was bothered by Caldwell's "grotesque" portrayals of poor whites, he recognized the potential for greatness in Caldwell's literary style and in his "real-life" knowledge of southern poor white life (156). As evidenced by Gold's critique of Caldwell's writing, reviewers such as Conroy were not the only critics willing to overlook Caldwell's unsympathetic representations of poor white life.

Because of these new political influences in Caldwell's life, though, recent critics such as Caldwell's biographer, Dan B. Miller, and Sarah C. Holmes have had trouble reconciling Caldwell's "grotesque" portrayals with his communist beliefs, especially since his follow-up novel, *God's Little Acre,* is as unflattering to poor whites as *Tobacco Road.*[12] Miller admits to contradictions in Caldwell's works despite also arguing that Caldwell's original plan for *God's Little Acre,* outlined in his 1931 application cover letter for the John Simon Guggenheim Memorial Foundation, specifically reflects communist principles (159). In the letter, Caldwell wrote, "[M]y aim is to write a full length novel of proletarian life in the South. [. . . N]o one with any degree of sureness has pointed out the direction that the masses must take in order to keep from falling below the deplorable standard of living [. . .]. And the problem, while acute to the masses, is of even greater significance, or should be, to the Nation at large" (63–64).[13] While Caldwell does focus on communist principles in *God's Little Acre,* especially when he includes the mill town strike as a subplot, he still defines his poor white characters, whether on the farm or in the mill town, by their inferiority and their sexuality. To explain Caldwell's decision not to follow the communist principles fully that he discussed in his application letter, Miller has suggested that Caldwell mixed his own "personal sensibility" with leftist ideals (159). Of course, the "personal sensibility" that Caldwell adds to *God's Little Acre,* once again, reflects his connection to the eugenics movement, specifically the theories of "socialist geneticists."

Caldwell's decision to incorporate "socialist geneticist" ideology is recognizable from the beginning of *God's Little Acre* because the Walden family does not have the same environmental roadblocks that Caldwell emphasizes in his story of the degenerating Lester family. Actually, in *God's Little Acre,* Caldwell seems to have once again followed his father's eugenic example by placing his new poor white family, the Waldens, in the same sort of modestly successful environment that Ira Caldwell attempted to create for the Bunglers. While the Lester family seems like "a Southern Gothic version of Goddard's Kallikak family, with Jeeter Lester presiding as patriarch over a collection of mental, physical, and behavioral misfits" (Keely 26), the Walden family does not seem to fit into the category of poor white because they do not really suffer economically and because none of the family members suffer from any of Kellicott's "Mendelizing" characteristics that would identify them as physically "inferior." As Wayne Mixon in *The People's Writer: Erskine Caldwell and the South* has pointed out, the Waldens are different from the Lesters because they own their own land, employ two black sharecroppers, and have an abundance of food (53).[14] While the Lesters battle each other for stolen turnips, the Waldens have more than enough food for themselves and for their guests, and just as their environment does not control them, the Waldens have also escaped the stigma of physical disfigurement that Ellie May and Sister Bessie must contend with in *Tobacco Road.* In *God's Little Acre,* Caldwell describes Darling Jill, Griselda, and Will as so physically "superior" that he creates a sense of erotic fantasy around them. Pluto idolizes Darling Jill so much that he thinks God put too much effort into creating her; Ty Ty describes Griselda as "the prettiest of them all" (Caldwell, *God's* 29–30); and Will has the appeal of a hero, "the carrier and symbol of a Power to which . . . all [do] homage" (Beach 243). Rather than suffering from poverty and having telltale "Mendelizing" traits, the Waldens live modestly and actually seem to represent ideal images of beauty and masculinity.

Despite the economic and physical differences between the Lesters and the Waldens, however, the "mental" and "moral" capabilities of the Waldens make the Waldens and the Lesters seem like versions of the same family. The Waldens actually display similar behavioral characteristics to the Lesters that put into question their physical and economic superiority. Just as the Lesters seem unaffected by violent activities, so too do the Waldens, and ironically, most of the Waldens' violent behavior is directed toward each other. At one point, Buck and Shaw, Ty Ty's sons, beat their brother-in-law, Will, over the head with a shovel (Caldwell, *God's* 97–99). Although Will is the recipient of this beating, he often beats his wife, Rosamond, when he and she are alone in the mill town (45). Jim Leslie, the only Walden son who moves to the city and marries a rich woman, also cannot escape the family's barbarous nature. When his family visits him in Augusta, Jim Leslie attacks Griselda, Buck's wife (127). Even Rosamond at times seems savage like her brothers and her husband. After finding Will in bed with her younger sister, Darling Jill, Rosamond tries to shoot Will and then beats his naked backside with a comb until it is "blistered" (60). Without regard to whom they are attacking or to the circumstances of the situation, the Waldens react violently and ambivalently, as if they consider violence a "normal" part of life and problem-solving.

The violent nature of the Waldens is often the product of their illicit sexual behavior, and although both the men and the women engage in seemingly obsessive sexual activity, the actions of the Walden women, just as in eugenic family studies, take precedence because they seem to disrupt the family the most. As the only single female remaining in the family, Darling Jill actually spends most of her time having sex either with the men who live in town or with her own extended family members. Ty Ty actually says that her excessive sexual desires just mean that "she is finally coming along at last," as if her desires are making her a woman (Caldwell, *God's* 16).[15] Even when Rosamond catches Darling Jill with Will, Rosamond does not stay angry with her sister for long. In fact, they begin hugging each other after Rosamond frightens Will away from the house, and Pluto sees them as "suffering a common bereavement" (61–62).

While Darling Jill's excessive number of sexual partners and her family's acceptance of her behavior put her and her family's "moral" values into question by eugenicists' standards, her sexual relationship with the albino gold diviner, Dave, reveals just how much her sexuality controls her (95–96). By having sex with Dave, Darling Jill has broken two types of social codes. As an albino, Dave bears a "Mendelizing" physical trait, seemingly marking him as genetically "inferior." Also, since Ty Ty compares Dave to "a coal-black darky" (81), Darling Jill actually commits a form of miscegenation, reminiscent of the actions of the poor white women in Estabrook's and McDougle's *Mongrel Virginians* and of Ellie May who does not care, or even notice, that black men watch her have sex with Lov (94–95). Ironically, Ty Ty is not upset by Dave's relationship with Darling Jill. He actually watches as Dave and Darling Jill have sex in the yard, never trying to stop them (95–96). Because Darling Jill, like Dewey Dell in *AILD, has* to have sex, regardless of whether her partners are family or considered eugenically "inferior," her sexuality has the potential to cause problems in her family and, also, in society.

Although Darling Jill is the most openly sexual female in the family, Griselda is the Walden woman who causes the most problems within the family. Despite the fact that Griselda is Buck's wife, all of the Walden men, except for Shaw, are unable to control themselves around her. Not only does Jim Leslie try to keep her in Augusta with him, but both Ty Ty and Will want Griselda for themselves as well. When Ty Ty talks to or about Griselda, he comments either on providing her with oral sex or on seeing her naked (Caldwell, *God's* 30, 137). He even says, "I spend all my spare time trying to slip up on her [Griselda] when she ain't looking to see them [her breasts] some more. [. . .] You can't sit calm and peaceful and think about nothing else till you see them again" (89). Will's obsession with Griselda leads him to act as violently as Jim Leslie does in Augusta.

Although Will initially seems to dislike Buck for staying on the farm, Will admits that he ridicules Buck because "Griselda [is] Buck's wife" (99). The desire Will has for Griselda even causes him to damage his relationship with Rosamond further because he continually talks about having sex with Griselda, even taunting Rosamond by saying, "It's all in the family, ain't it? [. . .] Buck wouldn't care much if I did get her. He can't use her all the time" (48). Because of Griselda, the Walden men's relationships and Will and Rosamond's relationship are continually disrupted by arguments and violence.

Despite how obsessed the men act about Griselda, however, she does not act as Darling Jill does. In fact, Will's anger at Buck and Griselda's marriage reveals how faithful Griselda is to her husband. Because of Griselda's lack of sexual activity throughout the novel, Caldwell complicates his typically oversexualized and dangerous portrayals of poor white women; however, with Griselda, Caldwell does not create another version of *Tobacco Road*'s Pearl either. Although Griselda does at times act "superior" to the other Waldens, she does not always separate herself from her family's acts. When Ty Ty talks about her body, Griselda appears embarrassed, but she also takes money from him, seemingly as payment for her beauty, and lets him watch her, at least once, as she undresses, while "glancing at him each moment" (Caldwell, *God's* 89–90, 137). Also, when Jim Leslie tries to kidnap her, Griselda simply says, "Oh, Jim Leslie is all right, Pa. [. . .] He didn't hurt me a bit. He didn't even scare me. He's too nice to be ugly" (127). Griselda's reactions both to Ty Ty and to Jim Leslie are troubling because, although her denial of their sexual advances makes her seem "superior," she also acts at times as if she condones their obsession with her, as if she expects them to want her, even occasionally encouraging their desire for her, as evidenced by her "glanc[es]" at Ty Ty and her kind words for the brutal Jim Leslie. Even though Griselda appears far more composed than the overtly sexual Darling Jill, Griselda's actions still make her seem like a problematic poor white female, especially since she did choose to marry into this seemingly "inferior" family.

Although Griselda's behavior with Ty Ty and Jim Leslie is contradictory, her unfaithfulness in the mill town is not. Griselda does not go to the town intending to have sex with Will; however, while she waits for Will to return from a strike meeting, she becomes increasingly entranced by the sights and sounds. Being in the town gives "her a pleasure she [has] never before experienced" because, as she listens to the "sounds, voices, [and] murmurs," she feels as though she is as "real" as they are (148–50). Back on the farm, Griselda feels trapped in a "closed" and "uninviting" atmosphere (148), but with this new "pleasure" and this new sense of reality, Griselda releases the sexual inhibitions that her contradictory actions with Ty Ty and Jim Leslie suggest she has been struggling with. Being in this atmosphere makes Griselda so sexually motivated that, when Will returns from the meeting, she feels "like running to him and throwing her arms around his neck" before he even speaks to her (150). When Will says that he is "as strong as God Almighty Himself," Griselda obviously agrees because she wants to "[get] down on the floor in front of him and [throw] her arms around his knees and [beg] for the laying of his hand on her head" (154). Instead of denying Will's sexual advances as she does Ty Ty's and Jim's, Griselda allows Will to dominate her by letting him "[catch] her and [drag] her" into the bedroom (157). Edward Wagenknecht has argued that Griselda has sex with Will because she is "overwhelmed with admiration for his heroic conduct" (161), but as evidenced by how she desires him immediately upon seeing him, Griselda seems to have just allowed her "real" desires and "pleasure[s]" to guide her finally. With Will in the mill town, Griselda feels free to become more open and inviting than she did on the farm.

Griselda's change in behavior from a woman who guards her sexuality to one who embraces her sexuality as a way to explore her "real" self corresponds with how Caldwell presents his other female characters in the mill town. In fact, Caldwell makes the town seem like a highly sexually charged environment that transforms women into uncontrollable sexual beings. Not only does Griselda seem out of control when she considers rushing Will as soon as he returns from his strike meeting, but even the sexually open Darling Jill begs Will for sex when she seduces him during an earlier visit in the town by saying, "Please, Will, [. . .] I can't wait" (Caldwell, *God's* 56). Rosamond also "kiss[es]" Will frantically after she tries to kill him when he has sex with Darling Jill (67). Just as the Walden women cannot control themselves in the mill town, the female mill workers also seem more like sexual beings than wage-earning familial supporters. In fact, because they work in the mills, Caldwell seems to make their sexuality more powerful than the Walden women's because it is related to their work and to the freedoms they gain from their economic independence. Unlike the male workers who have been beaten down by hard mill work and lack of nourishment, the female workers, according to Will, have gained strength from the mills and usurped the male workers by taking away their jobs: "They were never men, the people who entered the mill now; the mill wished to employ girls, because girls never rebelled against the harder work, the stretching-out, the longer hours, or the cutting of pay" (68). This economic freedom the women have gained is only understood by Will as an increase in sexual freedom, though, and according to Will, the women are so taken by their sexual impulses that they do not even care about the hard life the mill owners are forcing upon the workers. As a result, the women are described as "wild-eyed" and "firm-bodied girls with eyes like morning glories," and while the men want to change their working conditions, the women are "in love with the looms and the spindles and the flying lint" (69). The Walden women and the mill women are both driven and defined by their sexual desires in the mill-town atmosphere.

Will's overtly sexual description of the mill women reflects the views held by upper- and middle-class whites and even some working-class men who found women's economic independence dangerous because it led them to buy sexual attire and to smoke, drink, and date men in and out of their class (Hall et al. 223, 254, 219). Because Griselda, Darling Jill, and Rosamond also become more sexually uninhibited in the mill towns, however, Will's description of the women's sexuality as empowering as well as dangerous further complicates poor white women's sexuality. Although Griselda's and Darling Jill's sexuality causes familial and social disruptions because of whom they choose to have sex with, they are still, as evidenced by their sexual encounters with Will, subject not only to their desires but also to the men they desire. The mill women, though, are not just driven by their sexual desires; in fact, because they are involved in "public" work and do not have to depend upon men for financial support, their economic freedoms have given them a dominant position over the male workers, making their supposedly increased sexual freedom seem even more dangerous than the sexual freedom experienced by poor white women such as Griselda and Darling Jill (Hall et al. 154). For Will, the combination of the economic and sexual freedoms of the mill women is oppressive to him and to the other male workers who must wait "idly" outside the mill while the women work (Caldwell, *God's* 68–69). The working women's newly realized freedoms make them the dominant gender in the mill town and seemingly in the working class. The danger Will associates with these women becomes even clearer when he adamantly refuses to help Griselda, Darling Jill, and Rosamond obtain jobs in the mill (70, 164). At one point, Will actually "beg[s]" Darling Jill not to work in there (70). As a result of these mill town scenes and the varying degrees of poor white female sexuality presented in them, Caldwell seems to suggest that giving these women access to "public" work only gives them more power and makes them more dangerous than the sexually deviant women who are trapped in the "closed" and "uninviting" rural areas away from the freedoms of the town.

Despite his feeling of oppression as a result of the mill women's enhanced power and sexuality, Will attempts to gain strength and power from the women's open sexuality as a way to retrieve the power he feels he and the other male workers have lost. When Will has sex with Griselda, he uses the woman who has previously held sexual control over him, Jim Leslie, Ty Ty, and Buck to gain his own personal strength that he can use against the mill owners. He tears the clothes from her body, saying, "I've woven cloth all my life, making every kind of fabric in God's world. Now I'm going to tear all that to pieces so small nobody will ever know what they were. They'll look like lint when I get through" (Caldwell, *God's* 156). By ripping Griselda's clothes apart and having sex with her, Will seems to think he reclaims his patriarchal strength, not only over his family but also over the mill. The next day, his show of strength seems to have taken him out of his subordinate position just as he has hoped. Instead of the three Walden women fighting because he has had sex with all of them, the women show no anger towards each other. The three women actually work in unison to dress Griselda and to prepare breakfast for Will before he goes to turn on the power at the mill, co-existing as a new family unit (162). Even the female mill workers who previously dominated the male workers become subordinate to Will and the other men. As the men rush into the mills, the women still look "wild-eyed [. . .] with erect breasts," but now, the women are in the "mill yard" watching the men in the mill

(168). With their bodies "closely pressed" together and huddled next to the mill, the women are thankful to the men for relieving them of having to support themselves and their families on insufficient wages (168–69). The women are so emphatic about Will's power that they, like Griselda, worship him as he stands in the window above the female mill workers (170). Will has become the head of his household again, with three women this time, and "God Almighty Himself" to all the women who once took his and the other men's jobs. With the sexual power he receives from his encounter with Griselda, Will no longer feels subordinate to his wife, to the female workers, or to the mill.

Although Will's power helps him to regain control of his environment at least for one day, Caldwell seems to suggest that the sexual power that he gains from Griselda and that he equates with personal strength is not the type of power that can save Will and the lower class from persecution. Although Will intends to make the mill owners "look like lint," as he makes Griselda's clothes look, the mill guards kill him, and the image of strength he has built the night before with Griselda is shattered (Caldwell, *God's* 173). Not only does Will lose his strength, but so too do the other male mill workers. Without Will, the men become "weak," saying, "I don't reckon there'll be any use of trying to fight them without Will. They'll try to run now and make us take a dollar-ten. If Will Thompson was here, we wouldn't do it. Will Thompson would fight them" (174). Ironically, after the tragic ending at the mill, the women do not appear "weak"; Caldwell describes them as still looking "beautiful" with "erect" breasts and "faces [. . .] like morning-glories" (173). They do not even wallow in the tragedy of the day's events because the mill women come over to Rosamond's house and prepare dinner for the Walden women and Pluto (176). They even try to ease Pluto's fears about the dangers of the town (176). In spite of all the masculine superiority during the scene before Will dies, the men are not the ones who retain their strength. Even Darling Jill, the most sexually deviant woman in the novel, is seen as an empowered woman at the end of this scene because Pluto describes her as his "protection in a foreign country" (176). By putting his faith in the power he gains from his sexual conquest of Griselda, Will loses all of his personal power and destroys the other men's chances to act; however, the women, whom

Will thinks he finally has control over, retain their dominating and sexual strength in spite of his death.

The tragedy of the novel does not end in the mill towns; instead, the force of Griselda's sexuality, which has become enhanced in the open environment of the mill town, leads Buck and Jim Leslie to see themselves as totally dependent upon her. When the three women return and tell the men about Will's death, Buck knows almost immediately that Griselda has had sex with Will (Caldwell, *God's* 184). Since Will is dead, Buck cannot redeem his name by killing Will to show that he, not Will, is the "real man" (186), and he also knows that Griselda does not really want to be with him anymore; she would rather be in the open and inviting mill-town environment living with Darling Jill, Rosamond, and Will as a family (184). Buck's frustrations, though, are partially relieved when he kills Jim Leslie, who tries to kidnap Griselda again. Then, Buck walks into the fields, presumably to commit suicide (209). Although Jim Leslie is as desperate to have Griselda to himself as Buck is, neither man can truly have Griselda as his own anymore. When Buck walks into the fields by himself, his actions reveal that he knows he has lost Griselda. Before he leaves, he passionately "kiss[es]" Griselda and holds her "closely" to him, but he only holds on for a moment before he "push[es]" her away (209). Griselda is no longer the woman who turned away all but her husband's advances; now she is, as she tells Ty Ty when she returns home, "open[ed . . .] up" to the sexual desires she once tried to deny.

Although the violence at the end of the novel seems like the result of the Walden men's irrational views of power and desire, Caldwell, as Faulkner does with Addie Bundren, places the blame on the women for the family's failures, and ironically, Ty Ty is the character who condemns the women. After Will, Jim Leslie, and presumably Buck die, Ty Ty speaks about how his sons have died because they refuse to act like the women and because they insist upon "tak[ing] a woman or a man and hold[ing] him off all for yourself" (Caldwell, *God's* 208). He also says, "The good Lord blessed me with three of the prettiest girls a man ever had in his house [. . .], but he puts sorrow in my heart to pay for it. It looks like a good thing and a bad thing always have to go hand-in-hand" (207–8). While his comments seem to be aimed at showing the women's superiority, they actually condemn the women by highlighting their sexuality and their non-traditional lifestyle choices. By declaring the women too beautiful and, essentially, too sexual, Ty Ty forces the responsibility for the men's uncontrollable desires onto the women. He further condemns the women and their sexuality by focusing on how they willingly decide to share Will in an unconventional relationship, thereby creating a non-traditional family structure, reminiscent of Ira Caldwell's description of the Bungler family's break from the traditional nuclear family unit (332). Since the Walden men could not submit to the women's new "open" sexual structure, as Griselda has described it, then they resort to violence to try to maintain their monogamous relationships. Of course, the women's "open" sexual lifestyle that Ty Ty condones and even seems to applaud involved the type of sexual acts that caused eugenicists to put their focus on southern poor whites. As a result, instead of condemning his sons for not following the women, Ty Ty actually condemns the women who are unable to conform their desires to society's standards of acceptable sexual behavior.

In spite of the violent ending with the deaths of the men and with the dangerous survival of the sexually free Walden women, Caldwell, just as in *Tobacco Road,* does not condemn the Waldens completely; however, instead of blaming other factors for this family's inferiority, he focuses on the helpless and innocent side of the Waldens that makes them seem as if he is trying to show how his poor white characters are also suffering because of their inadequacies. Despite Will's adultery and brutal treatment of his wife, he also seems like a lost man who just wants to return to his job at the mill. Although the women of the family should have destroyed their relationships with one another by their sexual acts, they remain close to one another and try to protect each other throughout the entire deadly ending of the novel (Caldwell, *God's* 203). Then, when Buck shoots him, the women all come to Jim Leslie as he dies, and Rosamond comforts him as "his mother would" have if she were still alive (204). Even Ty Ty suffers at this traumatic outcome because he feels as if "[n]othing matter[s] any longer, because blood [has] been spilled on his land—the blood of one of his children" (206). The Waldens do have goals and aspirations and love for each other; they, like Addie and Dewey Dell, just seem unable to fulfill these goals or to remain faithful to one another because, as Jay Watson suggests, they find themselves constantly "in predicaments they can neither understand [n]or control" (287). Their "impotence" to "control" their lives leads the Waldens, according to Sylvia Jenkins Cook, to "turn to agricultural fantasies, orgiastic religion, and sexual license because they have no other means of giving voice to their longings" (Cook, *Erskine* 127). Even though the Waldens do have moments of hope for their futures and affection for each other, their lives seem drawn to destructiveness, and just as the Lesters of *Tobacco Road* seem destined to fail in their attempts to realize their aspirations of prosperity, strength, and love, so too do the remaining members of the Walden family.

Of course, by leaving the sexually "open" and seemingly dangerous women alive at the end of the novel, Caldwell also reiterates the problems that "inferior" poor whites, specifically poor white women, can cause for the survival of the nation. Not only have the women survived, but they are also the new dominant gender on the farm, just as the women are in the mill town. In fact, the final sounds of the novel are the excited voices of the women (Caldwell, *God's* 211). Since the Walden men have enhanced sexual desires and since Griselda, seemingly the most desirable of all the women, is now in touch with her "real" desires and "pleasure[s,]" the women still have the capability to entice other men who may become just as devastated by the women's sexuality as the Walden men. Of course, by allowing the Walden women to live, Caldwell also highlights what is missing in their lives. Despite the numerous sexual encounters throughout the novel, none of the women has any children. Even when Buck accuses Darling Jill of being pregnant since she has supposedly decided to marry Pluto, Caldwell never actually indicates that she is pregnant or that she is even going to marry Pluto (190). Moreover, unlike the two remaining couples in *Tobacco Road,* Caldwell does not even leave the women with suitable partners because Ty Ty seems afraid of sex and Shaw would rather chase women in town than stay at home (3, 110–12). The absence of children is also odd because part of the nation's fears about the South was the southern lower class's excessive fertility. By leaving the children out of the Walden women's lives, Caldwell has done what Faulkner could not with Dewey Dell. He has performed a literary sterilization. While no evidence suggests that the women were actually sterilized, Caldwell's presentation of the family's demise suggests that he may have wanted to focus on how the childlessness of poor white women would be best for the nation. Of course, even though the Walden women do not have children, their sounds of "excitement" at the end of the novel act as a reminder that they have still retained their dangerous sexual appeal (211).

REVERSING THE POWER

Like Caldwell's poor white novels, John Steinbeck's *The Grapes of Wrath* was immensely popular. By May of 1939, just one month after its release, *The Grapes of Wrath* appeared on the national bestseller list (Parini 219; Wyatt 3). Then, in 1940, Steinbeck won both the National Book Award and the Pulitzer Prize for the novel (Wyatt 4). His ideas for this novel originated from a series of articles he wrote for the *San Francisco News* in 1936 (Howarth 78–79). In preparation for these articles, Steinbeck gathered information about California migrant workers who had come from depleted southern farms in search of work, and like Caldwell, he experienced first-hand how they lived. First, Steinbeck visited the offices of the FSA and studied the photographs of poverty-stricken Americans, including the famous "Migrant Mother" photographs taken by Dorothea Lange (Hapke 29). After doing research at the FSA, he wanted to witness the plight of the migrants first-hand, so he visited "government migrant camps," "squatters' shacks, impromptu camps of weeds, cardboards, and pieces of tin [. . .], and workers' camps" (Benson 80, 83). Jay Parini notes in his biography that, on this journey, Steinbeck felt as though he witnessed "the front line of poverty" (175). When the articles appeared in the *News,* Steinbeck wanted to continue his focus on these migrant workers in a new project. Originally, Steinbeck did not intend for this new project to become a novel. Actually, he first intended to tell the migrant story as a documentary picture-book in the style of Erskine Caldwell and Margaret Bourke-White's *You Have Seen Their Faces* (Howarth 76–77). Photographer Horace Bristol even took the pictures for the collaborative book, but Steinbeck decided that the story should be told as a novel (76–77).[16] Regardless of the form of the book, though, Steinbeck focused his intentions on identifying and alleviating the devastating poverty he witnessed while conducting his research.

Although Steinbeck did not want to publish a documentary picture-book, he did release a pamphlet with accompanying pictures in 1938 before the release of *The Grapes of Wrath.* In this pamphlet, titled *Their Blood Is Strong,* Steinbeck included his 1936 *News* articles that first highlighted his interest in California migrant workers, and he included updated information about his subjects. Two pictures in the pamphlet reveal the degrading living situations of the migrant workers (Steinbeck, *Their Blood* 14, 24); however, as the title suggests, Steinbeck does not simply dwell on the degradation of his subjects as Caldwell does in *Tobacco Road* and *God's Little Acre.* In fact, the title itself, *Their Blood Is Strong,* becomes a declaration that he contradicts the perception that poor whites are genetically "inferior" and destined for destruction like the Lesters and the Waldens. Kevin Hearle has noted that, as an amateur biologist, Steinbeck had read the work of eugenicists such as Jan Christiaan Smuts and Ellsworth Huntington (249).[17] Parini found that Steinbeck also read the work of J. S. Haldane, father of "socialist geneticist" and *Science and Society* contributor J. B. S. Haldane (104). Like his son, J. S. Haldane paid a great deal of attention to environmental influences (104). While Steinbeck obviously had knowledge about eugenic ideas, the title of this pamphlet and sections of his later biological work, *The Sea of Cortez,* written with Edward F. Ricketts, suggest that the novelist's notions about eugenics differed from the work of eugenicists who only looked to the lower class to find evidence of genetic inferiority. Just as Steinbeck declares poor whites the "[s]trong" class in his pamphlet, he ridicules certain eugenic goals in *The Sea of Cortez* by writing that "hope" drives humans to think that "[m]an grows toward perfection" and leads people to overlook the effects the environment has on their ability to reach "perfection" (Steinbeck and Ricketts 72–74). Through his pamphlet, Steinbeck addresses the eugenic ideology of which he obviously had knowledge, but unlike Caldwell, Steinbeck does not place his poor white subjects in an "inferior" position, suggesting that he does not base "perfection" simply on class status.

By using eugenic terminology in his pamphlet title, Steinbeck both acknowledges the prevalence of eugenic discourse in America and subverts that discourse to create a new perception of poor whites so that he can make an argument as to why poor white migrants deserve assistance. Steinbeck's desire to transform this perception only begins with the title. He first acknowledges the arguments associated with the opposing eugenic viewpoint before going on to refute each claim. According to Steinbeck, upper- and middle-class whites despise migrants, and Steinbeck even lists the reasons why migrants are disliked: "that they are ignorant and dirty people, that they are carriers of disease, that they increase the necessity for police and the tax bill for schooling in a community, and that if they [are] allowed to organize they can, simply by refusing to work, wipe out the season's crops" (2). While this statement at first seems to affirm the negative perception that poor whites simply "are" a certain way, Steinbeck immediately replies to this perception with his own suggestions about what has caused the social downfall of the migrants. He admits that the migrants live in a "kind of sub-humanity," but he also says that their extreme poverty has taken away their "dignity and spirit" (9). Furthering this argument, Steinbeck also declares, "And if these men steal, if there is developing among them a suspicion and hatred of well-dressed, satisfied people, the reason is not to be sought in their origin nor in any tendency to weakness in their character" (9). Steinbeck wants his readers to look beyond the class-based eugenic perceptions of poor white migrants and to recognize the environmental conflicts in their lives.

While Steinbeck addresses eugenic arguments in an attempt to reconstruct public perception of his poor white subjects, he also uses them to reveal the hypocrisy of privileged whites desiring to degrade the migrants. On the first page of the pamphlet, he opens with a statement obviously meant to frighten upper- and middle-class whites: "There are at least 150,000 homeless migrants wandering up and down the state, and that is an army large enough to make it important to every person in the state" (*Their Blood* 1). Reminiscent of the words of Ira Caldwell, Steinbeck calls the migrants an "army," but Steinbeck's "army" is not Ira's "great army of delinquents" whose genetic inferiority threatens to take over the population ("The Bunglers" 383). Steinbeck's "army" is the creation of the elite whites' "[hate]" (*Their Blood* 2). Not only does Steinbeck focus on how this "army" is man-made rather than genetically made, he also shows the hypocrisy of subjugating lower-class whites. According to Steinbeck, poor white migrants now have the jobs once performed by immigrant laborers. The privileged classes felt justified in treating immigrants poorly because of their foreign status and because they could threaten them with deportation (25–28); however, these new poor white American migrants should not be treated in this manner, Steinbeck says, because they are a "new race" and because "the old methods of repression, of starvation wages, of jailing, beating, and intimidation are not going to work" (3). Even though Hearle has interpreted Steinbeck's use of the term "new race" as Steinbeck's possible adherence to white supremacy (247), the term "new race," in relation to the content of the pamphlet, seems to work as a reminder that lower-class white laborers are a different "race" from the foreign workers the privileged whites felt justified in degrading. Now, upper- and middle-class whites cannot justify their actions based upon the supposed racial inferiority of their workers because they are mistreating other white "American people" who previously owned their own farms and who are still "resourceful and intelligent" (*Their Blood* 2, 3).[18] By continuing to degrade lower-class white workers, though, prosperous whites have proven that they just want their workers, regardless of race, to feel "inferior and insecure" (12).

Along with debunking eugenic ideology and privileged whites' excuses for their behavior, Steinbeck also focuses on the renewal process that he sees as possible for lower-class white migrants. The migrants' renewal begins with the familiar altruistic mother figure. Steinbeck's emphasis on this 1930s American stereotype becomes apparent from the cover of the pamphlet. The picture on the cover is of a woman staring defiantly into the camera while breastfeeding her child. Even the nursing child glares into the camera, as if both he and his mother are accusing the readers. Throughout the pamphlet, Steinbeck uses other examples of strong motherhood when he writes about what the government camps provided for the migrants. Although the destitute lifestyles that lower-class whites have been forced to live have caused them to suffer a "loss of dignity," Steinbeck insists that this "loss" is corrected if the migrants are given a caring and friendly environment in which to flourish, and the government camps provide this type of environment, where "beaten, sullen, and destitute" migrants may become "revived" (*Their Blood* 16). When describing the rejuvenating experience of the camp, Steinbeck places the most emphasis on the women. A group known as the "Good Neighbors" acts as the welcoming committee for the incoming tenants. As the welcoming committee, the women assess and provide for the new campers' needs, clean their dirty clothes, and help them bathe (16–17). Essentially, the "Good Neighbors" act as surrogate mothers, helping their downtrodden fellow workers to regain hope. By focusing on a nursing mother and surrogate mothers, Steinbeck manages to take the altruistic mother figure into the California migrant camps, where mothers have become desperately needed.

Even though Steinbeck emphasizes the saving mothers of the migrant class, he also presents an opposing version of these mothers. Unlike the women in the eugenic family studies and Caldwell's oversexualized poor white women, Steinbeck's opposing images of motherhood condemn upper- and middle-class whites rather than women of the lower class. Other than the picture of the nursing mother on the pamphlet's cover, all of the other poor white mothers Steinbeck presents have either birthed stillborn children or do not have the ability to produce breast milk to feed their newborn babies (*Their Blood* 8, 22, 33). These suffering mothers and their children are plagued by "malnutrition" (22). Despite the extreme differences in the altruistic and the suffering mothers, presenting them together not only reveals the extent of the social injustice that poor white migrants must face, but it also reveals their strength and perseverance. Although the malnourished women cannot save their own children, they seem determined to save their fellow migrant workers, as evidenced by the women of the "Good Neighbors." These strong, persistent women provide a background for Steinbeck's final warning to his upper- and middle-class readers: "They [the migrants] are of the best American stock, intelligent, resourceful; and if given a chance, socially responsible. [. . .] They can be citizens of the highest type, or they can be an army driven by suffering and hatred to take what they need" (30). Through *Their Blood Is Strong*, Steinbeck obviously envisioned changing the nation's perceptions about poor whites and spurring his readers to treat the migrants with respect and with "dignity."

When writing *The Grapes of Wrath*, Steinbeck used similar techniques to those used in *Their Blood Is Strong*. Instead of denying the eugenic perception of poor whites as "inferior," Steinbeck once again organizes his story around this perception, and he acknowledges it mainly in the type of characters he creates. Focusing primarily on the Joad family, Steinbeck does not, as some reviewers and critics have said, create completely sympathetic characters.[19] In fact, his characters actually share some of the vices that Caldwell's controversial and "grotesque" poor whites have. Tom Joad, the first member of the Joad family introduced, immediately puts into question Steinbeck's supposed sentimentality because Tom is not just a loyal son but also a convicted murderer. Having just been paroled after four years in prison, Tom seems like the typical uncontrollable poor white male reminiscent of the Walden brothers (*Grapes* 16).[20] His brother Noah resembles the typical mentally challenged poor white because he "move[s] slowly" and is considered "stupid" (80). Steinbeck even includes references to his poor white male characters' strong and, at times, lurid sexual appetites. Tom Joad and Jim Casy, a former preacher traveling with the Joads, swap stories about their sexual conquests and their "a-lustin' after the flesh" (172). Steinbeck even creates a stock female character in Rose of Sharon. With a child on the way and a husband with no income, Rose of Sharon resembles Dewey Dell and the poor white women in eugenic family studies who are supposedly causing the destruction of American society. Rose of Sharon even seems as sexually inviting as the Walden women and the female mill workers with her "plump body—full soft breasts and stomach, hard hips and buttocks that [. . .] swing so freely and provocatively as to invite slapping and stroking" (97). These do not immediately seem like sympathetic characters deserving and desiring help from Steinbeck's economically stable readers.

Steinbeck allows his upper- and middle-class characters to voice the prevailing eugenic attitudes about poor whites. While on the road, the Joads are referred to as "bums" and "shif'less" by the business owners on whom they must depend for shelter and food (*Grapes* 187, 192). Along with these general derogatory terms, poor white migrants are also referred to by a specific name both to identify them and to ridicule them: "Okies" (205). One poor white man explains the meaning of the term by saying, "Okie use' ta mean you was from Oklahoma. Now it means you're a dirty son-of-a-bitch[, . . .] you're scum" (205). Later, the Joads hear this term again, but this time a white businessman uses the term much more aggressively, to dehumanize the migrants as well as demean them. He tells his son, "Them goddamn Okies got no sense and no feeling. They ain't human. A human being wouldn't live like they do. A human being couldn't stand it to be so dirty and miserable. They ain't a hell of a lot better than gorillas" (221). In one of the "interchapters," Steinbeck defines the term again, and once again the definition becomes increasingly more severe as compared to the last two.[21] This final, general definition highlights all of the negative characteristics that Steinbeck has given to members of the Joad family: "These goddamned Okies are dirty and ignorant. They're degenerate sexual maniacs. These goddamned Okies are thieves" (282). Thus members of the Joad family—Tom, Noah, Uncle John, and Rose of Sharon—become implicated in these destructive characteristics.

Although Steinbeck seems to pander to upper- and middle-class expectations, he actually uses these negative, expected qualities in his characters, as he does in *Their Blood Is Strong,* to reconstruct society's negative expectations of the lower class. Unlike the "[hybrid . . .] in-between" images of Bundrens, the "inferior" first impressions made by the Joads are proven false. Although Tom's criminal record makes him seem like a dangerous person, Tom explains that he only killed in self-defense (*Grapes* 28). Even later, when Tom kills a police officer, he also commits that act to protect himself because he has just watched as the officer senselessly killed Casy (386). Just as Tom does not turn out to be a deviant, dangerous criminal, Noah does not seem like a genetically disabled feebleminded man as Steinbeck's original description suggests. In fact, Pa Joad takes the blame for his son's "stupid" appearance because he twisted Noah as he came out of the womb (80). Rose of Sharon also escapes reproach because her marriage and pregnancy were not predicated on a lack of foresight or on sexual misconduct. Her husband, Connie, had planned to attend school and to move up into a middle-class lifestyle (165), and as an expecting mother she appears "demure and serious" instead of "provocatively" sexual (97). The Joads even have a legitimate response to the privileged whites' claims that they are typical "Okies." Pa Joad refuses to accept the label of "shif'less" because he says that his family did live a prosperous life once (188). Steinbeck emphasizes that the Joads did not waste their land and their privileges, as the Waldens did in *God's Little Acre* (12). Because of these explanations discounting the apparent "inferiority" of the Joads, Steinbeck, just as he does in *Their Blood Is Strong,* undercuts the upper- and middle-class voices who generalize negatively about these poor white migrant workers.

Just by including the degrading perceptions of poor whites, however, Steinbeck acknowledges their importance. Mimi Reisel Gladstein argues that, by nicknaming the poor white migrants "Okies," elite whites are making these poor whites seem "more immigrant than migrant" ("*The*

Grapes" 136). Although Gladstein only views this "immigrant" characterization as a way to delineate class status (139), the use of the term "Okies" also works to erase the migrants' status as whites. Comparing the migrants to "immigrants" or, in the terminology of the middle-class man, "gorillas," allows upper- and middle-class whites to separate themselves both economically and racially from the poor whites invading their California territory. Moreover, by focusing on the term "Okie," Steinbeck reiterates his statement in *Their Blood Is Strong* that privileged whites want the lower-class whites to consider themselves "foreign" and "inferior" (*Their Blood* 3). Tom Joad understands this attempt to undercut his family's self-worth when he says, "They're a-workin' away at our spirits. They're a-tryin' to make us cringe an' crawl like a whipped bitch" (*Grapes* 279). Steinbeck emphasizes the damage that this unrelenting ridicule can have by contrasting strong poor white migrants such as Tom to others who have begun to believe in their own supposed inferiority. A man who has "los' [his] eye" is plagued with an inferiority complex because his boss relentlessly ridicules him because of his disability; therefore, the one-eyed man walks around "dirty" and "stink[ing,]" immersed in "feel[ing] sorry" for himself (180). Some of the migrants living in the Hooverville camps also do not seem to believe that their lives have worth. While staying at a Hooverville, the Joads meet a man whom they refer to as "bull-simple" because, instead of leaving and saving all of his possessions from the police officers planning to burn the camp, he chooses to stay in his tent because he has lost all hope in his life (278). Unlike Tom, the one-eyed man and the "bull-simple" man have become the type of "inferior" people they are believed to be.

Despite the defeatist attitudes of some poor whites, the majority of the Joads embody a perseverance that works against the destructive familial images presented by Caldwell. In fact, just as Steinbeck seems to be usurping the prevailing eugenic ideology by hinting at the possibility of its truth and then dismantling it, he also usurps the power that the privileged classes wield over their poor white counterparts. Not only do their derogatory comments not destroy the Joads' spirits, but the Joads actually seem to believe that they can, with continual effort, gain power in the class war. Speaking with conviction, Ma Joad tells Tom, "Rich fellas come up an' they die, an' their kids ain't no good, an' they die out. But, Tom, we keep a-comin.' Don' you fret none, Tom. A different time's comin'" (*Grapes*

280–81). This empowering and seemingly prophetic speech echoes the sentiment of the title *Their Blood Is Strong;* however, while Steinbeck merely states the positive qualities of the lower class in the pamphlet, he seems to use Ma Joad's speech to issue a warning about overlooking the power that the migrant workers actually have. In fact, she essentially predicts a reversal of power among the classes, with the lower class becoming the privileged class. Ma Joad's speech has been connected both to Steinbeck's interest in Charles Darwin and to his "phalanx" theory. While these two critical perceptions merit attention, considering Steinbeck's and Rickett's focus on Darwin and the "phalanx" in *The Sea of Cortez,* these critical theories overlook Ma Joad's use of eugenic discourse in her speech.[22]

Just as Steinbeck subverts poor white stereotypes and class-based eugenic criticisms of poor whites, Ma Joad's speech subverts traditional "'bourgeois'" eugenic discourse in two ways. First, she defies the negative connotations associated with the excessive fertility of the lower class when she emphasizes that her class of people "keep[s] a-comin.'" Of course, according to Ma Joad, her class's reproductive ability reveals the true strength of her people because, despite what the lower class must endure, it is still constantly rejuvenating itself. Along with this positive focus on reproductive ability, Ma Joad's speech echoes the ideas of the Russian "socialist geneticists" who wanted to prove that lower-class people just need a suitable environment, free of class oppression, in which to flourish and to become dominant. Since the lower class has already proven that it can survive and thrive, Ma Joad encourages Tom to wait for a "different time" when their people will live in an environment in which they can prove their worth. Steinbeck even provides an example to prove that the migrants actually could prosper if given a suitable environment in which to live. In the government camps that they live in and govern by themselves, the poor white migrants enjoy a communal environment and work together to find jobs, to stay healthy, and to uplift each other socially and mentally (*Grapes* 253–54, 302). In fact, the only disturbances in the camp occur when outside police officers pay starving poor whites, who do not live in the camp, to infiltrate the camp activities and start fights (342–43). Because of how civilized the migrant-governed camps are, Steinbeck emphasizes that a change in environment could reveal the lower class's potential to become a strong ruling class, and if given a more stable environment in which to thrive, then the consistently growing lower class could actually become the dominant ruling class that some Russian "socialist geneticists" envisioned it being.[23]

While Ma Joad's speech echoes the ideas of the Russian "socialist eugenics" movement (Joravsky, *Lysenko* 262), Steinbeck's decision to use Ma Joad as the voice for the power of the lower class aligns him with the dominant American perception of the Depression, both eugenic and political, that women will either save or destroy American society. Unlike Faulkner's "unfit" mothers and Caldwell's sexually predatory and sexually oppressive poor white women, Ma Joad is highlighted as the base and the stronghold for her family and for other poor white families, and Steinbeck never even references her as a sexual being. Despite the fact that the Joads exist as a patriarchal family, Ma Joad is still referred to as "the citadel of the family," and she also acts as its emotional compass: "And since old Tom and the children could not know hurt or fear unless she [Ma Joad] acknowledged hurt or fear, she had practiced denying them to herself" (*Grapes* 76). Gladstein refers to Ma Joad as "the symbol of positive motherhood," a woman with "superhuman qualities" ("The Indestructible" 77–78). These "qualities" take a different form when she instead of Pa Joad becomes the leader of the family. Nellie Y. McKay argues that Ma Joad becomes the leader because women accept change better than men (53). Ma Joad actually says, "Man, he lives in a jerk—baby born an' a man dies, an' that's a jerk—gets a farm an' loses his farm, an' that's a jerk. Woman, it's all one flow, like a stream, little eddies, little waterfalls, but the river it goes right on. Woman looks at it like that. We ain't gonna die out" (*Grapes* 423). Unlike Addie, whose leadership only creates chaos for her family, Ma Joad shows the stable qualities that uphold her family even in such a turbulent time as the Depression. She refuses to allow her family to break apart (169); she will not allow her husband to give up hope that he will find a job (352); and she continues to believe that her class of people will survive. Her role as an altruistic mother extends into her role as society's mother, too. From her insistence that Casy join the family's traveling caravan to her generosity with food that is not even enough to feed her own family, Ma Joad reveals her commitment to universal nurturing (104, 257). She embraces her role as "citadel," letting her family as well as the other "Okies" know that their situation has hope.

Just as Ma Joad acts as the main driving force and mothering figure for her own family as well as other families, other women whom the Joads encounter on their journey to California also reveal these same strong, nurturing, and persistent qualities. Steinbeck emphasizes, in almost all of the novel's female characters, the ability to encourage members of the lower class and to help them remember and regain their self-worth, despite all of their struggles and the way in which privileged whites treat them. He even makes his fictional characters more authentic by basing them on the various women that he documents in *Their Blood Is Strong.* Sairy Wilson, the wife of Ivy Wilson and traveling companion to the Joads, resembles the malnourished, suffering women Steinbeck highlights in his pamphlet. Despite being terminally ill, Sairy musters enough strength to help the Joads as Grampa dies (136, 139, 142). Ironically, only after Sairy assists the Joads does Ma Joad notice Sairy's frailty: "[S]he [Ma Joad] seemed to see for the first time the pain-tormented eyes and the face that was haunted and shrinking with pain" (150). Instead of focusing on her own problems, Sairy focuses on helping her fellow migrants, and as a result, she gives Grampa "dignity" in his death and comforts the Joads in their time of need.

While Sairy resembles the women in *Their Blood Is Strong* who overcome their pain to help their fellow migrants, the women of the "Good Neighbors" group in the pamphlet are represented by a fictional band of government camp welcomers. The women in this group are actually the people who work the hardest to make the government camp the type of environment that poor white migrants can use to reveal their strength and their personal governing abilities, qualities that upper- and middle-class whites do not think they have. Since the government camp is governed by the migrants themselves, the women of the camp have set up various women's committees to ensure that all of the activities and the duties needed to keep the camp running smoothly and effectively are taken care of each week (*Grapes* 313). Apparently, the women's committees provide so much organization for the camp that the camp manager says he has been "worked [out] of a job" (304). As the welcoming committee, the women also have the job of making new campers feel at home in their new environment. Just as the "Good Neighbors" in *Their Blood Is Strong* help the campers regain hope and "dignity," so too do these women. When the Joads first arrive in the government camp, Ma Joad wants to interact with the other women, but she is upset because she and her family are not "decent" anymore as a result of their traveling (303). Despite Ma Joad's nervousness, the committee women put her at ease, and Ma Joad feels so welcome that she says, "I feel like people again" (307). Not only do these women act, like Ma Joad, as the strongholds for their class in the camp, but they also exude the comforting qualities of Sairy by giving the despondent migrants who come into the camp weak a new sense of hope and self-respect.

While Ma Joad represents the strong yet nurturing universal mother and Sairy and the women's committee reflect the female leadership qualities that Steinbeck witnessed while traveling to the migrant camps in 1936, Rose of Sharon, as a pregnant, single woman, brings the focus back to the eugenic ideology of the day. Although Steinbeck, at the beginning of the novel, subverts eugenic ideology by transforming Rose of Sharon from an overtly sexual woman into a pregnant, married woman focused intensely on "motherhood," he reassesses the social perception of her character when Connie leaves her. Without a husband and with a child on the way, Rose of Sharon becomes the type of woman eugenicists and the American public would have recognized as potentially dangerous: a poor, single mother. Rose of Sharon even imagines a horrible future for her child because she wonders about her own mothering abilities. In the government camp, a crazy woman named Lisbeth Sandry tells Rose of Sharon that, if she has committed a sexual "sin," she will lose her baby (*Grapes* 309–10). Rose of Sharon immediately becomes scared because she "hug-danced" with Connie (310). When Tom kills the police officer who has killed Casy, Rose of Sharon sees her brother's violent action as another reason to suspect the eventual doom of her child's life. She becomes "[hysterical]" over the fate of her baby; however, instead of thinking it will die, Rose of Sharon imagines that her baby will experience an even worse fate, abnormality: "Connie's gone, an' I ain't gettin' good food. I ain't getting' milk. An' now you [Tom] kill a fella. What chance that baby got to be bore right? I know—gonna be a freak—a freak! I never done no dancin'" (393). With all of these family indiscretions, Rose of Sharon begins to believe that, if the baby does survive malnourishment in her womb, it will most certainly be a "freak" rather than a "normal" child. Ironically, she seems more adamant about blaming her child's problematic future on herself and her family's supposed "sin[ful]" behavior than on her poverty.

In the end, Rose of Sharon's fears about the welfare of her child come to fruition when her child is born dead (*Grapes* 442). Rose of Sharon and the Joads, however, do not blame themselves for the death of the child. In fact, Steinbeck arranges a dramatic shift in their personal viewpoints, and of course, this shift is led by Ma Joad, who tells her family, "Don't take no blame. [. . .] They's changes—all over" (443). Ma Joad's comment begins a reversal of the familial attitude as self-loathing and self-degradation are replaced by anger and strength directed towards placing the blame on the upper- and middle-class whites who have taken away their "dignity and spirit." The death of the child has caused the Joads to quit looking at themselves as an "inferior" group and to begin focusing on how prosperous whites, by denying them adequately paying jobs and, at times, fairly priced food, have succeeded in killing Rose of Sharon's supposedly problematic child. Owens has argued that, when Uncle John sends the dead child down the stream in an "apple box," he sends "a messenger of death" to the other poor white migrants, letting them know that they "will wander no longer" (*Grapes* 446, Owens 139). As a "messenger," however, the exposed baby is also a way to show those miserly classes the fruits of their labor. Unlike Grampa and Granma whom the Joads buried, hiding their loss, the dead child will not be hidden as if he or she never died (*Grapes* 145, 240). Uncle John and the rest of the family want the upper- and middle-class whites, who make the Joads feel "inferior and insecure," to know that they have succeeded in ridding society of one more poor white mother's child.

Although Rose of Sharon does not have a baby to care for, her role as a mother does not end with the death of her child. Steinbeck ends the novel with Rose of Sharon breastfeeding an adult man who has not eaten for at least "six days" (*Grapes* 452–53). Her final actions have been discussed in connection with Steinbeck's political beliefs, with his focus on group dynamics, and with his desire to place women in leadership roles, but each of these critical theories about Rose of Sharon's act neglects the parallel with *Their Blood Is Strong.*[24] In his pamphlet, Steinbeck reports on three would-be mothers who, like Rose of Sharon, lose their babies due to malnourishment; however, unlike Rose of Sharon, these women do not even have the ability to "produce breast milk." Even though Rose of Sharon seems as though she should suffer the same effects as the three documented women, Steinbeck planned the ending in spite of what he had witnessed in the government camps. Responding to his editor, who wanted him to change the ending, Steinbeck insisted that he could not change it because he had envisioned it even before he wrote the novel (Steinbeck, "Letter to Pascal Covici" 166–67). Because of his insistence and his obvious planning of the ending, Steinbeck seems intentionally to have disregarded his first-hand knowledge of how a malnourished mother's body would respond. His disregard allows him, though, to make a final judgment on the eugenicists' conclusions about poor whites.

Unlike Rose of Sharon's dead baby and the Walden men of *God's Little Acre* who kill each other off, the men will survive, and the women, who have been stripped of their natural abilities to have children, will act as the caregivers to these men. As the men's caregivers, the poor white women really do become their class's saviors because Steinbeck's commitment to showing how the poor white migrants will survive is reiterated when Rose of Sharon "smile[s] mysteriously" while breastfeeding the man (*Grapes* 453). This look from Rose of Sharon is reminiscent of the "curious look" Ma Joad has on her face when she tells Tom that, while the "[r]ich" and their children "die, [. . .] we [the lower class] keep a-comin'" (281). With the women as their support, these poor white migrants assert themselves above the "inferior and insecure" label forced upon them, and unlike other poor whites who have returned home defeated by the ridicule of the privileged whites and unlike the Lesters and the Waldens who stay in their rural homes to their personal and economic detriment, the Joads announce, in this final scene, that they will continue to survive and that they will continue to "keep a-comin'" no matter what obstacles they must overcome.

Unlike *As I Lay Dying, Tobacco Road,* and *God's Little Acre,* Steinbeck's novel about poor white survival did not unleash a barrage of criticism about southern poor whites or elicit contradictory reviews about whether the novelist truly sympathized with his subjects. Instead, reviewers of *The Grapes of Wrath* questioned whether Steinbeck had gone too far in his positive characterization of the lower class compared with his disparaging depiction of the privileged classes that criticize rather than help the migrants. Some reviewers praised the novel for showcasing the honor still existing in lower-class life while others were distressed by Steinbeck's desire to challenge the social order. In a 1939 review for *New Masses,* Granville Hicks referred to *The Grapes of Wrath* as a perfect "illustration" of "proletarian literature" (22). Cowley applauded Steinbeck for his ability to "[rouse . . .] people to fight against intolerable wrongs" ("American Tragedy" 383). Clifton Fadiman, who had focused on "the phosphorescent rottenness of the [Bundren] family" in his review of *As I Lay Dying,* saw *The Grapes of Wrath* as a call to arms: "If only a couple of million overcomfortable people can be brought to read it, John Steinbeck's 'The Grapes of Wrath' may actually effect something like a revolution in their minds" ("Highway 66" 81). The "overcomfortable" people Fadiman referred to, however, did not always appreciate this novel. Marshall Maslin called the novel "brutally unfair" because of the harsh depiction of upper- and middle-class whites (3), and a reviewer for the Portland *Evening Express* called it "one-sided" ("Books" 6). Another reviewer, Robert E. McClure, even went so far as to defend America's "present social order," saying that it had "virtue" regardless of Steinbeck's presentation (8). With this mixed reaction, Steinbeck seems to have frightened some of his readers, not as Caldwell does with his degenerate poor whites, but with the social uncertainty that Steinbeck creates through his truly noble poor white characters, specifically Ma Joad. For the 1939 reviewers, the only confusion Steinbeck creates is whether this strong, poor white family, with Ma Joad as its base, is truly representative of a strong lower class that not only has the power to start a social "revolution" but also to become, as Soviet Marxist geneticists and Ricketts suspected, a viable force in society, the "deliver[ers of] our species."

Each author's presentation of rural poor whites seems directly related to the public concern about the detection and/or detention of the supposedly genetically "inferior." In the early 1930s, the public had become overwhelmed with this eugenic information through academics, politics, and entertainment, and as a result, Faulkner's and Caldwell's novels reflect the confusion in America about how to deal with the seeming generational degeneration that the public was led to believe had become an imminent problem. Interestingly, both authors do not completely condemn any of their characters. They are, at times, even reluctantly pointing out their characters' flaws. Although Faulkner and Caldwell follow the pattern of eugenic family studies, their characters' actions and reasons for committing those actions are not so straightforward as the actions in the eugenicists' studies. Addie's and Dewey Dell's adulterous behavior and illegitimate children should make them models of the sexually degenerate poor white woman, but their desire to correct these grievances keeps not only Faulkner but also most of the middle-class upstanding citizens from condemning them completely. Caldwell's Ellie May, Darling Jill, Rosalie, and Griselda seem to be just as much products of the dangerous anger-infused environment as they do sexual predators. As a result, none of these female characters seem like intentionally malicious intent women who deserve to be subdued.

Because these presentations are so confusing and contradictory, the questions arise as to why these authors do not strictly draw these families as either "inferior" or "normal." What Faulkner and Caldwell add to their "family studies" is actual human emotion and interaction, or at least their version of how they think a family of this lower-class status would act. The interactions between siblings, parents, and townspeople are drawn to include family histories, environmental and societal influences, and personal challenges. The eugenic studies did not analyze and present all the intricacies of what went into their subjects' decisions. As a result, their focus remained solely on the seemingly "inferior" actions. Faulkner and Caldwell, on the other hand, do not merely present a list of actions. By creating rounded characters, they, in essence, humanize these people that scientists during the early 1930s just wanted to categorize as either fit or unfit. Faulkner and Caldwell seem to be challenging their readers to decide for themselves how to deal with these examples of seemingly "real people" who are more than just society's potential destroyers. These authors do not, however, escape the ideology of eugenicists because, even though they highlight contributory factors, they do not ultimately justify and redeem all of their poor white characters, specifically the women. They seem unable to reconcile seemingly natural human deficiencies with the eugenic notion that these deficiencies could potentially destroy not just that family but the future of the nation. Despite the shadows over the futures of the Bundrens, the Lesters, and the Waldens left by Faulkner and Caldwell, the authors' inability, or perhaps unwillingness, to eradicate the families leaves their interpretations of their futures open. Faulkner does not abort

Dewey Dell's illegitimate child, and although neither the Lesters nor the Waldens have any pregnancy to show for all their sexual activity, Caldwell also does not definitively sterilize any of his female characters. Both authors are unwilling to cast that final judgment on any of these families.

Steinbeck's complete overrule of eugenic principles in *The Grapes of Wrath* is a complete shift away from eugenic ideology, even from the contradictory views presented by Faulkner and Caldwell; however, Steinbeck is also unable to separate his female characters from the dualistic stereotypes assigned to poor white women. Steinbeck clearly does not think that the lower class is made up of genetically "inferior" people destined to destroy America's future. For Steinbeck, the only factors for a person's actions, even those of the lower class, are family history, environmental and social influences, and personal challenges. The Joads are not driven by any hint of so-called genetically "inferior" predispositions. They are no contributing pieces of the Joad family puzzle that the author cannot reconcile with his humanized portrait of his subjects. Although Steinbeck departs so greatly from the eugenic ideology of lower-class inferiority, he does not do the same with the altruistic mother stereotype. With Ma Joad, Steinbeck has created a character who is still a model of strength, but by presenting her in this stereotype, Steinbeck, like Faulkner and Caldwell, has fallen prey to the culturally and eugenically defined labels of southern poor white women. Whether Steinbeck actually believed that strong altruistic migrant mothers such as Ma Joad existed or whether he used this culturally accepted stereotype to make his positive presentation of these suspected "inferior" poor whites acceptable to the public is the question that has not and, most likely, cannot be answered. What is known, however, is that Steinbeck's use of the altruistic mother stereotype and Faulkner and Caldwell's use of the sexual degenerate stereotype reached a wide range of Americans through all forms of entertainment. As a result, the stereotypes that poor white women had to contend with became even more a part of American culture and, therefore, even more of a social constraint.

The dualistic stereotypes were further driven by the nonfiction work that was increasingly prominent during the 1930s. In fact, as documentary work began to increase because of the Depression, these female images associated with sexual predators and altruistic mothers became the focal points of documentary photographs, oral histories, and sociological analyses. *As I Lay Dying, Tobacco Road, God's Little Acre,* and *The Grapes of Wrath* may have been four of the most popular and acclaimed works of the 1930s, but the copious amount of social documentary focused on the lives of southern poor whites helped to solidify the eugenic perception of poor whites, especially the perception of southern poor white women, because these tales were supposedly based on reality and could therefore be trusted as fact.

3

MAKING THE EUGENIC "MYTH" A REALITY

The Fictionalizing of Depression-Era Documentary Work

ALONG WITH WILLIAM FAULKNER'S, Erskine Caldwell's, and John Steinbeck's fictional representations, the Depression also provided a fertile ground for nonfiction works about poor white families. In fact, William Stott has argued that documentary work became "the primary expression of thirties America" (x–xi). The reality of the Depression proved much more dynamic and shocking than any fiction an author could create, and because of this real drama permeating American society, authors used "social documentary" to tell the stories of the afflicted and downtrodden citizens affected by this devastating historical event (Stott 20).[1]

New Deal affiliates, Communist supporters and sympathizers, and sociologists used documentary methods to create public and political sympathy for poverty-stricken Americans, and through their documentaries, they hoped to spur the nation into action. That action, however, did not just consist of calls for economic relief; it also raised the possibility of using eugenic "relief" to assist those affected. Documentary works tested the iconic "Mom" image used during this period by presenting mothers who had to face poverty surrounded by their often starving children (Rabinowitz, *Labor* 58). These images of Depression motherhood often created conflicting messages, though, because, while the mothers could be thought of as representatives of the nation standing firm in the face of despair, they and their children could also be thought of as economic burdens. As a result, the possibility of eugenic sterilization and segregation became a common feature of contemporary documentary work as authors suggested methods that might stop America's plunge into total devastation.

With the national interest in the South and how its economic failures and reproductive rate would affect the rest of the nation, many of the documentary authors focused their studies on this troubled region. Such works generally highlighted the effects of economic depression by focusing both on the tenant and sharecropping systems that continued to keep farmers from succeeding and on the ever-expanding families that farmers had. Since many of the tenant and sharecropping families could not escape their poverty, many of them looked at having children as a way to increase their labor force, thereby increasing their ability to support their families. The desire for a large labor force, coupled with lower-class women's lack of knowledge about birth control, made the prospect of having a large family almost inevitable. Large southern families, however, were not looked upon as economic necessities by others in the nation. Instead, the large number of southern children was thought of as an unsettling image of the future of America. Since the women of the Southeast produced so many children, "[t]he more than twenty-two million native white women of childbearing age were destined not only to be mothers of the next generation of southerners, but, to a significant degree, of the next generation of Americans" (Scott v). The cultural and social implications of this possibility pervaded documentary works about the South.

Because of the national implications of southern poor white motherhood, documentary authors put a great emphasis on the child-rearing abilities of these mothers and on the future capabilities of the children these women had. Just as in the supposedly documentary eugenic family studies, the "good" mother / "bad" mother theme resonated throughout these works (Gertrude C. Davenport 68–69). For every "Migrant Mother" and Annie Mae Gudger persistently keeping her family from falling into deplorable conditions, women such as Mollie Goodwin and Ivy Woods represented the problematic southern mother afflicted by excessive sexuality and insufficient maternal capabilities. If these mothers really were going to bear and raise the next generation of Americans, documentary authors intended to assess their capabilities even as they sympathized with their economic situation. The documentary work of Erskine Caldwell and Margaret Bourke-White, directly sponsored by New Deal programs, along with Margaret Jarman Hagood's sociological study *Mothers of the South: Portraiture of the White Tenant Farm Woman* and James Agee and Walker Evans's *Let Us Now Praise Famous Men,* put these families and mothers at the forefront of documentary work on the Great Depression, and each of these books takes the altruistic mother symbol of American hope and complicates it with the concerns of eugenic ideology.

FICTION OR NONFICTION

Erskine Caldwell, with his widely popular novels *Tobacco Road* and *God's Little Acre,* made a career out of writing about the lives of poor white southerners; in fact, this interest led him to continue his focus on them in a variety of documentary projects. His decision to follow his fictional tales with documentary works on the same subjects was made because of the backlash he was receiving from angry southerners who felt that the Lester family of *Tobacco Road* and the Walden family of *God's Little Acre* represented the worst possible examples of southern life (Miller 138). Since the Lesters live in a state of inertia and the Waldens act violently or sexually, these two families do not, in fact, create a positive image of the South trying to revive itself during the Depression. Caldwell insisted, however, that he had derived his fictional characters from reality. He hoped that his nonfiction works would justify his fictional characterization of poor white southern life (Cook, "Erskine" 375).

In February of 1935, Caldwell began his campaign to validate his novels by writing a series of articles for the *New York Post* detailing supposedly factual evidence of poverty in Georgia. While Caldwell did not hesitate to blame both the state and federal government ("Georgia Poverty" 97–98), he also used his propensity for "grotesque" imagery to degrade the poor people that his articles were meant to help (Miller 156). In fact, his first article, "Georgia Poverty-Swept, Says Caldwell," actually begins with "grotesque" images rather than an assessment of governmental policies: "Children are seen deformed by nature and malnutrition, women in rags beg for pennies, and men are so hungry that they eat snakes and cow dung" (97). His subjects appear degenerate and animalistic because of how they live and what they must do to survive, and they also seem helpless because of the role that "nature" takes in their lives. In Caldwell's statement, the children are victims of "nature" first and "malnutrition" second, and the images of the adult women and men only worsen the image he provides of the genetically and environmentally handicapped children.

While Caldwell surprisingly begins his first article in the series mimicking the eugenic ideas of his father, Ira Caldwell, by citing both hereditary and environmental issues that have caused poverty in the South, his final article epitomizes the brutal imagery that made southerners so angry with Caldwell. His first three articles keep tottering between the desperate need of poverty-stricken people forced to have "large families" of "six, eight, ten or more children" and the animalistic qualities that he sees in these large families ("U.S. Aid" 101), but in "Starving Babies Suckled by Dog in Georgia Cabin," the final article in the series, the image of poor white motherhood surpasses even the "bad" mother images in the eugenic studies. In this article, Caldwell tells the story of three families living together in a house with only two rooms (105). The mother of one of these families refuses to eat with the other three families because she insists that her absent husband will soon return with food (105). Ironically, this mother who has denied her children nourishment lies on the floor sleeping instead of caring for her children (106). Instead, she allows a dog to mother her children: "On the floor before an open fire lay two babies, neither a year old, sucking the dry teats of a mongrel bitch" (106). The children have obviously become dependent on the dog as a surrogate mother because, not only do they feed off of the dog, but they cry out to it and follow it whenever it leaves them (106). Although this scene may seem unnatural to *Post* readers, it is clearly not unnatural to the other children in the house because the two older girls in the room do not stop the dog from nursing the babies (106). In fact, at the end of this article, one of the older daughters raises her skirt to the fire, offering herself sexually if she could only have "a heaping dish of hog sausage" (107). Through this girl's desperate desire for food, Caldwell creates a vision of what the future holds for this family. With the babies and the dog lying near the now exposed girl, the possibility of another generation of children mothered by a "mongrel bitch" emerges.

By March of 1935, the *Augusta Chronicle* in Georgia started an ongoing debate about the veracity of Caldwell's *Post* articles, and that debate led reporters to start their own investigation into Georgia poverty. Caldwell's father, Ira, even went with the reporters on their investigative journey ("Investigation" 118). In the first article of the five-part series, the reporters admit that, although they did not find the specific people Caldwell describes, not even the mothering "mongrel bitch," they did find that such people do exist, but only as "a minute portion of the population" (118). Despite their insistence on the small number of people who are "wretched, living in want and squalor, victims of their own shiftlessness and ignorance," the remainder of the series focuses on this "minute" group. The next three articles seem like attempts to persuade those in power to approach white poverty and deviance as a serious social problem that must be fixed by scientific sterilization ("Investigation" 119). Although the investigators use the final article to chastise Caldwell for not saying, as they did, that the problematic group of people was small ("Erskine Caldwell" 130), they have essentially proven why Caldwell puts so much emphasis on these poor whites. These people the reporters refer to as "wretched" provide a frightening image that has, evidently, spurred them to call for action, and unlike Caldwell, who wants to help this group through eugenic and environmental action, the reporters consider "sterilization" the only way to help society rid itself of these "wretched" people who keep producing generations of families to continue this tradition of "squalor" (129).

The debate about his articles continued when Caldwell included parts of them in his 1935 documentary travel book, *Some American People.* Here he chronicles his trip across America by telling stories about people he meets who have been affected by the Depression. When traveling through Nebraska and Kansas, Caldwell found farmers hard on their luck but still trying to survive (61–66, 84–88). Later, in the section on Detroit, he recounts how automobile plant workers lose their fingers because the plant managers keep speeding up the assembly line (164–73). While these images are grim and horrific, they do not degrade the people about whom he is speaking; they are simply victims of a harsh economic system. But in the "Tenant Farmers" section of the book, Caldwell's tone changes. By reusing the "mongrel bitch" story in this collection, he separates the South's problems from the rest of the nation's problems. No honor exists in a home where a dog has become the surrogate mother for the children. The only relief that Caldwell offers the South is his admission, as requested by the *Augusta Chronicle* reporters, that "[t]hese conditions are not typical of the South" (230). While Caldwell complies with the reporters' request, he does not miss the opportunity to use their investigation against the South, too. Not only does he skew the results of their investigation to use it as evidence that degenerate conditions do exist in the region, but he also criticizes the *Augusta Chronicle* for only supporting "a sterilization program" (236). Caldwell argues that promoting environmental change in conjunction with sterilization is the only way to save this depleted section of the nation (236). Interestingly, though, Caldwell does not offer reproductive solutions to social problems in the other sections of his book. This image of poor white motherhood, seemingly justified by the *Augusta Chronicle,* reached many Americans because *Some American People* sold more copies than any other book by its publisher that fall (Miller 225).

After *Some American People* came out, Caldwell decided to do "a photo-text study" about sharecroppers in the South with Margaret Bourke-White (Miller 226–27). Bourke-White was one of the most successful commercial photographers of the 1930s. She took photographs for *Fortune* and for the newly formed *Life* magazine (227, 229); however, she saw making a documentary book with Caldwell as a way to focus her work on "the ever-deepening hardship and sorrow of the Great Depression" (Miller 228). Therefore, in the summer of 1936, Caldwell and Bourke-White began a tour of the South, talking with and photographing southerners and their families along the way (229). While their intentions seem noble, their methods reveal that they had their own personal interests. When taking the pictures of her subjects, Bourke-White specifically had in mind what expressions she thought they should have, so she would wait hours until she could capture this particular image (233). She was known for using "strained angles," arranging items specifically for effect, and posing her subjects in "satisfying compositions" (Shloss 598). Stott has referred to Bourke-White's photographs in *You Have Seen Their Faces* as captured "[f]aces of defeat" (220). Just as Bourke-White waited for her desired image of her subjects, Caldwell had specific ideas about what they should say. In fact, even though he conversed with the subjects of the photographs (Miller 233), he made up what they said from his "impressions" of them and used these make-believe conversations in the captions for the photographs (Caldwell, Interview 284). While Caldwell admits in the opening pages that he uses fictional captions, just by failing to use the southerners' own words he silences and, therefore, subordinates them in order to further his agenda. Sylvia Jenkins Cook has noted that writing the text in this fashion allowed Caldwell to call for "social reforms" while still emphasizing "the ironic and ridiculous aspects" of his subjects' lives as he does in his fiction (*Erskine* 283). The techniques used to construct the book immediately put into question both Caldwell's and Bourke-White's intentions for *You Have Seen Their Faces.*

Just as the purpose of the book, at first, seems innocently motivated, so do its contents. Miller notes, "The pictures were carefully chosen to represent an equal number of men and women, an equal number of blacks and whites" (237); however, the pictures of the poor white men and women differ in their presentation. While the men are usually pictured alone or at work, the women are often pictured in familial settings with either their children or their husbands but not both. Only in two pictures did Bourke-White photograph entire families together. In the majority of the family photographs just the mother is shown with the children, and Bourke-White even includes a photograph of a mother breastfeeding her child. This picture seems in direct contrast to the breastfeeding "mongrel bitch" of Caldwell's *Post* articles. The entire content of the photograph, however, disrupts the harmony of the mother/child image. An antique picture of what appears to be an affluent woman appears behind the breastfeeding mother, almost as if the woman in the photograph is staring over the poor white woman's shoulder, critiquing her mothering abilities. With these two contrasting images appearing together, the poor white mother becomes not just representative of the struggling South but also an image of how far the South has fallen. This picture taken in "Okefenokee Swamp, Georgia," corresponds with a picture that appears earlier in the book taken in "Clinton, Louisiana," in which a woman and a child appear sitting on the steps of a plantation house. As a result of Bourke-White's use of "strained angles," the pillars soar high above the mother and daughter, who look sullenly out into the distance. Caldwell's caption reveals that this pair now lives in an abandoned plantation house with other destitute families. Like the breastfeeding mother, this woman represents the lower class that has become increasingly prominent because of the vanishing southern aristocracy that once lived in this house and, presumably, that once helped to support the families inside of it, and the mother's child represents an even further unknown future.

Other mother/child photographs taken by Bourke-White highlight not the lower class's difference from the old southern aristocracy but also the inability of poor white mothers to care for their children. Unlike those taken with the old photograph and the plantation house as backgrounds, the photographs of just the mothers and their children place the focus not on their surroundings but on their physical and emotional appearances. One taken in "McDaniel, Georgia," is of a mother holding a dirty child, but the most memorable portion of this photograph is the appearance of the mother. Her face looks dry, worn, and wrinkled, and her hair appears uncombed and disheveled. This seemingly young woman, aged before her time, has a sneer on her face as her child reaches to touch her chin, leaving open the question of whether her sneer is meant for her child, her desperate situation, or both. Bourke-White follows this frightening image of poor white motherhood with another just as terrifying. While the other photographs draw attention to the mothers, this photograph taken in "Peterson, Alabama," focuses on a young child standing beside his seated mother, who is holding a baby. Although holding a plate, the young child looks incredibly ill without hair and with a protruding belly, seemingly because he is suffering from starvation. According to the caption, the family's cat has more to eat than the family. With these desperate images, Bourke-White seems to suggest that, as the mothers fall apart and lose hope, their children also suffer as they appear ashamed, desperate and hungry, much like their mothers.

These images work in conjunction with Caldwell's written sections that separate the photographic sections. Caldwell places a great deal of emphasis on poor white families and how their size affects their well-being. Following his argument in his *Post* articles, Caldwell begins his discussion about tenant families by saying that the present economic situation keeps them from changing their lives because they are forced to "[breed] families of eight, ten, twelve, fourteen, sixteen, and more, in order to furnish an ever-increasing number of persons necessary to supply the rent-cotton for the landlord" (*You Have Seen* 6). Later, Caldwell tells the story of Sanford and his wife, poor sharecroppers with six children who "are resigned" to their poor state in part because they have no way "to stop having [children]" (21). Another family with eight children just gives up hope because they continue to fail in their efforts to support them (30–31). He compounds the familial problems of his subjects by saying, "Ten million persons on Southern tenant farms are living in degradation and defeat" (48).

Caldwell's conclusion brings up effective ways to help these families. He argues that "the youth" of the South should have a chance "to succeed" (48). To explain his plan to help them "succeed," he first lists the suggestions made by various groups. He notes that some "[s]ociologists [. . .] stake their reputations on a plan for sterilization of the mentally and physically unfit among the tenant farmers; others want to increase education and health" (44). Other groups, such as "[p]oliticians," "ministers," and "[e]conomists," also have plans that Caldwell thinks are either self-serving or "radical" (44). Having listed these suggestions, he suggests forming a committee that "should be composed mostly of sociologists, economists, and southern agronomists" (47).[2] This group of "economists" and "agronomists," with essentially no defined plan, and "sociologists," who cannot agree on whether to sterilize or to educate the lower class, would supposedly help the tenant farmer "remove the animalism from his mind" (45). Maternal images and reproductive lists drive this documentary book to its final eugenically motivated conclusion.

Despite obvious fabrications in *You Have Seen Their Faces,* the American public embraced Caldwell and Bourke-White's message so much so that their book found its way "near the top of the national best-seller list" (Miller 237). Even though the book achieved a wide readership, critics remained conflicted about its message. Hudson Strode applauded the book as an "eloquent collaboration" and urged all southerners to buy a personal copy (75). Southern critics did not necessarily agree with Strode's excitement. In *Southern Review,* Donald Davidson noted that *You Have Seen Their Faces* contains a more "tame" presentation of southern life than Caldwell usually offers, but he questioned the book's legitimacy as a documentary (59). According to Davidson, Caldwell's facts about sharecropping are as fictional as his subjects' dialogues. The "[t]en million" sharecroppers Caldwell numbers could not possibly exist, argues Davidson, because the "1935 Census report[s] only 716,356 sharecroppers" (64). The larger figure allowed Caldwell to urge the need to create a new identity for the South by following the "sociologists[']" reproductive plan. W. T. Couch, who adamantly disagreed with Caldwell and who later edited another documentary work, *These Are Our Lives,* in an effort to discredit him, focused his entire complaint in his review of *You Have Seen Their Faces* on this reproductive plan. Couch takes offense at Caldwell's review of the failed suggestions on how to improve southern life, and with Caldwell's discussion of the "sociologists[']" eugenic approach. He also defiantly questions Caldwell's facts: "I would like to know who these sociologists are," implying that this portion of Caldwell's work is also fictional (Couch, "Landlord" 58). While Caldwell and Bourke-White's message encouraged a great many Americans, their focus on familial relations and "sterilization" programs also caused some concern about how Americans viewed the South; however, their views about how the South could regenerate itself would become a staple image of 1930s documentary expression.

NEW DEAL RELIEF

While Bourke-White's photographs in *You Have Seen Their Faces* negatively portrayed poor white southern mothers and their families, Dorothea Lange's 1936 photograph "Migrant Mother," taken for the Farm Security Administration (FSA), a New Deal program, became an iconic image of American motherhood and of the Depression itself because Lange, unlike Bourke-White, molded her image to create a portrait of a mother who measured up to eugenic expectations.[3] Ironically, Lange almost did not take this picture. In a 1960 article titled "The Assignment I'll Never Forget," Lange recounts how she at first passed by the migrant workers' camp on a highway in Nipomo, California. After driving a short distance away from the camp, she said that she felt compelled to go back, where she spent "less than ten minutes with the woman" (42, 126). When she left the camp, she had taken the picture that Roy Stryker, the head of the FSA, would later call "'the picture of Farm Security'" (qtd. in Wood 19). Lange captured an image of a woman at once thoughtful and worried, her chin resting on her hand and her furrowed brow seemingly providing evidence of conflicting emotions. On either side of the woman stand two children leaning on her with their faces turned away from the camera, and in her arms, a baby sleeps peacefully, despite being covered in dirt and wearing, like the other two children, tattered clothing (Lange, *Photographs* 77). Only in that 1960 article did Lange describe her encounter with the "Migrant Mother."

> I saw and approached the hungry and desperate mother, as if drawn by a magnet. I do not remember how I explained my presence or my camera to her, but I do remember she asked me no questions. [. . .] I did not ask her name or her history. [. . .] She said that they had been living on frozen vegetables from the surrounding fields, and birds that the children killed. She had just sold the tires from her car to buy food. There she sat in that lean-to tent with her children huddled around her, and seemed to know that my pictures might help her, and so she helped me. There was a sort of equality about it. ("The Assignment" 126)

Lange's words about the "Migrant Mother" portray the woman, later identified by reporters as Florence Thompson, as an unbreakable force willing to sustain her suffering children by any means necessary and as a mesmeric force capable of capturing not only Lange's attention but also her respect (Levine 25). Even with Lange's article, though, Thompson remains a mystery because the only real information provided about her comes from the picture. The 1960 article only reiterates the strength of the mother because the picture itself already declares her strength in the way the children are positioned around her. She acts as their firm base, holding them up in their pain.

Despite the continued references to how "Migrant Mother" represents idealized motherhood, this picture and its origins seem embedded in contradictions. Even though this one picture has gained such acclaim, Lange actually took six photographs of Thompson and her children.[4] James Curtis argues that these six photographs uncover "powerful cultural forces of the 1930s" such as "anxiety about the status and solidarity of the family in an era of urbanization and modernization" and "a need to atone for the guilt induced by the destruction of cherished ideals" (48). Not only does the progression of the photographs display these "cultural forces" but so also does the public's acceptance of the "Migrant Mother" photograph. According to Curtis, the other photographs do not have the same effect as "Migrant Mother" because of the defeated expressions they show on the faces of the children and the mother, because of the desperation of the living conditions shown, and even because of the number of children in the photographs (48–67). Two of the photographs actually appeared in print before "Migrant Mother." In March 1936, shortly after Lange took the photographs, three appeared in the *San Francisco News*.[5] The first picture that appeared in the paper corresponded with the headline above it, declaring, "Ragged, Hungry, Broke, Harvest Workers Living in Squallor [*sic*]" (Taylor 43). "Migrant Mother" was the third to appear in that March series published by the *News*. Unlike the first photograph, published with the "Squallor" headline, the "Migrant Mother" headline read "What Does the 'New Deal' Mean to This Mother and Her Children." The headline used for this photograph suggests that this family deserves help offered by the New Deal, seemingly because this third image does not portray them as subhuman migrants living in filth. In September 1936, Lange submitted the "Migrant Mother" photograph to *Survey Graphic*, and it was touted "as one of the outstanding images of the year" (Curtis 67). Since one of the purposes of the FSA was to present a "positive view of America" (Wood 14), presumably "Migrant Mother" better represented the "status and solidarity of the family" and the lost "cherished ideals" of America than the other photographs in the series.

As the acclaimed photograph in the series, "Migrant Mother" reveals certain aspects about what made an image a "positive view of America" in the 1930s. "Migrant Mother" does not present Thompson and her family as living in "[s]quallor" as the *News* headline suggests, and it also does not reveal aspects of the family's life that Lange obviously wanted to omit. One of the most obvious omissions lies in the number of children pictured with the mother. Thompson reportedly had either six or seven children (Hapke 30; Levine 26); however, none of the pictures taken by Lange presents all of the children at once. With only three of them present in "Migrant Mother," the mother's burden seems large but not without hope. Curtis notes that, during the Depression, "business and professional elites [. . . with] influence on public policy decisions" felt that "the ideal family contained no more than three children" (52). Also, Lange never mentions that Thompson is a "widowed" mother of this large group presumably because, as the 1960 article explains, she never asked (Hapke 30). Lawrence W. Levine argues that the FSA photographers did not ask questions about their subjects so that they could create their own versions of their subjects' lives (26). If Lange's caption and photograph had revealed these aspects of the mother's life, Thompson would not have been an acceptable portrait of American motherhood because, without employment and without a husband, Americans would have seen Thompson and her family as a drain on American society. By leaving out the details of the husband's whereabouts, people viewing the image could either assume that "he was working or at least looking for work" or, the truth, that he was no longer with the family (Curtis 51). Leaving the question unanswered, however, Lange was able to keep the viewers at least wondering where the father had gone and was able to elicit increased sympathy for her subjects (Curtis 51).[6] "Migrant Mother," in effect, emerged neither as the "desperate" mother of Lange's 1960 article nor as the real woman whose family situation created seemingly insurmountable obstacles. Thompson came to represent, according to Stryker, "'all of mankind [. . .] but all of the perseverance too'" (qtd. in Wood 19). While Stryker admits that he questions the emotions of Thompson in the photograph, he obviously does not question her universality. He, like others who have viewed and published this photograph, has no negative response to this carefully created image of Thompson and three of her children.

The omissions Lange makes in her photographs and the emergence of "Migrant Mother" into a universal symbol may not have occurred merely because of Lange's own personal biases or aesthetic choices. Photographers of the FSA had full knowledge of the eugenic ideology pervading American society in the early twentieth century. Each time Stryker hired a new photographer to work for the FSA, he required the new hire to read an acclaimed 1925 geography book, *North America: Its People and the Resources, Development, and the Prospects of the Continent as an Agricultural, Industrial, and Commercial Area* (Lesy, "Assigned" 114). Nancy Wood has actually referred to *North America* as "the bible" of the FSA (13). Lesy describes *North America* as "a well-designed, amiably written [. . .] heavily illustrated geography book," but he also says that it "displayed the prevalent racial and social prejudices of its era" ("Assigned" 114). The author of *North America*, J. Russell Smith, was an advocate of eugenic ideology. In the book, Smith examines the failure of positive eugenics and the failure of society to stop those "feeble in both mind and body" from reproducing (101, 808). He even goes so far as to say, "It seems to be a peculiar irony that while we breed our animals up, we breed ourselves down" (808–9). Curtis notes that the eugenic ideologies spouted by Smith are further reflected in the "cultural stereotypes" he promotes of groups he deems either acceptable or unacceptable in American society (8). Using the content of *North America* as a guide, the FSA photographers would have gained a sense of how to present a popular view of American life and the acceptable ways to promote a strong American future. A photograph of a destitute woman surrounded by six or seven children would not have evoked the sympathy that "Migrant Mother" did; instead, it would lead the viewer to question the plight of America in relation to this new generation of destitute children.

Looking at Lange's "Migrant Mother" in conjunction with the other five photographs she took that day and with the information surrounding Thompson's actual circumstances provides new insight into the popularity of this photograph; however, other work sponsored by Roosevelt's New Deal did not require outside resources to uncover the nation's problematic obsession with poor white mothers and the number of children they had. In 1939, the Federal Writers' Project (FWP), a Works Progress Administration (WPA) program, published *These Are Our Lives,* a collection of stories about real southerners during the Depression.[7] The unique aspect of this collection is that the stories actually came from the subjects themselves; the writers' job was simply to write the story as the subject told it to them. W. T. Couch, the editor of the collection and an adversary of Caldwell, insisted on presenting the stories in this authentic fashion: "Here, then, are real, living people. Here are their own stories, their origins, their more important experiences, their most significant thoughts and feelings, told by themselves from their own point of view" (Preface xiv). Until this publication, the FWP had generally only been used to put together state guidebooks that introduced Americans to their country, but since the government mandated that the FWP focus on "work which had social usefulness," Couch also wanted to use the FWP to create a new image for the South (Hirsch and Terrill xviii). As regional director for the southeast branch of the FWP and as director of the University of North Carolina Press, Couch felt that he had to defend the South from the negative publicity it received during the 1930s. At a 1938 conference in Washington, Roosevelt had referred to the South as "'the nation's No. 1 economic problem'" (qtd. in Leuchtenburg 104). With this quotation appearing in the *New York Times,* southerners, including Couch, feared that Americans would use it to justify the desperate images depicted by writers such as Caldwell (Leuchtenburg 109; Hirsch and Terrill xviii–xix).[8] By giving southerners of all social levels a chance to speak for themselves, Couch hoped to give the South a chance to "clarify and solve its problems" (Hirsch and Terrill xviii–xix).

To provide what he thought of as an accurate version of southerners, Couch put together a specific plan as to how he wanted the stories to be collected and written. Couch insisted that *These Are Our Lives* should present the reality, both the positive and the negative aspects, of southern life. While he wanted to show that the degenerate Lester family of *Tobacco Road* did not represent all southern families, he did not want to use the collection to deny that such families existed in the South (Hirsch 186). He felt that southerners had to face the problems of their region in order to solve them (186). To obtain these realistic stories, Couch gave specific instructions to his writers to "keep [their] own opinions and feelings in the background as much as possible" (Preface 418). Unlike Caldwell, who wrote his captions for his subjects in *You Have Seen Their Faces* based on his "impressions" of them, Couch wanted "the subject's mind to speak for itself" (418). While Couch insisted that his writers simply record the stories as told to them, he did provide an outline of what information they should try to obtain from their subjects, and just as Lange highlights family in her "Migrant Mother" photographs, Couch puts the most emphasis on gathering family information. The first piece of information listed for the writer to gather concerns the size of the family (Moore, "Outline" 420). While Couch also suggests in his instructions that a writer does not have to follow the "outline in a rigid manner," he requests that "the majority of stories should be about families," whether those stories focus on an entire community or a small part of a community ("Instructions" 417, 418). He encourages his writers to learn "the size of the family, the coming of children and the effect their coming has on the fortunes of a family" (418). His focus on families follows the trend of documenting the Depression, whether through fictional or nonfictional representations, as a familial experience. With the South's problematic, reproductive role in the nation's future, however, *These Are Our Lives* works in much the same way as eugenic family studies because Couch chooses to identify and to understand poverty-stricken people as products of their familial situations.

While Couch instructs all of his writers to focus on the families of their subjects, the collection itself reveals how important the family is to specific aspects of southern life. The book has four separate sections, "On the Farm," "In Mill Village and Factory," "In Service Opportunities," and "On Relief."[9] Although each focuses on the role of the family, "On the Farm" seems driven by the number of children in each story and how the families react to having children. While this assessment seems appropriate because farm families needed to be large to supply sufficient labor, the stories place emphasis on the hardships caused by the children without showing the communal affection of the family. In the first story in the collection, "You're Gonna Have Lace Curtains," John and Sarah Easton have six children. Sarah recounts that, when she got pregnant the third time, she tried to abort her baby to save her family from further turmoil (Hicks and Harrison 6). Although John and Sarah love their children, they are desperate because they cannot adequately care for them (6). In "Some Sort O' How," Bernice Kelly Harris tells the story of Joe Fielding and his family, a wife, and eighteen children, five of whom are not his biological children (39). Because Joe is raising his children and his family members' children, he cannot afford his own farm (40, 43). Instead, he must pay doctor bills and watch his children suffer from "tuberculosis," and his wife has become so despondent about their situation that she no longer goes out in public (39, 40). Another story in this section, "Lived Too Long," makes childbearing and motherhood almost seem like a death sentence. In this story, Lady, a married woman with fourteen children, has been diagnosed with breast cancer. The doctor told her that she contracted it by "nursing too many children" (Newman and Aswell 87–88). This diagnosis seems to suggest that Lady's children are responsible for her cancer, and they fail her further because none of them can help with the medical bills because they too have "lots" of children and "are poor" (89). The Eastons, the Fieldings, and Lady's family continue to suffer because of their large families, and the futures of their children seem just as bleak as their parents' lives.

Having a small family, by contrast, is viewed as the way to experience and enjoy a middle-class lifestyle. The final story focusing on poor white families in the "On the Farm" section, "I Saved My Money," recounts the life of John Sylvester Hinton. Despite growing up in a large, poor family, John only has four children with his wife because he believes that big families keep people from prospering (Matthews 94). With only four children, John owns "cars, stock, clothes an' food aplenty," and he has no debt (95). Some stories actually focus on people who, having escaped the farm and a large family, hope that they will never have to live that life again. Evelyn in "Snappy Feeding" works as a hotel desk clerk and a waitress, and her only ambition is never to have to live a life like her parents, who have eleven children (Yoe and Edwards 346). Interestingly, in the middle of the collection, as editor, Couch places "Plow Beams for Bills," the story of a country doctor named Robert Cain who actually talks about the excessive birthrate of poor women and how he thinks this problem should be handled. Dr. Cain remarks that, although he did not at first agree with birth control methods, his experiences with poor women bearing multiple children have changed his mind (Harris, "Plow" 273). Therefore he tries to educate women about birth control, and for those he deems to be "mental defectives" or to have "abnormal physical conditions," he waits for the "approval of the Eugenics Board in Raleigh" and then has them "sterilized" (274). As the "county health officer," Dr. Cain insists that both his poor white and his poor black patients desperately desire this help in keeping their families small (273, 274, 264). He wants to help the people he calls "frail women" and "helpless children" (273). Interestingly, this discussion about birth control and eugenics is the doctor's main focus, as if stopping poor women's ability to procreate is the most important part of helping them. According to *These Are Our Lives,* having a small family is the main way for poor southern families to reverse their fortunes and to live happy and fruitful lives.

Dr. Cain's story does not just dwell on the problem of excessively large families; he also focuses on what he sees as the sexual depravity of the southern poor. He begins his story by recounting his effort to convince a poor white young boy into marrying his pregnant girlfriend and how his intervention kept the couple's families from fighting (Harris, "Plow" 264–65). This same type of scenario appears again in " . . . And Costs." The justice of the peace talks about needing to preside over a case in which a boy seduced a fifteen-year-old poor white girl "with the mind of a child of ten" (Humphries and Aswell 306–7). Although he expects the boy to go to prison, the real tragedy for him lies in the fact that the girl will now have a baby that she does not have the physical or mental capabilities to care for and that the baby's father has already moved on to his next female prey (306–7). These two stories, told by two of the three middle-class whites included in the collection, express eugenic concerns about lower-class women's lack of sexual control and emphasize how poor people need outsiders, both in class and stature, to help solve their problems. Of course, this focus on the sexuality of poor people also pervades some of the stories told by lower-class interviewees. One of the first stories in the collection, "Get Out and Hoe," resurrects the "good" mother / "bad" mother theme of eugenic family studies. The narrator, Irma, reveals that she and her husband, Morrison, had a good life together until a sixteen-year-old "bad" girl, Amelia, stole him from Irma (Dunnagan 34). Although Morrison returned home eventually, he did not leave Amelia before he fathered a child with her. Along with Morrison's baby, Amelia has three other illegitimate children with two other men (35–36). In the end, Irma, a faithful wife and mother, forgave Morrison and even consented to live next door to "crazy" Amelia (35, 36). One of the final stories in the collection, "Till the River Rises," tells the story of a family broken apart by "a whore" (Yoe and Edwards 379). A nephew killed his uncle because both men were trading the "whore" back and forth, causing an obvious family disturbance (379). Fan Flannigan, the narrator of the story, suggests that this deviant woman be "burned to a crisp in the chair" rather than the nephew because Flannigan sees her as the real murderer (379). Poor families, thus, seem to have two problems working against them: reproduction and excessive female sexuality.

The collection's emphasis on families and reproductive sexual behavior emerges as a pattern, and as editor, Couch is largely responsible for creating this pattern. Although only thirty-five stories appear in the collection, interviewers collected over four hundred stories (Stott 204).[10] Couch chose to include only stories that he deemed of great importance because, even though this book was supposed to be the first volume in a series, he had no assurance that a second volume would get published (Hirsch 169–70). Jerrold Hirsch notes that Couch decided to leave out the story of the prostitute Bessie Mae Boatwright, despite the encouragement of William McDaniel, the Tennessee state director of the FWP, to include it. McDaniel felt that Bessie Mae represented part of the South's problems both socially and economically, but Couch felt that Bessie Mae corresponded too much with America's preconceived notions about the oversexualized South. Since Couch did not want to ignore the problems of the South, his decision to leave out the story of Bessie Mae designates a sexual boundary that he does not want to cross; however, it also puts into question the stories that he does include, especially as they relate to poor white women. Of the twenty stories portraying poor white life, only one, "Snappy Feeding," depicts a woman as anything other than a mother, and although Evelyn in "Snappy Feeding" enjoys her jobs, her main ambition is still defined by family because she mostly concentrates on not becoming a mother (Yoe and Edwards 346). With this focus on family and motherhood, Couch follows the tradition of the 1930s, but unlike Lange, he does not use his editing abilities to alter the reproductive abilities of the lower class in order to keep the emphasis on the social class's economic plight. Instead, he amplifies the reproductive problem by emphasizing the sexuality that increases reproductive rates. Stephen Fender argues that Couch only succeeds in "present[ing] a hapless, rootless, shiftless, and degenerate population[, . . .] improvidently producing numbers of children beyond their means of support" (144). Also, by including Dr. Cain's story in the collection, Couch provides his only solution to "the nation's No. 1 economic problem": only by slowing the birthrate, either through birth control or sterilization, can the South restructure its problematic identity. Obviously, the nation agreed with Couch's rendition of southern life because Jerre Mangione notes that *These Are Our Lives* "received stronger praise than any other single Project publication" (367).

A SOCIOLOGIST'S VIEWPOINT

In 1939, a young sociologist, Margaret Jarman Hagood, published *Mothers of the South: Portraiture of the White Tenant Farm Woman,* a study providing scientific evidence that seems to substantiate the statistical data presented by Caldwell and Couch. Hagood began this study while she was working on her Ph.D. in sociology at the University of North Carolina at Chapel Hill in 1937. Her dissertation provided "a detailed statistical analysis of the fertility patterns of native white women of childbearing age in the Southeast" (Scott iv). Because of her "statistical" findings, Hagood saw a need to understand "the social context of the statistics" concerning this particular group (v). She recognized that southern poor whites had become the subject of much debate as a result of Roosevelt's reference to the South as "the nation's No. 1 economic problem" and of documentary work about Depression-era poverty (iv, vii). Hagood wanted to provide what she saw as a more accurate, scientific description of these women's lives than those previously presented by politicians and artists. Of course, she knew that this meant battling an already entrenched view of the importance of poor white southern women to the future of American society. Hagood acknowledges this commonly held belief about America's future, in the beginning of her study, by quoting one of her academic colleagues who said, "'As goes the South, [. . .] so goes the Nation. More than that, [. . .] as goes the rural mother in the South, so goes the Nation!'" (qtd. in Hagood 3). Then, Hagood rewords the quotation based upon her findings in the study: "'As goes the Southern tenant farm mother, so goes a large part of the South and the Nation'" (3–4). As a sociologist, Hagood not only studied the alleged truths set forth in other analyses of southern poor white life but was able to supply authority to those claims.

Unlike Roosevelt or other documentary authors, Margaret Hagood does not simply make a claim about the national importance of poor white southern women without explaining why it is true. According to Hagood, southern tenants have become the "Number One problem" because the number of tenant farmers keeps increasing each year, because they keep falling economically and culturally each year, and "because of their increasing share of the reproduction of the people" (3). What other authors only suggest by reciting over and over the number of children in a family, Hagood states in simple terms; however, unlike her counterparts during the 1930s who focused on poor white women's sexual promiscuity and their inability to act as fit mothers, Hagood approaches these women's lives from a positive angle. James Tice Moore has recently argued that a noteworthy aspect of this book is Hagood's representation of these women that defies the standards of the time. Instead of degenerate poor whites, Hagood presents "competent, conscientious individuals who [take] pride in their roles as mothers and as co-laborers with their spouses in crop production" (Moore, "Review" 387). In fact, Hagood puts a great deal of emphasis on presenting a positive image that directly contrasts what is expected. She notes that "tenant farm [mothers]" have three jobs which they do unconditionally: raising children, keeping house, and "farming"

(92), and although "an overwhelming majority—seven eighths" prefers working on the farm to working in the house, the women still complete their expected duties (89). Also, Hagood spends a great deal of time focusing on her subjects' mothering abilities since, essentially, this part of their lives is the most in question. According to her findings, however, she argues, "In no particular do the portrayals of certain fiction writers seem more unrepresentative than in their belittling of family ties" (155). The children are not simply a means to gain unpaid labor; they also allow the women to take pride in themselves as mothers. The women in her study show an unqualified devotion to their children, partly because they believe that raising their children well connects them with the "ideology" of "the economic superior class" (86). By focusing on the positive aspects of these women's lives, Hagood creates a picture of poor white women devoted to supporting their husbands, to working hard, and to raising their children in a socially acceptable way.

While Hagood seems committed to showing the honor in poor white women's lives, she agrees that those lives do at times epitomize all of the negative connotations associated with her colleague's statement. She states that "tenant farm mothers embody many of the causes, processes, and effects of the general regional problems of an exploiting agriculture, overpopulation, general cultural retardation, chronological and technological lag" (4). For Hagood, the lives of her poor white female subjects represent why certain sharecroppers and tenant farmers do not have the ability to climb "the agricultural ladder" to become landowners (40). To lead into her discussion of how these women "embody" this problem of poor white economic and social destitution, she first acknowledges the ongoing eugenic discussion, noting that poor whites who fail to climb the "ladder" tend to get branded as "biological[ly]" inferior (40); however, Hagood argues that this "biological" explanation does not adequately detail the problem. Aligning herself with the environmentally conscious eugenics movement of the 1920s and 1930s, she begins relating the questions raised by the "socialist geneticists."

> In oversimplified terms there are three variables: "quality" of people, their environment [. . .], and their achievement. [. . . W]hat degree of quality can we infer in people whose achievement as measured by position on the

> tenure ladder is low, but whose environment [. . .] has been very disadvantageous? (40)

Like "socialist geneticists," Hagood does not think these questions can be answered until new standards of "achievement" and "adequate [. . .] environmental standards" are implemented (40). Only then will it become possible to understand the "relationship between the three variables" (40). As a sociologist, though, Hagood does not have the ability to change the standards of "achievement." Instead, she focuses on changing the "environmental" standards through the lives of poor white women, and just as other documentary works of the 1930s have done, she uses the size of the women's families as evidence against them. Although Hagood disassociates herself from the sexually predatory images of poor white women found in other works, she still aligns herself with eugenicists when she uses the reproductive abilities of the women to explain the poor white class's problems.

In fact, Hagood not only aligns herself with eugenic ideas, but she also employs some of their methods. Despite studying the lives of many different women, she focuses her study on two specific women who merit so much attention, according to Hagood, that she tells their entire life stories. The women she chooses and the way in which she tells their stories follow the pattern of the eugenic family studies because these women, Mollie Goodwin and Mary Hunt Simmons, have contradictory mothering experiences. Hagood presents the life of Mollie first. Mollie grew up in a sheltered, male-dominated environment in which she was not allowed to attend school regularly or to date (185, 190–91). To get away from these restrictions, she moved to town and began working in a cigarette factory (190). She moved to break the cycle of marriage, children, and male familial domination; however, when her mother and her brothers became sick, she had to return home (192). Back at home, knowing that she would never return to her factory job, she married an older man and now has three surviving children, only one of whom she considers to have the ability to have a successful life (194–95, 198). Mary, the focus of Hagood's second case study, has just the opposite approach to life. Unlike Mollie, Mary loves being a wife and having children (199–200). As a mother of nine, Mary insists that her children attend school because she wants to raise them to act as "respectable citizens," which she sees as entirely possible regardless of her family's lack of material wealth (212). While Mary represents the quintessential poor white woman who works hard to fulfill her three designated roles and never complains, Mollie represents the poor white women who are not suited for this life and who, when forced into this life, neither produce effective children nor nurture their children into effective adults.

While Hagood's choice of women explicitly reveals her desire to show contrasting images of poor white motherhood, the way in which she tells the stories also contributes to this dualistic imagery. Although both stories come from personal interviews conducted by Hagood, Mollie's life story reads more like a fictional creation than a documentary work. Unlike Mary's story, Mollie's does not refer to interviews or conversations that Hagood conducted with Mollie; instead, Hagood, rather dramatically, traces "the annals of the life of Mollie[, . . . a] tenant child," beginning the journey "more than a quarter of a century ago" (183). Reminiscent of Caldwell's captions in *You Have Seen Their Faces,* Mollie's supposed personal thoughts and fantastic descriptions of instances in her life are chronicled by Hagood with no specific references to Mollie as the original storyteller. For instance, Mollie's first encounter with female reproduction seems somewhat fictional because of Hagood's descriptive technique: "Mollie heard groans and knew her mother was suffering. Her own body began to ache. Her mother's sounds grew louder and louder [. . .]. Suddenly she thought she was having a baby. [. . .] She remained motionless for a long time, knowing and feeling nothing but a horrible fear of disgrace and dread" (187–89). This violent and terrifying scene is Hagood's description of Mollie's mother giving birth and Mollie simultaneously having her first menstrual cycle. Later, Hagood adds to the dramatic effect when she tells of how Mollie's coming-of-age moment was ruined by her reproductive ability. When Mollie's parents finally allow her to purchase and wear a new silk dress to a party, she starts her period early, ruining her dress and forcing her to sit alone all evening (189). Hagood refers to this tragedy as "[t]he loss of her life's triumph and [an] indescribable embarrassment" (189). From these scenes, women's reproductive ability seems more like a limitation than a gift. Mollie's plans for her youngest daughter, the only child she thinks can succeed, explain just how much she dislikes her domestic life because Mollie refuses to allow this daughter to do fieldwork or housework in hopes that she will do what Mollie could not, "get an education [and . . .] a job" and ultimately escape the farm (197–98).

These dramatic, horrifying images in Mollie's life story do not appear in Mary's story. Actually, the drama of Mollie's life is replaced by a structured image of Mary, and ironically, Hagood allows Mary to do what she does not allow Mollie to do, guide her own story. However, even though Mary gets to participate in telling her own story, she shares no inner sensibilities about her living situation. Instead of presenting herself as a woman with emotions, Mary presents herself only as a daughter, a wife, and a mother. According to the story, Mary spends all of her time "making a living by industry and [. . .] maintaining respectability" for her family (Hagood 200). Keeping "respectability" for her family depends upon Mary's ability to protect her nine children from "the pitfalls of sex sins" (200). Mary tells Hagood that her family members can attain "respectability" if they follow "traditional" standards "relating to sex" (217). As a result of this belief, Mary's approach to dealing with sex and female reproduction seems quite different from Mollie's story. The only discussions or thoughts Mary has about sexual issues relate to how she thinks these topics should not be discussed or thought about by her or her children. When talking to Hagood about her children, Mary recounts how she once found a birth control pamphlet in her son's pocket (214). She refers to the pamphlet as "dirty" and "awful" (215, 214), but she also says that she does not want her son to have an illegitimate child (214). Of course, Mary's inability to talk about sexuality corresponds with her decision not to talk about her family's economic "failure" since Mary's nine children and her inability or unwillingness to use birth control have contributed greatly to her family's poverty (217). Therefore, although Mary does not emphasize the negative aspects of her poor white life as Mollie does, she does spend a lot of effort denying important aspects of her familial life, suggesting that even this positive image of poor white motherhood requires some use of fiction, this time by the woman herself rather than the outside storyteller.

Although Mollie and Mary represent two versions of poor white motherhood, Hagood uses their common lack of opportunity to connect them to the lives of the other poor white women to whom she speaks. Mollie's lost opportunities come as a result of her inability to escape poverty regardless of how hard she has tried. Mary's lost opportunities come as a result of her unwillingness to recognize that the birth control information she does not want her children to have may well have kept her family from the economic "failure" about which she refuses to speak. Hagood presents neither woman, whether she has been forced into this life or has chosen it, as a horribly unfit mother; instead, she treats them and her other poor white female subjects as products of their social "environment[s]." According to Hagood, the women she has studied lack the time and the education to change their lives and their families' lives. Only a portion of them, especially those who mother ineffective children, seem to lack the "biological" ability to change their destitute situations (76, 44). Even the mothers of "feeble-minded" children are presented as innocent victims (53–55, 77). Concluding her study, Hagood states that, no matter how good a poor white woman is, she still has too many obstacles to overcome: "And even though the finest inherent vitality be granted and the intangible values of rural life admitted, the environmental handicaps, both biological and social, are sufficient to prevent these youth from attaining the 'quality' of population desired for American people" (244). She even echoes the sentiments of the "alarmist eugenicists" she wants to disassociate herself from when she says that these facts affect "nearly a million and a half tremendously important reproducers of the Nation's people" (244, 245). Like Caldwell in *You Have Seen Their Faces,* Hagood uses numbers to make her message compelling. Because of this "million and a half" group of innocent, yet still problematic, poor white "reproducers," Hagood sees America's future as ultimately in jeopardy (246).

END OF AN ERA

In 1936, the same year that Caldwell and Bourke-White began their study of rural poverty in the South, James Agee and Walker Evans also set out to study this section of the country. Agee had worked for *Fortune* magazine since 1932, and in 1936, Agee's managing editor at *Fortune,* Eric Hodgins, assigned him to write a story about Deep South sharecroppers (Hershey xi, xv). Hodgins allowed Agee to take photographer Walker Evans along with him to document the story visually (xv). Evans at the time worked as an FSA photographer, and as Carol Shloss notes, he had become well known because, when he photographed a scene, he refused to alter it and thereby change its purpose and voice (607). Agee appreciated this approach because it showed Evans's desire to "discover reality, not fabricate it" (Hershey xvi). When Agee and Evans set out to create a realistic account of southern rural life, they thought that their investigation would only take a month; however, Agee and Evans had to spend a month searching just to make connections with possible subjects (xvii). They finally met a group of men whom Agee refers to by the pseudonyms Fred Ricketts, Bud Woods, and George Gudger (xvi–xvii).[11] After meeting these men and their families, Agee and Evans felt welcome in their world and began their work. When Agee returned to *Fortune* magazine, he could not conceive of writing the story the way the editors wanted him to write it, but they also would not allow him to sell the story as his own to a publishing company (xix). Finally, in 1937, *Fortune* released the story to Agee, and Harper and Brothers picked it up (xx). Once again, however, the book never made it to publication because Agee refused to make the revisions that Harper required (xxv). Not until 1941 was *Let Us Now Praise Famous Men* finally published by Houghton Mifflin.

Despite Agee's attempt to create a realistic account of southern tenant life, the supposed reality of the text becomes overshadowed by textual contradictions that arguably reveal more about Agee than about his subjects. At the beginning of the documentary, Agee says that he hopes his book can help "rectify the unpleasant situation down South" (Agee and Evans 14), but he also admits that writing this book could be problematic because of how his subjects will be perceived through his words: "It seems to me curious, not to say obscene and thoroughly terrifying [. . . to] parad[e] the nakedness, disadvantage and humiliation of these lives before another group of human beings in the name of science, of 'honest journalism'" (7). Despite Agee's activist goal and recognition of potential problems, however, he is unable to avoid the pitfalls of portraying poor white southern life. Like Caldwell and Couch, Agee's own middle-class understanding of this group at times obscures the type of people his subjects actually seem to be. Linda Wagner-Martin has argued that, although this documentary is about "real" people, Agee has made his subjects into fictional "'character[s]'" (45). For Wagner-Martin, Agee's subjects become "'character[s]'" because he makes himself into a "'character'" in their lives as the "narrator/reporter" editorializing their thoughts and emotions (45). Paula Rabinowitz suggests that this aspect of the book "returns" the focus "to the middle class, enlisting the reader in a process of self-recognition" (*They Must* 51). While this intrusion by Agee into the narrative of his subjects could possibly force middle-class readers to survey their own interactions with people of the lower class, it also helps to reinforce American middle-class preconceptions about the lower class. As "narrator/reporter," Agee seems unable to disconnect himself from their stories, and as a result, at times he objectifies the poor white characters he wants to help.

Agee's initial objectification of his subjects emerges in his decision to follow the pattern of other Depression-era documentaries by centering his discussion of poor whites on their familial situation. Although Agee does not provide detailed lists of multiple families and the number of children in each, he does examine the potential of the children and the parents as he describes the three tenant families. He actually puts a great deal of emphasis on the children. While he recognizes that the children are "still in the tenderness of their lives," he also says that they act "like temperless and feeble-minded children" (Agee and Evans 78). Agee's decision to use this well-known eugenic term is not an isolated event in the text because he continues to reference the eugenic connotations associated with "feeble-minded" in other descriptions. He describes Ivy Woods's unborn baby as a "heavy-browed beast" (77). The Ricketts children, according to Agee, have "the grinning look of dogs" (386). Even the Gudger children, despite the fact that Agee has the most respect for their family, do not escape the animal descriptions. Although he refers to all of the Gudger children as "dogs" (66), he specifically says that Squinchy Gudger has "the comic and foolish look of a dog who has been dressed up by children" (280). Richard H. King has argued that Agee portrays his subjects as "proto-human and lack[ing] any significant measure of self-consciousness" in order to establish their "innocen[ce]" (223, 230). This animal imagery, however, works much like Caldwell's "mongrel bitch" story because Agee's animalized subjects seem unable and unworthy to "rectify" the South's "unpleasant situation." As a matter of fact, as "beast[s]" and "dogs," they actually seem like the reason for the "unpleasant situation."

Agee actually takes this focus on poor white children a step further in the "Colon: Curtain Call" part of the book. In this section, he describes the fictional life cycle of his subjects in an effort not to take away from their "sum total" (Agee and Evans 100–101); however, he fills this "sum total" with contradictory images because of the eugenic undertones permeating this part of the book. Like all new life, poor white life begins with all the "human possibility to build itself ruin or wonder" (101), and as an unborn baby, this life is "capable [. . .] of health, which is perfection, which is holiness [. . .] and is capable likewise of all harm to itself and to others" (101). The difference between "holiness" and "harm" exists in the "physical and mental" abilities of this unborn life (101). Agee does not deny that the outcome of the unborn baby's life also depends upon the environment in which the baby lives (102). However, although Agee admits this environmental chance at redemption, he asserts that this unborn life has emerged from "a chain [. . .] of sorrowful and demented flesh" (102). He continues this look into the ancestry of poor white life by focusing on the parents of this baby. According to Agee, the parents are "two [. . .] crucified people" who created "a crucifixion of cell and whiplashed sperm," therefore creating another "crucified" person" (102–3). As a product of these "crucified" people, the unborn baby already seems trapped in a "prison" before his birth has even occurred (103). In this "prison," the baby gets enveloped by "beaten blood," and he is growing towards "bondage" (103). Inside the womb, the baby must fight to survive by fending off "the blow of the bayonet in his solar plexus" (103). Finally born, the baby gets a chance "to find himself," but he takes that chance burdened by his parents, who may have the ability to "harm" him, and by the "beaten blood" he has inherited (103).[12] According to Agee's description of poor white conception to birth, this child, this representative of the future generation, must face a plethora of struggles both before and after birth.

Like the animal references, the type of language Agee uses to describe the "sum total" of poor whites' lives further complicates his presentation of the people he supposedly wants to honor. Using the term "crucified" to describe the parents has often been seen as Agee's way to reveal the "holiness" that he sees in this group. Michael Staub has referred to this "holiness" as Agee's "fierce insistence on the sacred indescribability of each life" (159). Even Lionel Trilling in his 1942 review of *Let Us Now Praise Famous Men* argues that Agee's only fault in the book is that "he writes of his people as if there were no human unregenerateness in them, no flicker of malice or meanness, no darkness or wildness of feeling, only a sure and simple virtue, the growth, we must suppose, of their hard, unlovely poverty" (102). The problem with this version of "holiness," however, actually lies in the term "crucified." While "crucified" does bring with it connotations of "holiness," it also suggests "defeat" and "torment," and according to Agee's description of poor white conception, this latter connotation becomes increasingly prevalent.[13] To assume that "crucified" refers simply to "holiness" would be to overlook Agee's other use of "fierce" language. The terms "whiplashed," "beaten," "prison," and "bondage" do not support this simple image of "holiness." This child must begin life in "torment," a victim of his own heredity and of the environment meant to protect and nurture him. While Agee's description does not unequivocally signal the "holiness" of this new life, he also does not deny that, despite the unfavorable conditions, the baby still has a chance "to find himself" in life away from the biological battle. Even this final chance at "holiness," though, depends upon the also "crucified" parents. Once again, Agee blurs the line between "holiness" and "harm" by the "defeat[ed]" language he uses and by the limited possibilities he offers to poor white children.

Agee concentrates a great deal on the parenting abilities of his poor white adult subjects. In fact, just as Agee seems to follow eugenic ideas in his account of the conception and birth of poor white children, he also follows the eugenic example of putting poor white women at the forefront of his parenting assessment. While the men work and provide for their families, the women emerge almost as the sole caretakers, and just as in eugenic family studies, their mothering capabilities dictate the author's view of their familial situation. When Agee is determining which family is suitable to stay with while conducting his study, he actually judges the suitability of the Woodses, the Ricketts, and the Gudgers by the matriarchal women in the family. Of all the families, Agee has the least respect for the Woods because their family name has been desecrated by the reputation of Ivy Woods and her mother, women he refers to as "dogs" (Agee and Evans 77). The townspeople have branded Ivy a harlot because of her illegitimate children, and she seems to have inherited this trait from her mother, who is also known for her explicit sexuality (79). Agee even says Pearl, Ivy's daughter, "already [shows] the signs" of following this family pattern (280). Ivy's husband is so cognizant of his wife's sexual transgressions that he refuses to let Agee and Evans stay in the same house with her (372). Fred Ricketts's wife, Sadie, does not have the undignified reputation of Ivy; however, Agee does not respect her. When Agee and Evans first meet the families, Evans wants to photograph them. Sadie washes her children so that they will not look too dirty, and although Agee appreciates this, he still only looks at her with pity because, to him, her "eyes" are full of "fury and shame and fear" and because he thinks of her as a "little crazy, terrified child" with a "[foolish]" husband (363–64). Only Annie Mae Gudger garners any respect from Agee, who actually admits that he has a fondness for her (398). Like Sadie, Annie Mae cleans her children before the pictures, but Agee says that Annie Mae has an "intense social and perhaps 'spiritual'" understanding of how her children should look to succeed socially (275).[14] Because of this "'spiritual'" understanding, Agee decides to stay with the Gudgers, who he thinks "still have a little yet earnest wish that anything shall be as pleasant and proper to live with as possible" and who he calls "the most nearly representative" of the three families (Agee and Evans xlv, 156). Only the Gudger family, with Annie Mae as its focal point, has managed, despite its poverty, to hold onto the "social and [. . .] 'spiritual'" values which Agee seems to respect.

Before the Gudgers reach this representative status, Agee presents a version of their family that not only problematizes his holy conception of them but also shows how susceptible even this poor white family is to the "harm" of life that he obviously sees in the Woods and Ricketts families. Once again, the focus falls on a poor white woman. At the beginning of Agee's account of his travels, even before he introduces and tells how he meets the three families, he first introduces the Gudgers, as if foreshadowing the praise he will give them later. He does not, however, focus on Annie Mae, her husband, and the children. Instead, he focuses on Emma, Annie Mae's sister, who is leaving Alabama to reunite with her estranged husband in Mississippi. Agee does not just present Emma as a member of the Gudger family; he presents her as a sexual "nymph" on the verge of destroying her sister's happy family life (Agee and Evans 372). In fact, he actually compares Emma's and Annie Mae's feminine qualities. While Agee describes Annie Mae as beyond her sexual prime, he describes Emma as overtly sexual (71). According to Agee, Emma is so sexually attractive that he, Evans, and George, Annie Mae's husband, all want to have sex with her: "[I]f only Emma could spend her last few days alive having a gigantic great time in bed, with George, a kind of man she is best used to, and with Walker and with me, whom she is curious about and attracted to, and who [. . .] have for her the mystery or glamour almost of mythological creatures" (62). Wagner-Martin remarks that, because of Agee's focus on Emma's sexuality, Emma becomes "a sexual object and nothing else" (49). Stott has argued that Agee's concentration on Emma makes her a real "woman" (302). Both of these assessments of Emma's character, though, overlook how Agee positions her in the story and in relation to Annie Mae. Emma must leave for Mississippi to meet her husband before the Gudger family can emerge as the family Agee most respects. Emma, who Agee says "emanates [*sic*] so disordering or witless violation," must leave so that George does not get drawn into this sexual woman's downfall just as Bud Woods must not invite Agee and Evans to stay with him to protect them from his wife or his wife from them (Agee and Evans 72). Also, she must leave so that Agee can focus his attention not on sexual pleasure but on creating a realistic view of his subjects. As a result, Emma emerges neither as a "sexual object" nor as a "woman" alone; she represents all that must be discarded from poor white life in order to save it. When Agee returns to the Gudgers in the last scene of the book, they are, without Emma, the representative and hopeful poor white family.

Without Emma present in the family, Agee's attention goes straight to Annie Mae, and although he has already introduced the Gudgers in his opening account of his fantasized affair with Emma, he provides a completely new view of them, especially Annie Mae, when he recounts his first visit to their house in the final scene of *Let Us Now Praise Famous Men*. When Agee compares Emma and Annie before Emma departs, Annie Mae seems pale in comparison, having lost her beauty and even her motherly ability. Agee describes her as "a scrawny, [. . .] delicate animal" with "delicately shriveled" breasts (Agee and Evans 57, 71). Annie Mae's "animal" qualities and "shriveled" breasts do not correspond with the "'spiritual'" mothering ability with which he later presents her. With Emma as her counterpart, Annie Mae's ability as a superior woman and mother seems lost; however, when Agee revisits his first night in the Gudger house without the presence of Emma, the person he is most keenly aware of is Annie Mae. Agee becomes entranced by her unspoken words and her posture (398). During this visit, Annie Mae finally becomes the "generous nurturing" mother who grounds the family unit and keeps them together (Wagner-Martin 49). Even Annie Mae's breasts no longer appear "shriveled" because she "nurses" her son Squinchy to give both herself and him comfort during a thunderstorm (Agee and Evans 402). Annie Mae becomes both an altruistic mother for her family and a mother figure to Agee. When Agee returns to the house to spend the night, she feeds and waits on him despite her tiredness (413). Later, Agee refers to George and Annie Mae as his "brother" and his "sister," and even more intimately, he calls them his "own parents" (415). Although he is speaking about George and Annie Mae both, Annie Mae's presence is what "honor[s]" him the most (418). Therefore, Annie Mae emerges as what Wagner-Martin calls "the central symbol for Agee's metaphor of family"; Annie Mae attains this position both because she holds her family together and because Agee accepts her as his surrogate mother (49).

Evans's photographs of the families correspond to and, at times, amplify Agee's depictions. The photograph of Annie Mae especially highlights how Evans accentuates Agee's narration. Evans adds another dimension to Agee's portrayal of Annie Mae as an altruistic mothering figure because Evans's portrait of her, without her family, conveys the personal strength that engages Agee when he meets her. Trilling suggests that, in the photograph, Annie Mae represents "a single concentrated phrase of suffering," but at the same time, her "gaze" also "checks [that] pity" because, unlike the shameful look Agee sees in Sadie's eyes, Annie Mae's eyes "[refuse] to" allow her to be looked at as an "object" (100–101). Agee even remarks about Annie Mae's photograph in his text, urging his readers to look into Annie Mae's "gentle eyes" because they represent a woman trying to survive and capable of living a better life than the one she has now (Agee and Evans 321). This altruistic image of Annie Mae formed by Agee in the text and Evans in the photograph is further highlighted by Evans's decision to place Annie Mae's portrait by the portrait of her husband, George. While George is unshaven and has on dirty clothing, Annie Mae has pulled her hair back away from her face and is wearing a clean, collared dress. These contrasting images suggest even further how much determination Annie Mae must have in order to maintain the type of standards that Agee respects. As a woman representative of the "social and [. . .] 'spiritual'" understanding poor whites can have, Annie Mae represents a positive "truth" of what life could be like for the suffering lower class of the South (Olin 95).

Evans further creates a dominant image of the Gudger family by how he has chosen to photograph its members. Peter Cosgrove notes that the only family not to have a group picture taken is the Gudgers; they are all photographed individually (348). As a result, even though the Gudgers and the Woods each only have three children further in the photographs, the group photograph associates the Woods family with society's belief that poor people are prone to "shiftless fertility" (348). According to Cosgrove, Evans reinforces this point by taking the Woods family portrait on the bed while he photographs the Gudger bed alone, covered in a white sheet. These two corresponding images create the idea that the Woods bed is "fertile" and the Gudger bed is "ascetic" (348). The photographs of the children also support Agee's positive portrayal of the Gudger family. While the Gudger children are photographed with clean faces and clean clothes, even in spite of the tears in their clothing, the Woods children appear stained, and one of the Woods children is actually exposed from the waist down in their family portrait. Unlike the Woods children, the Ricketts children are not exposed; however, their eyes seem full of the same "shame" that Agee has described in Sadie's eyes. Of all the children photographed, Maggie Louise, Annie Mae's daughter, seems like the one child—and presumably a future poor white mother—who has as much potential as Agee sees in Annie Mae. Maggie Louise is alone in the photograph in a white collared shirt with a straw hat covering her head. She, like her mother, gazes into the camera, seemingly without fear and without "shame."[15] This photographic representation of Maggie Louise corresponds with Agee's portrayal of her in the text because he feels such respect for her that he actually mentally apologizes to her for thinking of her sexually as he has Emma (Agee and Evans 401). Just as Evans uses his photograph of Annie Mae to accentuate Agee's portrayal of her, he also uses the families' children to reinforce Agee's assessments of the Woodses, the Ricketts, and the Gudgers.

Of course, who is left out of Evans's collection becomes just as important as how he photographs his subjects. In the family portraits, only the Ricketts family is photographed with the accurate number of children in the family. All seven of the Ricketts children are photographed in their family portrait. By contrast, the Woods are photographed with three children even though Ivy and Bud Woods actually have two children together and four children from previous relationships. Although only three of the Gudger children are photographed, George and Annie Mae actually have four children. Evans's inclusion of only three children is reminiscent of the "Migrant Mother" photograph taken by Evans's FSA co-worker, Lange, and of the way she photographed Thompson's family. Since America's "ideal family" was thought, according to "business and professional elites," to include only three children, Evans seems to be adhering to these ideas while at the same time trying to convey a difference of the way an "ideal" poor white family appears with the Ricketts family photographed on a dirty bed with an exposed child and the Gudgers photographed individually, separate and strong (Curtis 52). The most noticeable absence in the collection is a photograph of Emma. Although Emma holds such an important place in the first part of Agee's story, Evans includes no pictures of her. Cosgrove argues that Evans excludes her to "rebuke Agee's middle-class narcissism" (347), but just as Agee must get rid of Emma early in his narrative to put a positive focus on Annie Mae and the Gudger family, so must Evans. Without a photograph of Emma, Annie Mae emerges as the dominant symbol of poor white womanhood, with Maggie Louise ready to follow in her mother's footsteps. From the absence of children in the Woods family and the Gudger family to the omission of Emma, Evans not only makes a statement with how he photographs his subjects but also with whom he chooses *not* to photograph.

Despite the "'character'" portrayals and Agee and Evans's revisions and omissions of their subjects' lives, Trilling still referred to *Let Us Now Praise Famous Men* in 1942 as "the most realistic and the most important moral effort of our American generation" (102). This "moral effort," however, does not differ much in stance and content from the other documentary work of the period. While Agee never goes so far as to call for the sterilization of any of his poor white subjects, both he and Evans make judgments about the families by how they present them and how they alter their family histories. Agee certainly makes a distinction between which lifestyles signify "holiness" and which signify "harm," and like the other documentary authors, he places most of his emphasis on poor white women. While Annie Mae represents poor whites who want to defy their desperate situations and live improved lives, women such as Ivy, Sadie, and Emma represent a "few hundred [thousand]" poor whites who exist in "specialized anguish" (Agee and Evans 321). Furthermore, the Woods women and Emma also represent the excessive sexuality of the poor white class that threatens to corrupt the middle-class values of men such as Agee and Evans and the "social and [. . .] 'spiritual'" hopes of poor white families that want to change their life situations. This work, like *You Have Seen Their Faces, These Are Our Lives,* and *Mothers of the South,* emphasizes not only the economic plight of poor whites but also the eugenic concerns and social obligations society must consider when confronting this group of people.

Depression-era documentary work gained little recognition once the United States became involved in World War II. Because of the war, most Americans turned their attention away from poverty-stricken southern sharecroppers and tenant farmers (Hershey xxxii). Couch did not get to publish a second volume of *These Are Our Lives* because FWP funding was cut (Hirsch 175), and *Let Us Now Praise Famous Men,* which was not published until 1941, sold poorly despite the praise of critics such as Trilling (Hershey xxxii).[16] Although the popularity of documentary work about the lives of poor white southerners declined, the photographs and the texts written about their plight still helped to put their economic and social problems at the forefront of national discussion, just as *As I Lay Dying, Tobacco Road, God's Little Acre,* and *The Grapes of Wrath* did, but instead of fictional accounts, the photographers and authors of these documentaries presented what the American public considered to be factual accounts. Of course, the supposed factual nature of these works makes the poor whites' lifestyles seem even more problematic for the nation than the accounts created by Faulkner, Caldwell, and Steinbeck. Whereas characters such as Dewey Dell, Ellie May, and Darling Jill could be dismissed as fictional, Caldwell's "mongrel bitch" surrogate mother and Mollie Goodwin from *Mothers of the South* are presented as real problems in poor white life that must be dealt with before the southern lower class can be rejuvenated.

The only solution provided in these works to help these supposedly documented problems is eugenically motivated, and once again, with the focus on poor white women, the solution must come through them. With suggestions ranging from birth control to sterilization, doctors continually emphasized the reproductive abilities of these women, and although birth control is not invasive in relation to sterilization, even this tactic of "negative eugenics" was not presented as a positive solution simply to help the women. Even Margaret Sanger had said that the use of birth control in the lives of these particular women of the lower class would be a "respectable" means of "social control" (Grosskurth 410; Paul, *Controlling* 95, 96). As a result, this "respectable" suggestion to help these "frail women," as Dr. Cain from *These Are Our Lives* calls them, had become just another means of eugenic control over these women who did not meet society's standards of acceptable motherhood. Of course, eugenicists knew that birth control would not be effective if poor white women like Mary Hunt Simmons continued to tell their children birth control was "dirty" and "awful." Ultimately, unless women were altruistic mother figures with the universal mothering characteristics of Lange's "Migrant Mother" and of Annie Mae Gudger, then poor white mothers deemed insufficient faced the eugenic fate determined by Dr. Cain and by the sociologists Caldwell highlights in *You Have Seen Their Faces.* Just as the absence of Emma from the Gudger family provides hope, the absence of sexually degenerate women or unfit mothers from the lower class is the only hope that these documentaries provide for poor whites.

What Faulkner's, Caldwell's, and Steinbeck's fictional accounts and Depression-era documentary work fail to consider is the notion that poor white southern women do not always fit into the dualistic stereotypes of the altruistic mother and the sexual degenerate. With the increase of lower-class white women in the "public" workforce, these women's roles extended far beyond their mothering capabilities and their sexual desires (Hall et al. 154); however, their roles as laborers and financial providers are typically suppressed in favor of the stereotypes. While most Depression-era literature overlooks the dynamic qualities of poor white southern women, several novels written by women about the 1929 Loray mill strike in Gastonia, North Carolina, directly address the complexity of poor white women's lives and the injustice of denying them agency outside of these stereotypes.

4

UP FROM EUGENICS

The Gastonia Novels and the Redefining of the Southern Poor White Woman

BECAUSE THE DUALISTIC IMAGES of poor white women as either altruistic mothers or sexual degenerates appeared in "scientific" studies, government-supported publications, and bestselling novels and documentaries, American society had become infiltrated with these stereotypes in the late 1920s and the 1930s.[1] Placing poor white southern women in these stereotypes often required authors to overlook women's work as farm laborers and their entrance into the "public" workforce during this period (Hall et al. 154). Even authors such as Margaret Jarman Hagood and Erskine Caldwell, who do portray poor white women as laborers, frame the characters within the stereotypes. Hagood acknowledges, in *Mothers of the South: Portraiture of the White Tenant Farm Woman,* that poor white farm women work not only as mothers but also as fellow farmhands with their husbands and children (92); however, her discussion of the women's lives is still centered on their mothering abilities. In *God's Little Acre,* Caldwell describes the female mill workers in overtly sexual terms, thereby concentrating more on their sexual freedom than on their economic activity (69). By taking the focus off of the women's participation in labor, Hagood and Caldwell effectively erase the roles that women play in the male-dominated labor force.

Despite the absence or the dismissive literary representations of lower-class women's labor, the entrance of these women into the "public" workforce as a result of increasing industrialism and decreasing child labor allowed them to participate in a new role as financial providers, a role that actually expanded the altruistic mother expectations. Unlike Ma Joad in *The Grapes of Wrath,* who just provided emotional support for her family, women working in the mills had to support their families financially as well as emotionally. As familial financial supporters, they had to contend with decreased wages because of their gender (Hall et al. 67), and since they earned less than their male counterparts, women were often employed instead of men, thereby creating animosity amongst the men, some of whom left their families (Hutchins 28). The children of working mothers also suffered because mothers spent less time caring for them and because those families that depended solely upon a mother's decreased wages often went malnourished (Hall et al. 41). Young, single female workers who did not have to support families with their low wages still suffered because the ruling classes associated their financial freedom with sexual freedom, just as Caldwell does in *God's Little Acre.* Of course, their socially misconstrued financial freedom was also hindered as a result of the mill owners' gender-based wage system (Hall et al. 219).

In spite of what these women had to face, they did not simply accept their meager working conditions. Although Caldwell's female mill workers do not actively participate in the labor strike that the male workers begin (*God's* 168–69), many mill women did participate in the labor movement. They fought against their poverty and, when applicable, their children's poverty, as active participants in labor strikes, advocating for higher wages and shorter work days. Because women made up a higher percentage of the workers due to the gendered wage system, women actually led many of the labor strikes (Hutchins 213, 219). The women's participation had to be qualified, however. Although working mill mothers and single working women both participated as labor activists, the mill mother's activism was generally more accepted by communist labor leaders and society leaders. Since the activism of working mill mothers could be directly linked to the welfare of the children rather than to the rights of women laborers, their activism was more accepted than the activism of female workers who had no dependents to support (Hutchins 58). As a result, labor issues affecting the lives of female workers, whether they had dependents or not, were often overlooked both by the CPUSA and the upper and middle classes. The CPUSA continued to focus on the altruistic mother figure, and the ruling classes used the activism of the unmarried working women as another reason to label them as sexual miscreants and troublemakers. As a result, even the labor activities of women were diluted through the dualistic stereotypes.

Despite the lack of attention given to working women in most Depression-era literature and in working-class spheres, four female authors did address these issues associated with women's roles in the labor movement. Mary Heaton Vorse, Myra Page, Grace Lumpkin, and Olive Tilford Dargan all wrote novels based upon the Gastonia mill strike that drew national attention in the late 1920s and the 1930s.[2] With the 1929 Loray mill strike in Gastonia, North Carolina, as the setting and foundation for Vorse's *Strike!* (1930), Page's *Gathering Storm* (1932), Lumpkin's *To Make My Bread* (1932), and Dargan's *Call Home the Heart* (1932), the authors center their stories on the struggles of female protagonists who must contend not only with labor struggles but also with society's expectations of how they should act. Sylvia Jenkins Cook argues that Vorse, Page, Lumpkin, and Dargan highlight three noteworthy aspects of poor white women's struggles in the labor movement: "why they changed from the most docile workers to the most recalcitrant workers, what place was available for them in the organization of unions and in Communist leadership, and [. . .] how they were to reconcile their traditional pride as the bearers of large families with the increasing poverty, squalor, and disease" of their living environments (*From Tobacco* 99). These novelists examine women's struggles in the labor movement not by denying the stereotyped roles but by grounding their protagonists in the dueling dynamics of motherhood and sexuality. Vorse, Page, Lumpkin, and Dargan focus on how these women's lives are too dynamic to be forced into stereotypical representations. The authors reveal through their poor white female union and working-class leaders that the altruistic mother and sexual deviant stereotypes are too confining to portray adequately the daily challenges that these women face. All four novelists emphasize the complexity of their female characters' lives by dealing directly with women's involvement in the labor movement and with the subjects of birth control, abortion, and eugenics. But, unlike Faulkner and Caldwell, these authors use these subjects not to highlight the women's deviance but, instead, the women's desire for control and independence. By centering their works on female labor activism and by complicating the stereotypes with confrontational topics, Vorse, Page, Lumpkin, and Dargan show how poor white southern women cannot be limited to society's expectations of them.

These authors not only had to deal with women's working-class status in conjunction with society's expectations but also with society's perception of the poor white class and specifically of mountain poor whites. As evidenced by eugenic family studies and the work of authors such as Caldwell, poor whites were generally associated with laziness, ignorance, and obsessive sexuality. Wes Mantooth has argued that, because of the literary perception of "backwardness among poor [s]outhern whites," the Gastonia novelists faced the difficult task of creating realistic poor white characters who would understand the communist movement (10). To accomplish this task, the authors focus on "gradual movement toward Communist values" rather than on an instantaneous understanding of those values (10). Because the characters must develop at a "gradual" pace, all of the novels, with the exception of *Strike!,* showcase the entire life sequence of their female protagonists.

Contending with society's version of mountain poor white life also proved to be difficult. Jacquelyn Dowd Hall has noted that, in the nineteenth century, the basic "'idea'" about mountain life had become "split" ("Women Writers" 18). Poor white mountaineers were stereotyped as either "isolated, unspoiled Anglo-Saxons in an increasingly polyglot world" or as "peculiar hillbillies" who lived like "barbarians" (18). Regardless of which definition people agreed with, this group was most often represented as people stuck in the past—for better or for worse (18). Reconciling the public perception of poor whites as feebleminded and the supposedly "independent" spirit of the mountaineer with the creation of a female-centered core in a paternalistic environment added to the level of difficulty Vorse, Page, Lumpkin, and Dargan contended with as they wrote these novels. Despite the difficulties associated with creating dynamic poor white female protagonists, however, the authors seem to use their texts to show the hindrances of the stereotypes associated with poor white women and to show the potential that these women could have if allowed to exist in spaces beyond these social expectations.

GASTONIA HISTORY

The Gastonia mill strike began in the spring of 1929 because of the changing dynamic of the mill workers and because of poor working conditions at the mills. Originally, "farmers and sharecroppers" were recruited to work in the mills, and their docile demeanor allowed the owners and managers to run the mills without any regard for the life of the worker. Much like the Lesters of *Tobacco Road* and the Joads of *The Grapes of Wrath,* most agricultural poor whites had been left without the ability to farm and had been forced off of their land. They "quietly and sullenly accept[ed] long work hours, low pay, and the necessary employment of all women and children" (Cook, *From Tobacco* 87). When the mills began recruiting "hill folk," however, the owners encountered a group of people who were not necessarily willing to work at all costs. Workers from the mountains had moved from an "independent existence in a society where poverty was the rule to a servile position in a society where poverty was the exception" (87). Coming from an "independent" lifestyle, the mountain workers did not accept the "paternalism" of the mill villages as the former farmers did, and they did not accept being cut off from the rest of the town simply because they lived in the mill-owned and -operated village (87). The animosity felt by these new "independent" workers increased because of the mills' implementation of the "stretch-out" (88). After World War I ended, the declining price of cotton caused the mills to lose money. To offset these losses, owners and managers cut wages and forced workers "to tend two or three times the number of looms that they had formerly looked after" so they could employ fewer workers (88). Workers finally reached their limit; not only were they making less than they ever had, but with the stretch-out, they were also working harder and in more dangerous conditions than ever before.

By March of 1929, Fred Beal, a communist organizer from the North, came to Gastonia to organize a group of workers for the National Textile Workers Union. The mill owners immediately tried to counter his efforts (Cook, *From Tobacco* 88). Shortly after Beal began his organization activities, mill workers suspected of colluding with him were fired, and as a result, the famous Gastonia strike began. The strike lacked a definite leadership plan because Beal wanted to focus on improving the workers' conditions and the CPUSA in New York wanted to use the strike as a way to expand their revolution nationwide. In the midst of the intraparty fighting, the mills brought in scab workers and the National Guard to protect them, and as a result, the number of strikers dwindled to a mere two hundred by May. Only when the mills began evicting families from their mill village homes did the strike become revitalized (88). Amidst the increasing violence, two high-profile deaths took place that brought national attention. In June of 1929, Orville F. Aderholt, the Gastonia chief of police, was killed when he and some of his officers forcibly gained entrance into the union headquarters (Mantooth 2). Then, in September of 1929, Ella May Wiggins, a mill worker, mother of five, and ballad singer for the union, was killed on her way to a union meeting (2). Aderholt's death prompted the arrest of fourteen union organizers, and after a trial, a mistrial, and a second trial, six union organizers were sentenced to long prison terms. The convicted organizers escaped the sentence by fleeing to Russia while on bail awaiting an appeal (Cook, *From Tobacco* 89–90). Wiggins's death, although witnessed by at least fifty people, gained none of this attention from the Gastonia authorities, and her murder went unsolved (89). The already weak strike could not handle the additional stress and demoralization that came with Wiggins's death and the union convictions, so the "rebellion collapsed" (Hall et. al 215). Proletarian writers, however, used the Gastonia strike to expand their message to the South in an effort to create a united working-class front that crossed regional boundaries.

Wiggins's death, although ignored by Gastonia officials, became increasingly important to the proletarian authors who saw her as a representative not only of the problems that female mill workers faced but also of the tragedy in all mill workers' lives. Vorse, Page, Lumpkin, and Dargan actually include representative Wiggins figures in their novels. In *Strike!,* Vorse introduces Mamie Lewes as the Wiggins figure. Page includes Wiggins as an actual character in *Gathering Storm* as a way to explain the political evolution of the novel's main female protagonist, Marge Crenshaw. Wiggins is represented by Bonnie McClure in Lumpkin's *To Make My Bread,* and in *Call Home the Heart,* Dargan creates a pseudo-Wiggins character in Ishma Waycaster. Including representative Wiggins characters allows the novelists to legitimize their works as "documentary novel[s]," to garner support for their downtrodden subjects, and to place an emphasis on the struggles of the mill women.[3]

As a worker in the mills, the Wiggins faced struggles that corresponded with what many other female mill workers faced; however, because of her ballads and her union work, she became a voice for all of the despondent workers. Although Wiggins came to the mill with a husband to help support her and her children, her husband eventually left, supposedly because he could not handle the disappointment of the poverty caused by the mill conditions (Hall et. al 226). As a result, Wiggins had to raise five children by herself, supporting them solely with her gender-reduced wages. Like many other women in the mill, she also faced the tragedy of losing children because, although she only had five living children, she actually gave birth to nine (226). With all of her responsibilities, Wiggins would not seem as though she would give up her wages for a greater cause, but she did precisely that. She even took on various leadership roles in the union; she encouraged strikers as a ballad singer, worked as a "secretary" for the union, lobbied for workers' rights in Washington, D.C., and recruited black workers for the union (226–27). Her role as a singer, though, is what made her famous. In her "most powerful and best-loved" song, "Mill Mother's Lament," Wiggins "drew on her own experience, appealing directly to other women in their roles as mothers or potential mothers and attacking the mill for depriving women of the means to carry out their responsibility for nurturing human life" (Hall et al. 226).

Although the ballad directly addresses the challenges that mill women faced, it also appeals universally to the working class with its focus on poverty, harsh working conditions, union relief, and class unification, especially in the final stanza, which highlights unions and the help they can provide to the working class.[4] Wiggins's lesser-known achievements as union worker, lobbyist, and racial unifier also solidify her standing as a female activist who transcended her role as a mother to focus on a variety of labor issues, whether they affected her rights as a mother of five or not. Because Wiggins appealed to so many and brought such encouragement, many of the mill workers attended union meetings just to hear her sing (Hall et al. 226).

The ballad singing that made Wiggins so famous, though, not only connected her to the plight of the mill community but also to cultural capital in America, thereby expanding her universality as a symbol for proletarian authors. Having been born in the mountains before moving to the mill town, Wiggins could be connected to the "ballad tradition" of the Appalachian Mountains (Whisnant 243). This mountain "ballad tradition" had been a focus of collectors and scholars of folklore since the late nineteenth century. Tracing the mountain ballad's origins back to "'English and Scottish popular ballads'" that original settlers in America had brought from their home countries, scholars began gathering and publishing these ballads, which came to be referred to as "Anglo-Saxon folk music" (54, 113, 243).[5] With the high cultural heritage associated with the origin of the ballads, mountaineers were considered part of this noble "tradition" (57). In fact, mountain ballad singers had a reputation for honesty, loyalty, and generosity because these traits were supposedly reflected in the high "social and moral value" of the ballads (54). Mill-town ballad singers such as Wiggins presumably used this "tradition" as a way to help fellow workers retain their mountain heritage and to help them "cop[e] with the challenges that were already upon them and the changes that lay ahead" with the increase in industrialism (153). Because of Wiggins's connection to this culturally revered tradition, highlighting her role in the strike was a way of exposing working-class grievances while at the same time establishing a sense of cultural respectability in the workers' lives and making them seem like sympathetic victims rather than the "barbarians" some upper- and middle-class whites considered them to be (Hall, "Women Writers" 18).

Although Wiggins's struggles and union activities make her an appropriate representative for working-class rights, the authors' decision to use a woman as their main protagonist breaks certain standards of the striking working-class community and of CPUSA ideology. Laura Hapke notes that, although women played a large role in the Gastonia strikes, their involvement has largely been ignored both by male documenters "directly after the strike" and by "commentators" who have continued to write about the strike since the 1930s (149). Other women, aside from Wiggins, have generally not been recognized for their participation in the strike (149). Hapke even notes that Wiggins only garners a "half-sentence" from most historians (149). Even the Communist Party did not promote the status of women in the labor movement. The CPUSA focused on advancing the plight of the entire lower class with an extra focus on males, as evidenced by Mike Gold's vision of the proletarian author as male, thereby creating a masculine image of labor.[6] Despite the absence of a female working-class voice in historical representations and in the political voices of the working class, Vorse, Page, Lumpkin, and Dargan ground their novels in the female working-class voice, specifically the voice of Wiggins, and even though their representative characters may be the main focus, the authors use that character as a way to highlight how other poor white women, regardless of their marital or motherly status, are capable of holding leadership positions in the working class just as Wiggins did before her death.

JUDGING THE WOMAN WORKER

In 1930, Mary Heaton Vorse published *Strike!,* the first novel written about the Gastonia strike. Working as a journalist, Vorse traveled to Gastonia to gather information for an article, but during her time there she also began writing a novel about the people she met and the events that occurred.[7] As a writer and as a controversial thinker, she had written articles about labor struggles across America, women's social roles, and the plight of the lower class, so by writing a novel about the strike, Vorse was able to combine all of the topics she thought were important and to legitimize them by connecting them to a historical event that had garnered a great deal of attention.[8]

From a young age, Vorse did not view her future as being bound to the roles of wife and mother. Growing up in Massachusetts, she had a strained relationship with her mother; in fact, Dee Garrison notes in her biography of Vorse that Ellen Heaton, Vorse's mother, neglected her six children, especially Mary, her youngest child (*Mary* 3, 11). With this example of motherhood before her, Vorse decided that she would devote her life solely to work (17). Despite her plans to remain a single, working woman, she did marry, and she eventually had three children. While traveling and writing stories about America's labor struggles in the 1920s, Vorse rarely saw her children, having placed them in boarding schools or with relatives (170). In 1924, she actually wrote an article, "Why I Have Failed As a Mother," for *Cosmopolitan,* in which she questions her personal choices. Confused about whether a woman could ever be both a worker with "independence" and a responsible mother, she asks with a sense of hopelessness, "Must there always be a double failure?" (345). Many of her creative works also concentrated on whether women could successfully have a career and a family without feeling like "double failure[s]"

(Garrison, *Mary* 41–42). Despite her confusion about her own life, her commitment to writing about these issues suggests that she understood that the questions she posed for her own life coincided with the questions other women asked about their lives.

Not only did Vorse question society's maternal expectations, but she also questions in her articles the negative mainstream perception of the lower class. While eugenicists helped to perpetuate the idea that lower-class people were innately feebleminded and sexually perverse, especially poor white women, Vorse's articles reveal a sympathetic view of lower-class men and women. In a 1929 article about the Gastonia strikes that appeared in *Harper's Magazine,* Vorse defends the mill workers by linking their illiteracy not to choice or to their inability to learn but to "necessity," since they and their children must work rather than attend school (Vorse, "Gastonia" 117). Despite their illiteracy, Vorse argues they still have "a direct quality, a completeness about them" (117). Later, in 1933, Vorse reported on the Scottsboro case in which nine young black men were convicted of raping two poor white girls (Vorse, "How Scottsboro" 148). Although the charges against the young men were untrue and the girls who made the accusations, Victoria Price and Ruby Bates, had dubious sexual reputations, the men were convicted simply because of their race (149, 152). Instead of condemning the girls for their sexual misconduct and their lies, which destroyed the lives of the nine defendants, Vorse shows how the white girls too were victims because of their poverty. Vorse refers to Price and Bates as "part of a great army of adventurous, venal girls" who prefer a sordid life riding the rails to "the crowded shacks at home and the uncertain work in the mills" (152). Unlike the "great army of delinquents" referred to by Ira Caldwell in his eugenic Bungler articles (383), Price and Bates are not described by Vorse as ready to destroy America; they are women "who [have] had all kindness and decency ground out of [them] in [their] youth" (Vorse, "How Scottsboro" 152). For Vorse, the stereotypes of poor white men and women as degenerate and perverse do not account for the struggles they have faced due to extreme poverty.

In *Strike!* Vorse explores both of these controversial concepts, centering her version of the Gastonia strikes on how female activists relate to the male strike leaders and union workers. Since Vorse lived in Gastonia during part of the strike, she spent her time "circulating among the strike workers, taking affidavits, meeting the women, [and] reporting the scene for several New York papers and the Federated Press" (Garrison, *Mary* 222). By spending time with the union leaders and the workers, she gathered firsthand information about the union's working dynamics. Vorse found that a great deal of tension existed between the male and female union workers and strikers.[9] Union leader Beal felt discouraged by his female workers, who did not acknowledge him as a leader, but the female union workers did not respect how he and other men refused to join with the women and children on the picket lines (Garrison, Intro. to *Strike!* xi–xii). The male workers and union leaders also worried about the freedom and the power that the women gained not only by working in the mill but by working for the union. Many of these women no longer accepted a subordinate position in society or at home. When Vorse writes about this tension in the strike, she highlights three types of female workers who helped to organize and to strike for their fellow workers: young, single mill workers; vigilant union organizers; and activist working mill mothers. Separating the women into these categories allows Vorse to highlight what kind of female involvement the male leaders and union workers accepted and how the men interpreted the women's involvement.

Vorse's *Strike!* seems at first to be dominated by male characters; however, she uses her prominent male figures to emphasize the social expectations concerning women involved in the strike. Although the details of the strike come from Vorse's own actual experiences in Gastonia, Vorse uses two male reporters, Roger Hewlett and Ed Hoskins, to narrate the story. Garrison has said that Vorse felt that the male reporters "would legitimize her views in a way a woman character would not" (Intro. to *Strike!* xv). Of course, using male narrators also allows her to present the female strike workers as she thinks men saw them. Roger and Ed do not just see the women as proactive strikers or union organizers; they also continually pass judgment as a way to understand why the women have become involved in the strike or have become successful in their union roles. Vorse also focuses attention on the actions of male union leaders to compare and contrast the leadership capabilities of both sexes. Since the male leaders qualify for their positions based upon their sex, their weakness as leaders suggests another way in which the female workers are unfairly held back. Ferdinand "Fer" Deane, a fictional version of Beal, is the ineffective leader of the union who often fails to meet his followers' expectations. Even Roger refers to Fer as "lacking," and Fer acknowledges his weakness, admitting that he would rather be working in a union in the North, where he had always lived before moving to Gastonia (Vorse, *Strike!* 7). Throughout the strike, he continually shows up late for meetings and provides little organization for the workers. The male strikers prove to be just as ineffective as Fer. They do not usually walk with the women and children on the picket lines because the men do not want to face police brutality (92). Joseph R. Urgo has argued that Vorse portrays the men in *Strike!* as individualistic while the women are portrayed as "inclined to collectivist principles and true Communism" (70). As a result, the male characters are primarily figureheads while the women generally take prominence in the strike and in the novel.

Despite their willingness to fight for workers' rights, the female strikers do not generally garner respect from their male counterparts. In *Strike!*, young, single women actually have to face two criticisms about their strike efforts, criticisms that the real single female strikers had to face in Gastonia, according to Garrison (Intro. to *Strike!* xvi). First, because they have no children or husbands to fight for, their activism is generally viewed as self-aggrandizing. Cactus Kate, one of the few young female strikers identified, walks on the picket lines and follows all the orders Fer gives to her, but both Roger and Hoskins dismiss her as destructive and self-involved, an "absurd and melodramatic little figure" (Vorse, *Strike!* 36). Hoskins argues that Cactus Kate and the other young girls have become so focused on "the limelight" that they actually "harm" union efforts rather than help (37). Despite Roger's and Hoskins's comments, though, Vorse emphasizes that Cactus Kate's actions for the strike, while possibly "melodramatic," are in fact effective. At one point, Cactus Kate even succeeds in threatening and humiliating officers who have resorted to violence to subdue the strikers whom the court officials refer to as "little girl[s]" (40). Along with critiques concerning their possible self-motivation for striking, young female activists also contend with slander concerning their supposed sexual motivations. Garrison notes that these women had to contend with the public perception that their activism, if not motivated by self-promotion, was motivated by their promiscuity and their defiance of "middle-class norms and masculine controls" (Intro. to *Strike!* xvi). Roger actually describes some of the young, single female strikers more as groupies than as political activists because of their relationships with Fer. First, Fer attracts Kate Trent, and later, he begins associating with Lissa (Vorse, *Strike!* 42, 103). Roger describes both women as sexual and simplistic, even though Fer never openly has a sexual relationship with either of them and both of them actually work diligently for the union. In fact, when no one in town wants to sell the union land to build a headquarters, Lissa convinces family friends to sell land to the union (124–25). Because Vorse does not diminish or exclude these women's accomplishments for the union, Roger's and Hoskins's criticisms of them seem motivated by their preconceived expectations of the women rather than any actual "harm" they cause the fellow strikers.

Just as the young, single mill women are described by the men as self-motivated, so too are those working as union organizers. Instead of being viewed by the men as "harm[ful]" to union efforts, however, female union organizers are seen as overly ambitious, too concentrated on personal glory. As union organizers, both Irma Rankin and Doris Pond work vigorously for Fer to help the union. Both women, though, feel resentment towards Fer because they must compensate for his weak leadership skills. Irma actually criticizes Fer for his lack of organization and his lack of personal involvement by calling him "obstinate and [. . .] lazy" with "no imagination" (Vorse, *Strike!* 8). While Roger also considers Fer a weak leader, he considers Irma "arrogant" for criticizing Fer so openly (11). Doris is also considered too critical later in the novel when new male leaders take over for Fer after he is arrested. When Doris disagrees with the men's plan to hold a meeting at a dangerous time, they tell her to "[s]hut up and keep out" of union affairs (196). Any open verbal disagreement by Irma and Doris results in their total dismissal by men who feel threatened by the women's opinions.

Of course, just as the supposedly flighty and promiscuous young, single women prove to be effective activists, Irma and Doris also prove through their actions that their criticisms of Fer and the other male leaders are well founded and that they want what is best for the union, not for themselves. Irma and Doris organize most union functions without the help of "lazy" Fer, and although Fer runs when a town mob attacks strikers, the two women stay and fight with their fellow workers (Vorse, *Strike!* 86, 155).

Even when the meeting that Doris warns the male leaders not to have ends in the murder of Mamie Lewes (the representative Wiggins figure) by the mob, Irma and Doris do not gloat that the men should have heeded Doris's warning (202). Instead, at the end of the strike, after Fer has been arrested, Irma and Doris show their complete dedication to union efforts when the new male leaders order the two women to relocate to the North to raise money for the union (223). Despite the women's supposed "arrogan[ce]" and self-promoting ambition, they accept their assignment, once again highlighting that they work only for the glory of the union. Even this sacrificing act by the female organizers is diminished because, after Fer is killed, Roger criticizes Irma again, saying that, if she had died instead of Fer, she would have expected a "martyr's crown" (223). Vorse, though, does not leave Irma wallowing in the self-congratulatory "martyr's" role in which Roger places her. Instead, Vorse notes that Irma will fall in line with other union officials in creating a "legend" of Fer's work for the union, omitting his "faults" as a leader, because his "legend" has the potential to increase support for their cause (235). Despite Roger's and the male leaders' views of the women, Irma and Doris are actually dedicated to their service and to the prospering of the union, even if that means breaking gender expectations and criticizing male leaders.

Despite their dedication to the strike, young, single women and single female union leaders are not described heroically by Roger and Hoskins; in fact, the only female activists who hold a high status within the union and with the reporters are the working mill mothers. Although most of the mothers are never referred to by name, they are the women who march on the picket lines with their children, demanding better lives for their children than they have had (Vorse, *Strike!* 26), and they are the women who suffer because the town mob destroys union relief supplies meant, according to northern papers, for "women and children" (63, 70). While the other women are criticized because they are perceived as only trying to improve their personal situations, mill mothers are applauded because they fight for their children. Praising the mothers for the sacrifices they are making for their children diverts attention from other labor issues affecting women workers such as their decreased pay and longer work days. The many mill mothers who appear throughout the events of the strike are represented by Vorse's version of Ella May Wiggins, Mamie Lewes, and even the focus on Mamie's efforts is directed towards her sacrifices for her children. Although Mamie's course toward union activism is charted from her decision to join the union to her ultimate sacrifice for it, she does not join the union for herself but, instead, for her children. Mamie lives in a shack outside of the mill village with her four surviving children (6). Now that her husband has deserted her and she has buried four other children, she sees the union as her only hope for her remaining children to survive (5–6). As a ballad singer, her contribution to the union, in contrast to the single women's contributions, seems neither self-serving nor sexual. Singing a version of Wiggins's "Mill Mother's Lament" that does not include the final stanza on union activist efforts for workers' rights, Mamie connects with other women because of the grief she feels for being unable to provide for her children (53). Listening to Mamie's songs, the mill mothers come together with a unified goal to save their children and generate an incredibly "powerful vitality" (53). With their children's futures driving their will, the mill mothers seem like the only unstoppable force in the union and the only faultless female force.

Mamie's success emerges partially as a result of her untainted persona that withstands temptation from personal agendas and from sexual desires, and this persona is a reflection of the altruistic mother stereotype. When Dewey Bryson takes over Fer's leadership position during the trial, he attempts to entice Mamie into a sexual relationship. Unlike Fer's relationships with Kate and Lissa, however, Dewey looks at Mamie as a heroic figure because she appears "young and happy and playful" in spite of all she has endured (Vorse, *Strike!* 166). Instead of being "arrogant" and critical like Irma and Doris, Mamie places all of her reverence with the union for saving her from living "like a dumb beast" (166). According to Mamie, the union has given her strength to tell her story through her songs, giving her life meaning. Dewey appreciates Mamie because she does not expect to gain personal privilege from her actions, and he also respects her even more because she puts the union above their growing personal relationship. In fact, when Dewey tries to make their relationship intimate, she says, "We got too much to do to get mixed up this way" (184). When she is killed, as Wiggins was in real life, Mamie becomes a heroic "mother" figure to all the strikers, just as Dewey saw her (202).[10] After her death, Dewey actually refers to Mamie as "the victim that the mob demanded" because, as the representative mill mother, she represented the real power of the union, a power that Dewey knows, despite his leader status, he did not even represent (202). Her death becomes world news (202–4), and later, when Fer and other union men die in the strike, her death is discussed in conjunction with theirs as the motivation "to bring solidarity to the whole South" and finally create a strong union (235). Even Roger is so spurred by Mamie's death and the men's deaths that he vows "to go" with the "class of the workers [. . .] wherever they went, whatever their destination might be" (236).

Vorse's presentation of Mamie indicates that even she is acknowledging the power of these stereotypes. Although Vorse is breaking down the stereotypes by making the young, single mill women and the female union organizers positive figures, she gives her readers the stereotypical altruistic mother figure when she creates for Mamie an alternate version of Wiggins's career and personal life. By excluding the final stanza of "Mill Mother's Lament" from Mamie's version of Wiggins's ballad, Vorse makes Mamie seem less politically radical and keeps the focus on her poverty and children. Changing the details of Wiggins's personal life also has a de-radicalizing effect. Unlike Mamie, Wiggins did have an affair with a union leader named Charlie Shope, and they had a child together (Hapke 160).[11] Hapke suggests that Vorse kept Mamie's relationship with Dewey platonic in an attempt to keep Wiggins's image pure (160). This alteration also successfully distances Mamie from the sexually destructive poor white women of eugenic studies prone to having adulterous relationships and illegitimate children. As evidenced by how Vorse uses Roger and Hoskins to condemn female independence and sexuality, and by the content of her magazine articles, Vorse knew what Americans wanted from their female heroes. Sinclair Lewis proved Vorse correct by focusing his review of the novel upon Vorse's strong mother characters and the sympathy they evoke. In fact, Lewis used Vorse's mothering images to chastise Herbert Hoover for his presidential policies by encouraging Hoover to recognize that his policies were not hurting the socialists and the communists but causing "the slavery of just such woman as once mothered a little boy named Herbie and gave him cookies" (Lewis 474).[12]

Although Vorse's alteration of Mamie's life does make her character into the altruistic mother stereotype, Mamie's character who, as evidenced by the review, gained national attention also allowed Vorse to showcase female characters who actually do dismantle the stereotypes. The young, single women and the female union organizers break out of society's stereotypical box because of the power and poise that they offer to union efforts. They are only stereotyped by the male narrators, not by their actions in the novel. In fact, even though the young, single women and the female union leaders do not garner the esteem from their work that Mamie does, Vorse uses their characters to show how their contributions to the strike, although great, were discredited because they did not fit society's expectations of how women should act. Moreover, these women are not an afterthought in the novel. They are dominant figures who are meant to be noticed and who, as the male narrators suggest, are impossible to ignore. As a woman who struggled with her own success and with societal expectations, Vorse obviously understood the problems these women faced. She also seemed to understand that these women would not be readily accepted because society was already familiar with the dualistic stereotypes that supposedly defined poor white southern women. However, Mamie opens the door for the other women to be viewed as they actually are, and Roger and Hoskins become representations of society's preconceived misconceptions about women who are not like Mamie, but who are just as vital and necessary to society's positive domestic growth. Even Vorse's obvious modification of Wiggins's personal life seems like a way for the novelist to show the hypocrisy of these stereotypes because she evidently believed her readers needed to see an altered version of Wiggins in order to accept her historical significance. As a result, Vorse may pander to her readers with the character of Mamie, but she also challenges her readers to view these women beyond the stereotypes and to look at their contributions and accomplishments, instead of concentrating just on their sexuality and their mothering capabilities.

DETERMINING THE ENEMY

In 1932, Myra Page, a woman who grew up with and studied poor whites, created an intimate version of the Gastonia strike in her novel, *Gathering Storm: A Story of the Black Belt,* which focuses on the struggles and the personal growth of one southern woman, Marge Crenshaw.[13] Although Page grew up in a middle-class Virginia family, she maintained a connection with members of the lower class through her teaching and her research (Baker xviii). After graduating from college, she taught in a school predominantly attended by children of working-class parents. She then left Virginia to attend Columbia University, but after completing her master's degree in sociology, she returned to Virginia and began working for the Young Women's Christian Association (YWCA) in 1920 (42–43, 52). Despite her dedication, she was asked to leave her position because she defied YWCA policy by telling the workers about unions (52). In 1921, she moved to Philadelphia, took a job in a factory so that she could better understand the life of the workers whom she kept trying to help, and became increasingly involved with the Amalgamated Clothing Workers' Union (56). Because of her class background, though, Page felt disconnected from the lower-class people she worked with at the factory and in the union, so in 1924, after being offered a fellowship at the University of Minnesota, she returned to school and began her Ph.D. in sociology (Mantooth 21). Following her desire to help lower-class workers, she decided to write her dissertation on southern textile workers with her main focus on their "'children and their work'" (qtd. in Baker 73). She conducted her study in Greenville, South Carolina, and in Gastonia, living in the mill villages so that she would not feel isolated from the workers (Baker 74, 78). After completing her Ph.D., she published her dissertation in 1929 as a book titled *Southern Cotton Mills and Labor* (Mantooth 22). Although the book contains some statistics, she mostly includes personal conversations that she had with male and female workers.[14] Using the details of this book and her own memories of mill village life, Page wrote about the Gastonia strike in *Gathering Storm.*[15] As a result of her firsthand knowledge, Page creates more of a complete portrait of the mill women's struggle than Vorse does in *Strike!*.

Through the character of Marge Crenshaw in *Gathering Storm,* Page combines all that she learned from the women she studied for her dissertation. The women in the mill villages all feared they had doomed their families for generations to come by "bequeath[ing] to their children and their children's children the heritage of being 'mill hands'" (Page, *Southern* 34), but even though they despised this "heritage," they knew of no other opportunities for their children (21). According to what the older mill women had observed, the only young people who had a chance for a good life were the young girls who wanted nice clothing and wanted to have fun. These girls, reminiscent of the young, single girls in *Strike!,* were labeled "the new generation" by Page, and instead of linking this "new generation" with images of sexual miscreants, as eugenicists and Vorse's male characters had done, Page presents them as "good union fighter[s]" who desire to achieve the elusive happiness not usually found in the mill villages (15). Generally, the "new generation" of girls wanted to avoid marriage, children, and sex because they saw how other women suffered, and they wanted to focus solely on union activities (16). In *Gathering Storm,* Marge embodies the "new generation" of future "union fighter[s]"; however, Page does not keep Marge's character locked in this youthful idealistic state that separates her from sexual activity and family. Marge becomes a "good union fighter" because, as she gets older, she focuses not on her sexuality and on the family that supposedly represses her, but on the mill owners who take away her chance at happiness. As a result, Page seems to explore how the "new generation" of mill women can evolve in their thinking to become potential class leaders.

As a future "good union fighter," Marge learns what type of woman she wants to become by watching and learning from her grandmother and mother. Granny feels responsible for her family being stuck in the mill village with no prospects for a better life; however, her motives for moving her family from the mountains to the village reveal that she thought the mills would bring good fortune. After being visited by a mill recruiter, Granny convinced her husband to move because she wanted their children to get an education: "Your folks and mine live and die ignorant 'n down-trodden. You want our chillen should be the same?" (Page, *Gathering* 15). When Granny and her husband began working in the mills, they realized what a mistake they had made. The owners treated the workers "like no-counts" and made the children work rather than let them attend school. Continuing her outspoken ways, Granny participated in a strike in the 1890s, which gained the workers increased wages, regular work hours, and a promise that children under ten would not have to work (24). When the novel begins, Granny is too old to work in the mills, but she still sees her struggles in Marge, her namesake, who already looks "peaked" from her work in the mill (10). Because Granny has witnessed what the working class can do if it works together, she constantly reminds Marge not to give up hope: "For we may be po,' hard-workin' people, Marge, but thar ain't better blood or char-*ac*-ter in all of the two Carlynys than's on cotton hills" (27). Granny may have brought her family to work for people who do not respect them, but she refuses to let her family members lose respect for themselves. According to Granny, her people are actually "better" biologically and socially than their upper-class counterparts, a sentiment John Steinbeck would emphasize later in his 1936 work *Their Blood Is Strong*.

Sally, Marge's mother and Granny's daughter, does not have the perseverance that Granny has. All of the negative parts of Sally's life have come, in her opinion, as a result of the mill, and instead of trying actively to change her situation, she feels trapped. Since the age of sixteen, Sally has been married to a worthless man who comes and goes whenever he pleases, usually leaving Sally pregnant when he departs (Page, *Gathering* 26–27). While his acts are irresponsible, his problems reflect most mill men's problems because they feel displaced in the mill villages (23). Since Sally only lived in the mountains for a short time, she does not know of the hardships that Granny moved them away from, so to Sally, the mountains represent her lost happiness (45). Sally's romantic view of mountain life keeps her from ever imagining a better life in the village. From these two women, Marge learns what she does and does not want out of life. Listening to Granny, Marge knows that, whether she lives in the village or the mountains, she will face pain, so Marge must fight rather than dream of a better place where opportunities do not really exist (Mantooth 25). Watching her mother live as a "shadow" has made Marge think that part of her fight for happiness is the ability to avoid marriage and motherhood because, to her, these choices lead to failure (Urgo 82).

Instead of trying to change the system by striking as Granny does, Marge focuses her attention on not becoming like her mother. She declares to herself, "She'd not be like Ma and the other women. Life was bad enough without a string of lil'uns coming along as regular as the seasons, weighing you down and sucking your spirit" (Page, *Gathering* 101). She even thinks of sex as "a forbidden, evil thing" because it only produces children (102). What she soon realizes as she gets older is that, while she may not think of marriage as desirable, she cannot stop herself from falling in love, and when she does fall in love with Bob Gregory, Marge begins to rethink her commitment to remaining single and abstaining from sex (110). Because of Bob, Marge realizes that love offers the only hope she has while living in the mill village and that giving Bob up would mean giving up her happiness. As a result of this realization, she finally understands the real reasons that her mother always looks unhappy. Marge thinks, "Why wasn't thar a way for poor folks not to have so many children? The rich didn't have them" (163). With this question, Marge finally begins to become the type of "new generation" woman who may actually help her people because she is no longer looking at marriage and children as the cause of her unhappiness. Instead of thinking about "motherhood as a threat" as Urgo suggests (82), Marge realizes that not having a choice about "motherhood," as the "rich" obviously do, is the more destructive "threat" to her future happiness. This questioning by Marge directly defies eugenicists' notions that poor white women are reckless procreators, having children without thinking about the consequences, and unlike Margaret Sanger and Dr. Cain from *These Are Our Lives,* Marge does not desire birth control so that she can adhere to the "negative eugenic" campaign.[16] For Marge, birth control is a personal choice based on her own reproductive desires. Of course, understanding that she has been denied her choice cannot stop her from having children, so when she can no longer deny Bob marriage without losing him completely, she marries him and immediately becomes pregnant with her first child (Page, *Gathering* 171).

Since Marge does not really want a child, her anxiety about her unborn baby is already high, but her fears are worsened by the fact that Bob and the other male workers have gone to war and that she now has to work even harder. In fact, Page describes Marge as so "heavy with child and drugged with labor" that she does not have the strength to worry about Bob's safety (*Gathering* 171). Her situation is further worsened by the fact that, while the price of living has increased because of the war, the amount of money she makes has not, so with her already decreased wages based upon her gender, she anticipates how much worse her life will become once the baby arrives (173). Because of this fear of extreme poverty, Marge becomes so desperate not to have a child that she attempts to abort her own baby, reminiscent of Dewey Dell's actions in *As I Lay Dying.* Unlike Dewey Dell, though, Marge acts as her own doctor. First, she tries "old-fashioned, useless methods" such as bathing in "hot mustard"; then, she prays for God to take her baby; and finally, she tries to abort her child physically by using "a long carrot, shaved down on one end to a sharp point" (174–76). For Marge, abortion is not a way to save her child from her poor mothering abilities and a life of genetic weakness, as Havelock Ellis suggested.[17] Instead, she would rather face the guilt of killing her child and the risk of killing herself with her invasive tactics than face a life with no escape from poverty. Ironically, though, despite her initial "resentment" towards the baby she fails to abort, she discovers that she loves the child, whom she names Roberta (174, 178). No sooner does she allow herself to love the baby, however, than Roberta dies, because Marge does not have the adequate nourishment to breastfeed her properly (181). Like Rose of Sharon's baby in *The Grapes of Wrath,* Marge's baby is also "killed" by a society that will not provide her with the birth control that the "rich" have or with the economic means necessary to support the child she loves. Marge now does not just ask why she cannot have birth control; she also asks why, even if she wants a child and works hard, she cannot care for her child. After the death of Roberta, Marge no longer focuses on not becoming a mother; instead, she becomes involved in union efforts as a way to fight for her right to have a family and to care for her family adequately, a right she believes the mill has taken from her (186).

Although the tragedy of losing Roberta spurs Marge to blame the mill rather than her child for her loss, she does not really understand how much she and the other workers need to band together until the mill takes all she has. Having moved from North Carolina to South Carolina after Bob returns injured from the war, Marge joins her first strike, but unlike Granny's efforts as a striker, Marge's are neither fruitful nor steadfast. Although she and Bob and the other workers strike, the union that supposedly supports them actually discourages the workers' efforts. The union delegates encourage the workers to return to the mills, calling the company their "best friend," and ultimately cause the strikers' efforts to fail (Page, *Gathering* 225). Rather than continuing to fight, she and Bob move to a different part of North Carolina to start their lives again (227). In their new location, working conditions are worse, and eventually, Bob dies because his mill work exacerbates his war injuries, and their new son, Bob, dies too (220, 241, 253). Cook has argued that the deaths of Bob and her children free Marge to become a committed activist (*From Tobacco* 121); however, the deaths become her burden, not her freedom. The loss of her family actually causes her to become an activist because her previous lack of determination has allowed her supposed "best friend," the company, to take away, once again, all she has ever loved. Since her family has essentially been murdered by the mills, Marge becomes incredibly determined, and instead of joining a union she may not be able to trust, she starts her own. With her new determination, Marge sets out to reclaim her happiness and to win true freedom from the mills.

As a union leader, Marge must first learn how to lead, and while she does gain encouragement from Tom, her brother, she learns about leadership from Ella May Wiggins, whom Page includes not as a historical reference but as a character. After the union is started and some workers, including Tom and Marge, lose their jobs in the mill, a meeting is coordinated, and Marge is one of the featured speakers. Marge knows that what she has to say is "something her people had to know" (Page, *Gathering* 284), but because her issues are so different from the male leaders' issues and because she has not had previous opportunities to lead, she has no example to follow. Only when Marge becomes close friends with Wiggins does she finally gain a mentor. Wiggins has an "infectious" energy that makes Marge feel as though they have a "deep-going" connection (303). For Marge, Wiggins "symbolize[s] the will to win" (335). Believing in Wiggins helps Marge to believe in herself and helps her to share her story. After listening to Wiggins sing at a meeting, Marge takes her turn on the stage and finally tells about her heartache caused by the mill, beginning with Granny's story of how her family originally came to the mill town and ending with how the mill has taken Marge's family: "The mill takes all, 'n gives nothin.' . . . It took my youth, it took my babies. It took my man. One thing it can't take—that's my fightin' spirit" (336). Just as Wiggins's ballads connect her struggles to the life stories of the mill women in the audience, Marge tells her family's story as a way to connect to the audience. Because they all share similar experiences, Wiggins and Marge bond themselves to the crowd, creating a lower-class familial "fightin' spirit." Their relationship also reveals how one female leader, Wiggins, can spur other women to believe they can become leaders. Hapke argues that Marge is a Wiggins figure used by Page to showcase the historical character of Wiggins (163), but Marge actually seems to represent all the women Wiggins encouraged to fight against oppression. Because of Wiggins and Marge's relationship, Marge finally finds her voice so that she can encourage other workers to stand up and fight.

Wiggins has given Marge such great confidence in her leadership abilities that, when Wiggins is killed on her way to a union meeting, Marge's confidence only increases. Once again, the mill has taken away someone she loves, but this time Marge believes that she has the power to stop the suffering (Page, *Gathering* 360). In fact, she and other union leaders join together and decide to attend a communist convention in Cleveland, Ohio, to hear about their fellow workers' struggles and to share their own stories (363). Hapke argues that Page betrays the cause of southern mill women because she "removes [Marge] from the life of the southern woman on strike," distinguishing "the South [as . . .] a problematic place in which to be an educated woman militant" (166); however, the Cleveland convention, with its diverse attendants, allows Marge to expand her understanding of why she must return to her home and encourage women as Wiggins encouraged her. At the meeting, Marge speaks with a nursing mother who is a union member from Pennsylvania (Page, *Gathering* 369–70). The women dream together that they can help create "a power that nothin' can halt" (370–71). She also talks with Tom's new wife, Bessie, about how, in Russia, women get time off work to care for their new babies (372). Talking to these two women about women's power and rights, Marge realizes that women, not just in her region, but globally, face the same struggles she does and that, if she continues her efforts, young women just beginning their lives will have the chance to have the family she lost, or maybe even have the choice not to have a family at all (372). This final image of the nursing child represents a new beginning for the lower class, a future in which the women work together to defeat the hierarchical social system. Marge embodies this future when she realizes how important her story will be in helping other women keep the happiness she has lost: "Marge could feel the lash of wet wind, the tremor of rushing bodies. . . . She was riding the gale! Not swept along, but deliberately, joyously a fore-runner, a marshaller of the gathering storm" (374). No longer blaming her mother, her sexual desires, her children, or herself for her troubles, Marge is ready to lead a "new generation" of women, from all regions, including the South, into a world where they can have fulfilling lives with families, careers, and self-respect.

Marge's success as a leader of the working class provides a promising picture of the abilities of poor white women that transcends the altruistic mother and sexual degenerate stereotypes. In fact, Page, unlike Vorse, totally abandons both of the prominent stereotypes, even as they relate to how other characters view Marge. As a leader and as a class representative who has lost her entire family to poverty, Marge does not fit the dangerous, over-sexualized stereotype at all, and although her political activity is partially based upon her desires for her children, her ability to think globally about workers' rights and to act as a "marshaller" in the effort to obtain these rights places her in a position of power so that she can supply much more than emotional or hopeful support to her class. Instead of acting as a helpmate for the men who lead the cause, she is now the leader. She is only able to reach this independent leadership position in her life because she learns to let go of all that society tells her that she must accept about herself as a woman and as a member of the lower class. In fact, when Marge embraces her power, she asserts herself as not being defined by her sexuality, her family, or her economic stance; instead, she asserts herself as an independent "fightin' spirit" whose voice and activities can change not only her life but the lives of all the other hurting people in her class.

Although *Gathering Storm* provides such a positive message about working-class rights and poor white women's leadership capabilities, the novel was generally dismissed both by reviewers and by readers. In fact, Page's positive message about the growth of the lower class coupled with her focus on communist principles are the major reasons why the novel was largely ignored.[18] While *Gathering Storm* was reviewed by few, those reviewers agreed that the book lacked any merit. A reviewer for *The New Republic* complained that Page tried to cover too much territory (290), and a reviewer for *The Times Literary Supplement* described the novel's failure by writing, "Propaganda defeats itself in fiction" (905). When *New Masses* asked Sherwood Anderson to review Page's novel, he refused because, although he disliked it, he would not write anything negative about it (Baker 239).

Page defended the novel years later in interviews saying that, even though reviewers thought of it as "'melodramatic,'" it was "'the absolute truth'" to her (qtd. in Baker 112). She felt as though the novel "'gave readers a true picture of the period'" (116). However, as the reviews suggest, her forward vision of the poor white southern woman may have been too much for the American public to accept. She represented a new definition of poor white womanhood that lacked a reference point. As a result, Page's "[p]ropaganda" extended beyond her political ideas to the very heart of America's need to stereotype these women. Page's unapologetic and unrelenting versions of the new poor white southern female leader showcase her feeling that this new definition is exactly what America needed and her willingness to cover that territory to reveal it to those who insisted on maintaining those stereotypes.

OVERCOMING EXPECTATIONS

Of the four female-authored Gastonia strike novels, Grace Lumpkin's *To Make My Bread* garnered the most appreciation from the left. A well-known communist sympathizer in the 1920s and 1930s, Lumpkin used communist principles to help mold her novel, and *To Make My Bread* represented these principles so well that in 1932 Lumpkin was awarded the Maxim Gorky Award for writing the "best labor novel" of the year (Sowinska viii). The novel garnered positive reviews despite being labeled as "propaganda" by reviewers, as *Gathering Storm* had been. Unlike Page's novel, however, reviewers thought *To Make My Bread* had great artistic merit, which allowed the content of the novel not to get mired in politics. A reviewer for the *New York Times Book Review* referred to the novel as "propaganda" with "dramatic conflict" ("A Novel" 7). In *The Nation,* Robert Cantwell admitted that the novel was "propaganda" but indicated that at least it was "very good, very effective propaganda" (373). Reviewer Cyrilly Abels called *To Make My Bread* "an honest, sincere picture, well set and well developed" (740). Perhaps the most flattering critique of Lumpkin's novel came from Vorse, the author of *Strike!.* She declared it "the best" of the Gastonia textile mill novels ("Grind" 104). Because the novel was so well received, Lumpkin became a prominent figure in the CPUSA; a second edition was published in 1933; and in 1934, parts of the novel appeared in an issue of *Working Woman,* a female-oriented communist magazine (Sowinska xiv). In 1936, the novel was even adapted into a play,

Let Freedom Ring: A Play in Three Acts (Hall, "Women Writers" 22). Because of its success, *To Make My Bread* made its mark as one of "the first great contributions to the American proletarian novel" (Sowinska xxii).

Lumpkin's middle-class childhood and interactions with poor whites provided her with examples to draw upon for her mountain characters. Although Lumpkin was born in Georgia in 1892, she spent a great deal of her childhood in North Carolina and South Carolina (Sowinska viii–x). Her father wanted to rebuild his family's wealth, which had been lost during Reconstruction (viii). To achieve this goal, he moved his family to South Carolina in 1910 and attempted to farm. Lumpkin and her sister, Katharine, became acquainted with the poor white children in their South Carolina town because they went to school with them (ix).[19] Later, Lumpkin took some education courses in college and went on to work as a school teacher for children, for poor adult men and women at night, and for the government. During the summer months, she spent time in the mountains of North Carolina and stayed with mill workers (x). Lumpkin's constant interaction with members of the lower class allowed her to become knowledgeable about the poor whites on whom she would focus *To Make My Bread.* She wrote articles for "a monthly Quaker publication," *The World Tomorrow; New Masses;* and the CPUSA's "official newspaper," *Daily Worker* (xii–xiii). In the midst of her burgeoning writing career, Lumpkin was sent to the South by the party, and while in the South, she, like Vorse, "observe[d] and participate[d]" in the Gastonia strike (xii). When she returned home to New York, she decided, as Page had done, to use the strike as an outlet to tell the stories of all the poor white people she had interacted with since childhood.

In Lumpkin's version of the Gastonia mill strike, women are once again at the center of the story; however, Lumpkin challenges Vorse's and Page's presentations of poor white mill women as willing activists who eventually decide to fight the oppression of the mills that restrict them and their children. Instead, Lumpkin focuses on how women such as Emma and Bonnie McClure must overcome the paternalistic ideology they encountered in their mountain homes and in the mill town and on how these women must channel their desire for better working and school conditions for themselves and for their children into a desire to fight for workers' rights. To highlight Emma's and Bonnie's potential to become leaders, Lumpkin adds another main female character, Minnie Hawkins, who closely resembles the eugenic "moron" girl.[20] Unlike Vorse and Page, who focus on female characters who do not conform to the dualistic stereotypes, Lumpkin uses the sexually degenerate Minnie to reveal how this type of woman could be problematic for proletarian efforts. Although authors of eugenic studies portrayed the "moron" girl as dangerous to mainstream American society, Lumpkin presents Minnie in contrast to Emma and Bonnie as a way to emphasize how potentially dangerous the "moron" girl could be to lower-class women's efforts to gain equality in the home and in the workplace and to workers' efforts to gain class equality. By mixing representative poor white progressive women with stereotypical "eugenic" representations of sexually destructive poor white women, she seems to admit that she, too, considers some poor white women dangerous; however, by not placing her complete focus on Minnie, she also asserts that most poor white women do have the potential to surpass society's expectations.

Just as in *Gathering Storm,* the McClure family in *To Make My Bread* moves from the mountains to the mill town, and as the family moves, the novel's focus moves from Emma's life to Bonnie's to highlight how the women's experiences change in different settings. Both women's lives center on motherhood, but the importance of their mothering roles differs in each setting depending upon what other roles the women play in their familial and work environments and upon each woman's views of her own abilities in relation to these environments. When Lumpkin introduces Emma as a widowed mother at the beginning of the novel, Emma is described as "a strong woman" who has the endurance to take care of herself and her children without the help of any men (11). This initial description of Emma changes, however, when her father, Grandpap, comes to help the family when Emma is about to give birth. With Grandpap in the home, Emma's two sons, Kirk and Basil, no longer look to Emma for guidance because they see Grandpap as the head of the home. Their dependence upon Grandpap becomes solidified when they witness Emma giving birth to her last child, John. During the birth scene, Kirk keeps his focus on Grandpap the entire time since he is horrified by his mother. Kirk actually begins to think of her as "a stranger, a sort of beast" (13), and when Grandpap delivers the child, Kirk compares Grandpap's actions to the "slaughtering" of a pig (13). As a result of this event, Kirk views his mother and childbirth as bestial and Grandpap as a dominant force over his mother. Kirk is even alarmed by the product, his new brother John, who has come from his mother's pain. To Kirk, John is an "echo of the storm outside" the cabin, a disturbance that has infiltrated his home because of his mother (13). As a result of this event, Emma no longer seems like "a strong woman," especially to her older sons.

Unlike Marge's grandmother in *Gathering Storm,* who helps make decisions for her family, Emma has no power in her family because she is constantly dominated by men. First, she must answer to her father, and when Grandpap is sent to prison for selling alcohol, she then bows to the will of her older sons, Kirk and Basil (Lumpkin 87). Even after Kirk dies and Basil has moved away to attend school, Emma still does not get to act as leader of her family. Despite his absence, Basil acts as the head of the household, selling his family's cabin without regard to Emma or his two younger siblings, Bonnie and John. As a man, he feels justified in selling their home to pay for his second year of school (121). Emma, who accepts Basil's decision because he is now the family patriarch, cannot even ask for her share of the money owed to her by Hal Swain. She must wait for Grandpap to return from prison so that he can get the money (122, 127). Because of the repression she feels in the mountains, Emma desires to move to the mill town, where she believes her family will become "rich" since men and women could both work while the children attend school (38, 136). For Emma, the mills represent an opportunity for her children to get a good education and for her to gain economic autonomy as a woman, equality that she obviously has never enjoyed in the mountains.

When she arrives in the town, however, her hopes of equality are lost quickly. Since Grandpap is too old to do mill work and the managers only rent homes to families with two workers, Emma, John, and Bonnie must board with their family members, Ora and Frank McClure (Lumpkin 157–58). Although Emma originally dreams "of round silver dollars dropping into her lap and of buying good food and fine things in the stores," she knows when she arrives there and looks at the desperate and "fearful" workers that her dreams may never come true, and as she suspects, they do not (195). She makes little money, and part of what she makes she gives to Grandpap, who then spends it on alcohol (201). Bonnie and John eventually have to drop out of school to help support the family once Emma becomes sick with pellagra (252). Later, as Emma lies dying, having struggled with pellagra for years, she feels as though she has wasted her life. She tells Ora, "I wanted so much, Ora, t' give my young ones a chance in life and see them have things that children should have. But I have made only misery and unhappiness for myself and them" (307). Emma's life in the mountains, dominated by her male counterparts, and her inability to find her own place in the mill town as an independent woman cause her to mourn not just for her lost life but also for what she perceives to be the lost futures of her youngest children, Bonnie and John.

Emma's already desperate life becomes even more difficult to endure when her family is disrupted by Minnie, a feebleminded, sexual "moron" girl. Although Urgo describes Minnie as a victim by referring to her as a "whore driven to prostitution by social forces beyond her control, and by making the mistake of loving too many men" (72), Lumpkin actually describes Minnie much like Faulkner describes Dewey Dell, as a woman afflicted by her own uncontrollable desires rather than by "social forces." In fact, Minnie seems to wish that people could see this sexual force inside of her so they could understand why she acts as she does: "The others seemed to know so little about what happened in her. They could not understand that sometimes with one man, sometimes with another, the heat came up in her and made her dizzy and blind so she scarcely knew what happened" (Lumpkin 102). Like the sexually perverse women of eugenic studies, Minnie seems like a victim of a generational affliction because her mother committed adultery and was known in their mountain community as a woman who tried to seduce every man she saw (44, 92). Because of Minnie's seductive ways and her unparalleled beauty, all of the women envy her (42), and most of the men want to have sexual relations with her. At one point, Minnie is having an affair with both of Emma's oldest sons, Kirk and Basil, and with Sam McEachern, another young man in the community (65, 71). The eugenic concerns about Minnie reach a high point when, while involved with all three of these men, she becomes pregnant with an illegitimate child (79, 93). Instead of being described as a "strong woman," Minnie really does seem to embody the description that Emma uses when she refers to Minnie as "poison ivy" (92).

Unlike the sexually dangerous women in eugenic family studies such as Goddard's *The Kallikak Family,* Minnie's sexuality does not destroy the reputation and family line of an upper-class man whom she has seduced. Rather, her "poison[ous]" sexuality almost destroys Emma's poor white family. Although Kirk and Basil know that Minnie is having sexual relations with both of them, they are so completely infatuated with her that, instead of leaving her alone, they take their frustrations out on each other (Lumpkin 76). Eventually, their affairs with Minnie lead to the breakdown of the McClure family. Basil leaves town to go to school because of Minnie's pregnancy (79). Kirk does not flee; instead, he attempts to save Minnie from her desires by bringing her into the McClure home. He knows that, if he abandons her, she is so full of "temptation" that men will flock to her "like buzzards over a carcase [*sic*]" (89). Emma knows that Minnie will "ruin" Kirk, but as a subordinate woman, she "give[s] in" to her son's wishes and allows Minnie and her child to stay with them (92). As Emma suspects, though, Minnie leaves Kirk for her former lover, Sam, and when Kirk tries to take her back, Sam kills him (110–11). Mantooth argues that Kirk's attempt to retrieve Minnie "evokes mythical images of lone outlaws who bravely take problems into their own hands" (86), but Kirk seems more like a fool who gives his life for an unworthy woman. Minnie's destructive presence continues to haunt the McClure family even after she leaves because Basil uses Kirk's death as a way to strip his family of their home, thereby forcing them into the mill town. Even Emma suffers from Minnie's sexual nature because, though she recognizes the danger Minnie brought to her family, she "give[s] in" to the paternalistic ideology that made her believe she had no choice but to follow Kirk's desires. In the town, her guilt over Kirk's death continues to plague her so much that she puts her family further into debt just to have a picture of Kirk drawn (224). For the McClure family, Minnie becomes a destructive force that breaks their familial bonds either through anger, death, or guilt. In fact, she almost brings "ruin" not just to Kirk, but to all of the McClures.

Although Lumpkin presents Emma as a victim of paternalistic mountain ideology and Minnie as a sexual deviant set to destroy poor white families, Lumpkin presents Bonnie, Emma's only female child, as a progressive woman. Tracing Bonnie's life from childhood to adulthood, Lumpkin reveals how Bonnie surpasses her mother because she garners the independence, the respect, and the equality that her mother desired yet never received. As a young girl, Bonnie is described by the men in the family as the type of "strong woman" that Emma wished to be seen as. The men see her not just as a hard worker but also as a leader, especially for her younger brother, John. After watching Bonnie work more diligently than John, Grandpap declares that Bonnie's behavior is an example of how a true "woman" should act (Lumpkin 24). Later, she reveals her heroism and her leadership skills, saving John's life when they encounter a snake (16). Her actions also reveal how selfless she is because she willingly injures herself to keep him from injury (16–17). In the mill town, she continues revealing her selflessness and her leadership capabilities. When the two McClure families move into a home together, she takes over the role of caretaker for Ora's children, a role that Sally, Ora's daughter, had fulfilled before marrying and returning to the mountains with her husband. No one tells Bonnie that "she must take Sally's place"; she just knows that she is needed (180). Spending part of her childhood in the mountains has taught her that she must be a hard worker and a willing caretaker, but since she escapes the mountains before she becomes overburdened with the oppression of paternalism that her mother had to face, Bonnie has never had to accept a subordinate position to any male. Even as she accepts "Sally's place" as the family caretaker, she knows that she is only fulfilling this role for the present rather than for the rest of her life (180).

Even though Bonnie's selfless actions as a child and as a teenager connect her with the altruistic mother image as she puts others' needs before her own, these selfless traits help her to feel confident in her personal abilities and help her to realize her role as a leader. As a mill worker, a wife, and mother of her own family, she becomes a leader for her family and for other workers, and unlike other altruistic mother figures in Depression-era literature such as Ma Joad and Annie Mae Gudger, Bonnie does not just act as an emotional caretaker. Hapke argues that Bonnie has a "passive identity as a mill mother enmeshed in family trouble" until she is near the end of her life (162); however, Hapke overlooks the fact that Bonnie really has no time to act "passive[ly]" because her husband, Jim Calhoun, leaves for war before Bonnie gives birth to her first child, and then, after returning from war, he abandons his family (Lumpkin 275, 283). As a result, Bonnie's responsibilities increase as she becomes both caretaker and financial provider. In the midst of all this responsibility, she is never described as worn down or resentful because she must work in the mills and as a caretaker for her children: "Loving was as natural to her as the breath she took into herself without thought" (315, 322). Like the working mothers in *Strike!* and in *Gathering Storm,* Bonnie gains personal strength and self-entitlement because she learns that she has the ability to support her family on her own. Her role as an active and independent woman extends into her mill work and her views of other women as well. She feels connected to the single, young female workers who seem carefree because, despite having children, she feels like part of the "new generation" of mill women, described by Page in her dissertation, who want the right to "enjoy themselves" (318). Because she does have children, though, she is also able to connect with the mothers, who like herself, worry about their children's future welfare. As a result, Bonnie becomes a voice for all the female workers as a ballad singer, writing and singing songs about the plight of mill women (342–46). Since Bonnie does not feel repressed by men and her life circumstances, as Emma did while she lived, Bonnie uses her freedom both to embrace motherhood and a leadership role among her fellow workers.

Bonnie's leadership abilities and her feminine independence are tested in the mill town by Minnie, just as Emma was tested by her in the mountains. Although Minnie flees with Sam into the mountains, she reappears in the town, and this time, instead of creating problems as a sexually indiscriminate mountain woman, she creates problems as a socially and politically influential prostitute who is being used by upper- and middle-class men to disrupt lower-class solidarity. In the mill town, she tries to create another love triangle with Basil and John, who has grown into a mature young man. Unlike Basil, John resists her advances (289). The upper- and middle-class men in town, however, think John has slept with Minnie, and therefore, they think of him as a safe and manageable worker (290). He seems to confirm their opinion of him when he joins the town lodge and begins drinking and spending time with Minnie and other suspicious women; in fact, he spends so much time in town that the mill manager makes him "section boss," expecting John to snitch on his fellow workers who are involved with unions (290, 294, 298). When Bonnie learns how John has been acting, she does not respond passively as Emma did to Kirk about Minnie. She urges John to take control of his life, rather than "bootlick[ing] all the higher-ups" (302). Even though she offends him and belittles him by chastising him, making her seem like Irma in Vorse's *Strike!,* her efforts are not interpreted as "arrogant," as Irma's are. Shortly after their conversation, John quits his job and begins working with Bonnie in the union. In a final effort to persuade John away from the unions, Minnie tells him, "[S]omething bad will happen. [. . .] I beg of you before it's too late—to give in" (368). Because of the strength of his sister who refuses to "give in" to his authority as a man, John does not "give in" either. With Bonnie's guidance, he refuses to be the next McClure man to fall for Minnie's destructive sexuality.

When Minnie warns John of danger, her words are reminiscent of Emma's lack of self-confidence, and they predict a final scene that will determine whether the lower-class workers will remain united in their cause or "give in" to the pressure of the town. Upper- and middle-class men in town move Minnie into the mill village with the workers and employ her as a spy (Lumpkin 369). Because of Minnie's information, "something bad" does happen when Bonnie is shot and killed at a meeting before singing one of her ballads (373). By making Minnie the catalyst for Bonnie's murder, Lumpkin not only reinforces the sexually destructive stereotype of poor white women, but she also adds a new dimension to their dangerous potential. Minnie's deviance and uncontrollable desires are not just creating an "inferior" new generation of "delinquents" as eugenicists suspected; she is murdering those who are strong representations of the lower class, seemingly only making this class weaker. Lumpkin's stereotyped portrayal of Minnie distances her from the other Gastonia novelists and may be one of the reasons that her novel was the best reviewed. By using a character such as Minnie, Lumpkin does not totally stray away from the socially accepted sexual deviant image of poor white southern women, as Page does; she certainly does not even challenge the stereotype, as Vorse does. Her "propaganda" is, for the most part, embedded in the stereotypes.

Although Lumpkin uses the stereotypes to create her message, she does challenge eugenic and social expectations with Bonnie's life and eventually her death. Bonnie's death does not mark the end of the first revolutionary movement in the state, as the mill-owned newspaper claims (383). Instead, it "is just the beginning" (383–84). Bonnie's funeral becomes a union meeting because, to the workers, her death represents how mill workers are treated. Her funeral is not just a time for all mill workers to come together; it is also a time for Bonnie's influence on other women to materialize fully. At Bonnie's funeral, Ora, Sally, and Zinie, John's wife, all gather around her grave, and then Sally takes on Bonnie's role when she leads the funeralgoers to sing one of Bonnie's songs (382). While she lived, Bonnie worked with each of these women to help the union and the workers (342), and as they gather to mourn her loss, their commitment to the union effort reveals that Bonnie has helped them become independent women like her. Emma may have died without hope; Bonnie may have fallen because of Minnie's destructive influence and because of other poor whites still dependent on the ruling classes; but with the final image of Ora, Sally, and Zinie singing, Lumpkin implies that the seed of poor white female strength has only begun to grow and that a new version of the poor white woman as activist has started to spread.

CHALLENGING THE IMAGE

Like Vorse, Page, and Lumpkin, Olive Tilford Dargan also wrote a novel, *Call Home the Heart,* based upon what she witnessed while in Gastonia during the strike and based upon what she witnessed in her childhood and adulthood when she lived in the South (Mantooth 129). During her early years as a teacher, she lived in multiple states across the South (Shannon 434–35). Later, she lived in the North and in England for a number of years attending school and developing her writing career. Dargan moved back to the South in 1916, bought a farm in North Carolina, and housed and cared for nine tenants (438–39). She also assisted poor, young married women who had already become overwhelmed by "poverty and incessant childbearing" (440). Anna W. Shannon argues that "Dargan's art was strengthened by her engagement in the struggle for survival on behalf of her mountain neighbors" (439). Of course, she had become intrigued by the plight of the working class and by women's rights well before she moved to North Carolina. While traveling outside of the South, she became acquainted with members of the CPUSA (433–34).[21] She read *The Woman's Journal* and *The Call,* journals that would have introduced her to articles written by Margaret Sanger that presumably informed her about "female sexuality" and birth control (437). Dargan also read the work of eugenicists such as Julian Huxley.[22] All of these different experiences and ideas she was exposed to affected how she wrote *Call Home the Heart.*

Dargan, like Lumpkin, follows the life of her female protagonist, Ishma Waycaster, from the mountain to the mill town.[23] This connection between Lumpkin's and Dargan's novels is the most significant similarity *Call Home the Heart* shares with the other female-authored Gastonia novels. Unlike the other novels, though, the plight of the workers and the strength of the women in the strike efforts in *Call Home the Heart* are secondary to Dargan's focus on the inner, personal struggles faced by Ishma. Unlike the various types of female activists in *Strike!,* Marge in *Gathering Storm,* and Bonnie in *To Make My Bread,* Ishma does not struggle with gaining the courage to act or with learning how to act; she struggles with whether she has the moral ability to act on her own behalf and on the behalf of her fellow workers. Barbara Foley has referred to Ishma as Dargan's attempt to create "an exemplary working-class protagonist" (395); however, as a seemingly unfit mother and as an adulteress, Ishma does not fit the model of an appropriate female striker advocated by the male reporters and union leaders in *Strike!*—the altruistic, morally upright mother desiring to save her children. Ishma desires to save herself above all, but since she, like Marge in *Gathering Storm,* does not have the knowledge about birth control to manage her fertility or the money and the skills to save herself from poverty, Ishma's life seems hopeless to her because she cannot do what Marge is eventually able to do: embrace her roles as wife and mother. Moreover, despite her seemingly genetically and sexually destructive traits, she is not like *To Make My Bread*'s Minnie either. Unlike Minnie, Ishma is overly conscious of how society negatively views her, and because she cannot fulfill society's maternal and sexual expectations, her life is shrouded in guilt. Dargan uses Ishma's fears about herself to highlight the effect of stereotypes about motherhood on poor white women who have the potential to act as leaders in their communities but hold back because their personal lives do not match society's expectations.

From the beginning of the novel, Dargan presents Ishma as a persevering young woman who, although trapped in a subordinate position in her mountain home, always tries to improve herself and her living situation. At a young age, Ishma learns that to succeed in her family and in the mountains, she must work diligently and give of herself freely: "Six days of the week Ishma was merely a family possession, giving herself so effectually that no one suspected she was giving; so entirely she did not suspect it herself" (Dargan, *Call* 1). Although Ishma's name actually means "waste," she does not intend to "waste" her life submitting solely to her family or to the endless work of the farm; instead, she gives as much as she can without sacrificing her own desires.[24] Because she proves herself to be such an efficient worker, she must stay at home and work instead of going to school, but instead of accepting this decision as the end of her education, she finds other ways to learn. Ishma learns to read by reading the Bible to her grandmother, and after her grandmother dies, she learns by studying her cousin Sam's school books (8). Even when she has no guidance and no school books, she teaches herself by reading history books and novels (9). Sam's teacher is so impressed by Ishma's intellectual abilities that he has the monthly magazine *Woman at Home* sent to her for three years (10–11). Although Ishma's work ethic and intellect distinguish her as a woman with great potential, her desire for self-reflection in the midst of a life that demands so much of her really sets her apart. On the seventh day when Ishma purposefully does not work, she takes the day to herself, climbs to the top of the mountain, and sits there all day looking at her world (1–2). At the top of the mountain, away from the drudgery of her life, she "replenish[es] her fount," giving herself hope that her life will not always be this endless procession of work and sacrifice and that she will not always be just a "woman at home" (1).

At the bottom of the mountain with her family, Ishma's "fount" is continually diluted by her family members—specifically her sister Bainie and her mother Laviny—who act as obstacles to her hope for a better life. Like Marge's mother Sally in *Gathering Storm* and Emma in *To Make My Bread,* Bainie and Laviny live like "shadow[s]" mired in the drudgery of the choices they have made and in their subordinate female roles. Bainie is old before her time because she has married a worthless man, Jim Wishart, who only seems to work at giving her more children for whom to care (Dargan, *Call* 7). Because Jim is lazy, his family's scale of living falls each year, and Bainie has become so despondent about her life that she even treats her children cruelly (7). Bainie's life almost seems like a complete replica of her mother Laviny's. Laviny married a man the townspeople referred to as a "'roamin' feller,'" and they had seven children, only three of whom survived (6). As a wife and a mother, Laviny acts so cruelly toward her family that, after her husband has a stroke and becomes paralyzed, she comments that she actually likes him better now that he cannot walk because she knows he will not leave (21). Despite her own sad existence, Laviny continually says that her life philosophy is, "A gal she must marry, an' a wife she must carry" (20). What Ishma must face with her mother and sister that Marge and Bonnie do not face with their mothers is the extreme cruelty that she endures because she expects more from her life than Bainie and Laviny have achieved. Although Ishma takes care of Bainie's children and works for lazy Jim, Bainie dislikes Ishma because of her "ambitious strength" (17). Laviny "punish[es]" Ishma for her desire to learn because Laviny thinks that learning too much leads to death or to mental disability (8). Since Ishma withstands this pressure from her family and continues to excel in whatever she attempts, Margaret Cheney Dawson noted in her 1932 review of the novel that Ishma defeats "slovenliness and ignorance" to become the "sole prop of a big and shiftless family" (5).

Despite Ishma's efforts to escape the desperation that plagues her sister's and mother's lives, she falls prey to her love for Britt Hensley and, as a result, to the type of life she never wanted. Since Ishma has to give all of her savings to help her family in a time of financial need, she has to settle for staying in the mountains (Dargan, *Call* 60).[25] She marries Britt and, like Bainie and Laviny, begins having children (64, 69). Although she does not originally want a husband, she really does love Britt; however, her mothering instinct never emerges. Shortly after marriage, Ishma has a boy, Ned, and twins. Urgo has argued that Ishma thinks of these children as "one shackle after another, preventing her escape from the mountains" (78). Her children do not really hold her back, though, because she cares so little for them that their lives seem almost inconsequential. When the twins die of the croup, Ishma mourns for a short time and then immediately sets her focus back on escaping the mountains (Dargan, *Call* 88–91). Ishma cares so little for Ned that she actually gives him to Laviny, crying "tears" of joy to be relieved of her mothering duties (124–25). Only when she becomes pregnant a third time does she feel "shackl[ed]" because she sees no end to the perpetual cycle of pregnancy (114). In fact, she actually sees her life as full of "barrenness" because Ishma feels that only the independence she does not have will make her life full, not children. She even feels guilty for the "barrenness" she feels with her family (150). Ishma, despite her love for Britt, cannot reconcile herself to motherhood because she never gains a desire to love and care for her children.

To escape the fate of Bainie and Laviny and the guilt she feels, Ishma decides to run away to the mill town with Rad Bailey, a former suitor with a large savings. She believes that, by leaving with Rad, she will escape the drudgery of her life as a mother and as a worker for her family. Instead, she finds that she has caused herself more pain than she originally felt living in the mountains. Not only does her adultery ruin her reputation among her mountain neighbors, but it also ruins her image of herself. Her fellow church members, who once saw Ishma as exceptional, vote to excommunicate her (Dargan, *Call* 160). In the mill town, she feels so ashamed of her behavior that she rarely leaves the home of her boarders, Pace and Genie. Ishma claims that her unborn child keeps her from seeing the town, but she actually does not go out because she does not think she is worthy of this new life: "Was it great? Was it fine? Was it glorious? Whatever its value, she knew it could not be worth the price she had paid; the price which she would never get through paying" (179). Ishma sees herself as forever tainted because of the choices she has made to give up her children and her husband, and she knows that her weakness will haunt her for the rest of her life. The one time she does leave the house, her experience is cut short when she goes into labor (187). Because of what she has done to Britt and her children, Ishma thinks she deserves her exile from mill-town life. Since she refuses to live a life she does not want to live as a mother and a wife, a life that other poor white women in her life have consented to, regardless of whether they wanted to, her mountain neighbors declare her unfit and unholy, and she has even lost her self-respect.

Although Ishma's move does not give her true independence because she is still bound to a man and still has a child to mother, the mill town offers her opportunities to further develop her intellect and her work ethic without the same pressures she experiences in the mountains. Unlike in the mountains, where Ishma could not control her fertility, the doctors in the town teach the lower class about birth control; however, the women still do not have control of their reproductive capabilities because they still must get permission from their husbands to use birth control. When Rad expresses interest in having children, the mill town doctor, Derry Unthank, tells Rad about birth control, but Ishma can only get Rad to follow the doctor's orders by explaining that, if they had children, she would feel "wickeder" than she already does (Dargan, *Call* 196). While Ishma must belittle herself to stop what she once saw as a never-ending cycle of pregnancy, the freedom she now has gives her time to develop the exceptional qualities that previously helped her stand apart from her seemingly "shiftless" family. As in the mountains before she married, Ishma spends her time caring for other people. Ironically, she helps mill women who are suffering from overwork and from the ill effects of excessive childbearing. Since Ishma is able to help these women only because her adulterous indiscretions have helped her to escape her expected role as mother, though, she remains haunted by "incessant inner questionings" (198). As evidenced by her statement to Rad concerning her desire not to be any "wickeder," Ishma still has a negative opinion of herself, and although her work with the mill women should make her feel better about herself, their suffering only reminds her of her socially unacceptable actions.

The shame that Ishma feels as a result of her broken commitment to Britt is constantly reinforced by their child, Vennie, for whom she still must care. Unlike Ned, who is a healthy and growing boy, Vennie is described as "a little scrub of a kid" because she suffers from "diseased nerves" that cause her body to wither and her hair to fall out (Dargan, *Call* 196). Ishma takes full responsibility for Vennie's affliction, citing her decision to leave Britt as the cause of Vennie's downfall and further marking herself as the "bad" mother highlighted in eugenic studies. Because Vennie needs constant attention due to her poor health, she actually becomes a physical "shackle" to Ishma. Since Ishma must constantly care for Vennie, Ishma cannot return to work, and she cannot visit the ill mill women (192, 199). Ishma accepts that taking care of Vennie is "part of her punishment" for her indiscretions (231). Even this notion of "punishment," however, does not make Ishma into a loving mother, and without the desire for motherhood, Ishma once again fails in her efforts. Lost in her thoughts of how the child is suffocating her, Ishma thinks, "But what did Vennie matter? Was her life forever to be bound up in a child's? Was her horizon always to be Vennie's horizon? Was she never to reach the world?" (231). While

Ishma ponders how Vennie holds her back, Vennie runs into the street and is killed by a car (233). Like her reaction to the death of the twins and to losing Ned, Ishma does not mourn long because, to her, Vennie remains "insignificant" (243). Hapke argues that Dargan "conveniently" kills Vennie so that Ishma may pursue her dreams (167), but Vennie's death condemns Ishma just as much as it frees her to work. Now, Ishma sees herself as an adulteress, a child abandoner, and a murderer—a woman overrun with the negative eugenic characteristics of poor white sexually deviant women.

Although Ishma does think of herself as "free" without Vennie to care for, she spends her "free" time trying to mend her personal image of herself. She convinces Rad they should abstain from sex until they have enough money to marry (Dargan, *Call* 266). She begins to work in the mills, and in her spare time, she still cares for the mill women and their daughters. Not only does she resume her role as caretaker to the women, but she also joins and begins to recruit for the national Textile Workers Union (277–78). Ella Ramsey had told Ishma before Vennie's death that she wanted Ishma to work as a recruiter because of how the mill workers respect her (221). Ishma had felt encouraged when Ella had said, "[I]t's a shame fer a woman like you not to count" (227), but with Vennie to care for and her own low self-esteem, Ishma never felt that she could "count" the way Ella felt that she could. Without Vennie and without fear of being impregnated again by Rad, Ishma becomes the type of woman she has always desired to be, and ironically, just as she did before she had Vennie, Ishma becomes a surrogate mother for all the ill women and children, revealing once again her exceptional qualities. Derry, the town doctor, even refers to Ishma as "the great Earth-mother" (294–95). In spite of how respected she becomes, though, Ishma still seems to doubt her self-worth and her personal qualifications to help others. She even describes herself with the eugenic term "feeble-minded" at one point when she must decide whether to spend time with Rad or to attend a union meeting (279). Just as she does with her children, she feels trapped by her relationship with Rad, whom she also does not love. Although Ishma wants to believe that she can make a difference and that Ella and Derry are correct in how they view her, she is unable to look beyond the deviant image she has of herself and respect herself as the independent woman she wants to be, so even when she works hard to change her self-image, she still feels hampered by her inability to fit into her expected maternal role.

Ishma's feelings of unworthiness become overwhelming the night she returns to the mountains. Throughout her time living in the town, Ishma has continued to consider herself unworthy. Her insecurities have increased because she has failed as both a wife and a mother and because she has never truly felt worthy enough to help her fellow members of the lower class. On this night, though, Ishma intends to prove her self-worth, at least as a union worker, by breaking down the racial boundaries that she has been taught are keeping the union from achieving victory (Dargan, *Call* 354). To prove she is a champion of the working class across racial lines, she sets out to save Butch Wells, a black man working for the union, from being lynched. She does succeed in saving Butch, but her dream of solidifying her worth falters when Butch's wife, Gaffie, attempts to hug her (383). She feels repulsed by the black woman, trapped in her embrace, reminiscent of how her children made her feel. Ishma does not want physical or emotional contact with this black woman whom she considers part of a "'lower' race" (Alaimo 124). Immediately after she pushes Gaffie down, however, Ishma realizes that she has failed to get beyond her "innate" prejudices and thus to live up to the title of "great Earth-mother" (Cook, "Critical Afterword" 455).[26] As a result, she flees back to the mountains, disparaging herself along the way and completely stripping herself of any self-worth her union activities have allowed her to retain: "I know what I am now. I'm an animal. I haven't got a little Neanderthal woman in me. She's all of me. I'm nothing else. That's clear. And I'm not going to do a thing about it. I didn't make myself. I'll be as I was made. I wanted to slap that woman and I slapped her" (Dargan, *Call* 385). Instead of proving that she is a worthy person, Ishma feels as though she has finally proven that she is completely unworthy of the independent, fruitful life she dreamed of as a child in the mountains.

By returning to the mountains, though, Ishma has only returned to a life that she formerly did not want. She, too, recognizes the irony of this decision when she reunites with Britt, and they have sex at the top of the mountain, her former place of renewal (Dargan, *Call* 428). While Britt sleeps beside her, she wonders how she can reconcile these two sides of herself (432). She wonders if she truly is "a beast [. . . ,] ashamed and apart" or a woman full of "desire" finally quenched by the return to Britt, the man she loves and whom she feels comfortable with now that she knows about birth control. Cook has argued that, by returning to Britt, Ishma has failed as an activist because she has chosen "one human being" over "humanity" (*From Tobacco* 107); however, Ishma actually refocuses her life on "humanity" when she returns to Britt and shows her true personal strength. Although she has no answer to which person she actually is, she still intends, with Britt to assist her, to help her people by bringing mill children to the mountain to renew their spirits, once again becoming a surrogate mother figure (Dargan, *Call* 430). Instead of continuing to belittle herself because of her negative self-perceptions, she allows herself to be a woman who does not fit the altruistic mothering role that she thinks she is expected to play or even the activist mothering role that the female protagonists in the other Gastonia novels fulfill. She tells Britt, "I'm not looking back. It's the future that's going to be so hard to forget. The future of all men and women and little children" (429). In spite of failing at being a wife, a mother, and a progressive southern union organizer, Ishma, in this moment, refuses to let her failures keep her locked in a "Neanderthal" existence. Though she may not epitomize the altruistic mother figure, she remains dedicated to helping fellow members of the lower class. Britt confirms her decision when he also chooses to overlook her faults, even saying that her "heart [. . .] don't belong to time" (430). Back with the man she loves, Britt, and now in control of her fertility, Ishma declares that her life will not be a "waste," and she decides to continue her efforts to help the lower-class women and children she cared so deeply for in the mill town.

In the sequel to *Call Home the Heart, A Stone Came Rolling* (1935), Dargan confirms that Ishma continues her efforts to help members of the lower class; however, instead of helping mill workers by bringing their children to the mountains, she goes back to the mill town, with Britt, to help the workers organize and strike for their rights. Her time in the mountains has given her a new sense of confidence that makes her seem like a totally different woman than the one who fled first from and then back to the mountains in *Call Home the Heart.* Back in the town, she takes a job in the mill to feel close to the workers and to organize a union and a strike (Dargan, *Stone* 121, 202). She even seems to have defeated her racial prejudices that kept her from embracing Gaffie in *Call Home the Heart.* Not only does she help save another black man from racial violence, but she also walks alongside black workers in a union funeral procession, proclaiming their equality as oppressed people (294, 405–6). Although Ishma has changed, she does not become a leader, as Marge does in *Gathering Storm* or Bonnie does in *To Make My Bread,* without first facing her past. When the townspeople hear rumors about her adulterous relationship with Rad, they declare her unfit (340–41). Her affair with Rad even causes her to lose Britt in the end because he dies trying to defend Ishma's honor (343). While this public disavowal would have crushed Ishma completely in her former days, she does not allow the event to destroy her. Instead, she rejoins the strike and is arrested fighting for what she believes is right (406–7). Instead of being defined by other people's expectations, she defines her own sense of self, and despite losing her husband and her freedom, she feels as though she has finally gained her independence because she believes in her ability to fight for a greater cause (411). Her strength is solidified when the strikers, who previously shunned her because of her relationship with Rad, free her from jail and help her to realize fully her role as a leader (412).

The ending of *Call Home the Heart* has sparked much discussion among reviewers of the 1930s and even among contemporary critics. Dawson disliked the conclusion because she wanted "a heroine instead of a woman," even though she liked that Ishma does not just become a "mouthpiece" (5). Archer Winsten, in his 1932 review for *Bookman,* appreciated the ending for the very reason that Dawson disliked it. To Winsten, the conclusion allowed Dargan to show how "feminism" can enter into the world of the "mountaineers in field and mill town" (319). Hapke, in her recent critique of the novel, has argued that Ishma's failure to stay in the town is Dargan's way of keeping Ishma from becoming "a heroine" and usurping the "legend" of Wiggins's real-life sacrifice (169). For Dawson and Hapke, Ishma is lessened by the fact that Dargan makes her just "a woman" rather than "a heroine." While Hapke and Dawson both criticize the book for this quality, the fact that Ishma is a "woman" is what makes this book "feminis[t,]" as Winsten argued. Although obviously a caring woman when dealing with the children and families of people who need her help, she is plagued throughout her life by a feeling of inadequacy because she does not want children of her own. As a result, she fails at being the altruistic mother that Laviny, Bainie, Britt, and Rad expect her to be, and she almost fails at her marriage with Britt because she fears the children their love will bring. Then, when she cannot immediately free herself of her lifelong racial prejudices, she concludes that she really must be the degenerate person that eugenicists, society, and the church have labeled her. When Ishma gets on the train to return to the mountains, she gives up because she cannot be the "heroine" that even she expects herself to be. She is not Mamie Lewes, Marge Crenshaw, Bonnie McClure, or Ella May Wiggins. At the top of that mountain lying next to Britt, however, Ishma evolves into a new type of "heroine" and a new version of Page's "new generation" of lower-class women. By returning to the mill town later in *A Stone Came Rolling* to continue the efforts she had abandoned, she becomes a social activist, not for her children and her family, but for herself and for her fellow members of the lower class.

Although Ishma disappointed some reviewers and perhaps even some readers because she did not fulfill their expectations, Dargan's new version of the social activist emerges as a more realistic representative than any of the other women in the Gastonia novels. Dargan does not hide Ishma's activist purpose as Vorse does in *Strike!* when she deletes the final union call-to-arms stanza of "Mill Mother's Lament," and she certainly does not appease her readers with socially acceptable characters, as Lumpkin does with Minnie. Furthermore, Dargan even sets Ishma apart from Marge in *Gathering Storm,* the only female Gastonia character who is most like Ishma, because Ishma does not need to travel outside of her southern home or come in contact with international union organizers to further her abilities as a leader. She has even managed to gain control of her reproductive capabilities because of her knowledge and access to birth control. Ishma's strong leadership capabilities are innate qualities that she has always possessed, even during her most desperate times. As a result of these significant changes to the female Gastonia character, Dargan creates a woman who is easier for readers to identify with than the other female authors do. The readers do not have to suppose Ishma's struggle and success; Dargan clearly states them. The readers also do not have to look for inspiration outside of themselves and their surroundings. Their families, their communities, and their own individual lives can serve as the greatest inspirations for a better future. For poor white southern women, Ishma's life represents a much more feasible blueprint to follow than the other women's lives, even if the readers do not share her distaste for mothering. Ishma is not a reprehensible deviant, a worldly woman, or an incomprehensible saint. Instead, she is a leader, a failure, a lover, a friend, and a caretaker, and sometimes she plays all these parts on the same day. Ishma embraces all these parts of herself by the end of *Call Home the Heart.* Dargan, through Ishma, seems to encourage her female readers not to feel the need to be perfect "heroine[s]" but, instead, to strive to be their best and to define their own sense of self-worth in spite of their seemingly insurmountable faults. As a result, Dargan challenges her readers with a woman who completely dismantles both stereotypes and who could potentially represent any woman desiring to make a difference in her own life and in the lives of others.

REVISING THE CRITICAL RECEPTION

Despite their differences in presentation, each of these female novelists challenges the stereotypes of poor white southern women as altruistic mothers and sexual degenerates. Vorse focuses on the activist efforts of young, single women as a way to discredit the notion that poor white women without children are simply sexually motivated or power-driven. She also seems to acknowledge, through her alteration of the facts of Wiggins's life, that in order for society to accept poor white women's activism, the women need to project altruistic mothering qualities, placing their children's futures before their own needs. Page examines how such women, because of oppression and poverty, have been stripped of their right to act as loving wives and protecting mothers; however, even without families to fight for, they remain activists fighting for future workers and their rights to familial and economic security. Lumpkin focuses on how independence can encourage these women to gain personal strength that gives them the courage to confront all of their adversaries, whether those foes come from the elite classes or their own lower class, and to influence all workers, male or female, to fight for their labor rights. Dargan explicitly attacks both the sexual degenerate image and the altruistic mother image when she allows Ishma, an adulterous woman and the opposite of the altruistic mother, to continue fighting for herself and her fellow workers. In 1934, E. A. Schachner, "an influential Communist journalist and editor," wrote an article about Page's, Lumpkin's, and Dargan's versions of the Gastonia strike (Elfenbein 193), and he actually cited the collective feminist effort of the novelists as a reason to place their works at the forefront of proletarian literature as "the first truly revolutionary novels to be written in the United States" (Schachner 68). He even applauds the fact that the novels are written by "Southern nonproletarian women" because he thinks these women are "more progressive, more sensitive to oppression, and more equipped with the necessary culture" than male writers because they, like poor white southern women, also have to strive for independence in a paternalistic society (60). Therefore, according to Schachner, these novelists are not only challenging the dualistic images that define poor white women but also liberating themselves from the "bourgeois man-made codes" set by their class and, ironically, by the CPUSA (66).

The works of Vorse, Page, Lumpkin, and Dargan really do seem like "truly revolutionary novels" compared to the 1930s Gastonia novels written by male authors. While the female authors focus on the roles that women play in the strike and in union organization and on breaking down the stereotypes associated with poor white southern women, Sherwood Anderson and William Rollins utilize the stereotypes when portraying working-class female characters in their versions of the Gastonia strike. In fact, in Anderson's *Beyond Desire* (1932) and in Rollins's *The Shadow Before* (1934), the altruistic mother image and the sexual degenerate image are used to diminish the women's role as activists. In *Beyond Desire,* Anderson actually compares young female mill workers to "little mothers" and their machines to "children who need constant attention" (52). By portraying the women's work as a form of mothering, he places all working women, whether they have children or not, in a maternal role and further distances them from labor activism. When not describing the female mill workers in maternal terms, he describes them in sexual terms, making the women appear not only attracted to all classes of men but also to each other (Anderson 95–96, 97, 101). The only identifiable female activist, Molly Seabright, is a mix of both the altruistic mother and the sexual degenerate. At one point, she is described as a mother to the "looms" (288), and later, she is described as sexually attracted to the looms and her work, reminiscent of Caldwell's "wild-eyed" and "firm-bodied" workers who are "in love with the looms" in *God's Little Acre* (Anderson 298; Caldwell 69). In fact, Molly is just as inactive in the labor strike as Caldwell's female workers because she is preoccupied with the illegitimate child she is going to have as a result of her sexual relationship with the foreman (Anderson 298–99). The only true activist in *Beyond Desire* is a man, Red. Unlike the women authors, Anderson does not even acknowledge the role that women played in the Gastonia strike. Instead, Anderson puts the focus back on the stereotypes generally used to define poor white southern women.

In *The Shadow Before,* Rollins does not totally dismiss the activist efforts of the female workers as Anderson does in *Beyond Desire;* however, his female activists are still mired in the dualistic stereotypes attributed to poor white southern women. The female strikers in *The Shadow Before* actually hold important union positions and assist in union organization, but their roles in the union do not provide the same stabilizing effect as the women's roles in *Strike!, Gathering Storm,* and *To Make My Bread.* In fact, their contributions to the union are often compromised by their sexual desires. Micky, a young female mill hand, is a strike leader who is driven more by her lust than by her desire to help the union. Although she is having an affair with Harry, the mill owner's son who has joined the strikers in their fight for workers' rights, she really lusts after Ramon Viera, a Portuguese mill worker. Because Ramon wants to win the favor of the owners and operators to get a more prestigious job in the mill, Micky thinks that, if she tells him some of the strikers' plans, he will commit to being in a relationship with her. Her plan, however, does not work. Even after Micky informs Ramon that Harry is going to burn the mill, Ramon still does not commit himself to Micky (Rollins 344–45). Ramon simply stops Harry, who then commits suicide, distraught over his failed plan. In the end, Micky is left with neither man (382). With such a focus on Micky's sexuality and how it distorts her union efforts, Rollins diminishes the efforts of female activists, implying that their sexual appetites will override any desire they have for working-class rights. Although he acknowledges the activism of female workers, Rollins echoes the sentiments of the male journalists, Roger and Hoskins, in *Strike!* who suggest that activist women have the potential to cause more "harm" with their efforts than good.

Despite how differently the female authors present their poor white female characters, this major difference in the novels has not always been considered by either reviewers or critics. In the same 1934 article that praises the female-authored novels, Schachner also praises Anderson's *Beyond Desire,* grouping it with Page's, Lumpkin's, and Dargan's as one of the "first truly revolutionary novels" (68). Although Urgo considers Rollins's novels to be absent of "all feminist" issues, he finds some redemptive qualities in *Beyond Desire* because he sees Anderson's focus on sexuality as "sympathetic to feminist perspective" (81). Just as these comparisons lessen the female authors' efforts to expand poor white women's roles in society, the four female-authored Gastonia novels, although considered "revolutionary" by Schachner, are, ironically, criticized for how they present their female working-class characters. Recent critics such as Urgo, Hapke, and Cook criticize *Strike!, Gathering Storm,* and *To Make My Bread* because they think that Vorse, Page, and Lumpkin portray their women as typical, altruistic mother figures. Of all the Gastonia novels, *Call Home the Heart* is usually the only novel that "stands apart" to critics as valuable (Urgo 77).[27] Its value, however, is a product not of Ishma's independence from social expectations and personal denigration but of the novel's supposed "considerable artistic merit" (77). Because of the critical reception of these four novels, the authors' "progressive" accounts of female poor white characters are still being diluted by negative social images.

Strike!, Gathering Storm, To Make My Bread, and *Call Home the Heart,* however, are not insufficient feminist tracts, parallel achievements with *Beyond Desire,* or only valuable for "artistic merit." They "[stand] apart" from other poor white literature of the 1920s and 1930s, including Anderson's and Rollins's versions of the Gastonia strike, because Vorse's, Page's, Lumpkin's, and Dargan's female characters actually do surpass the stereotypes of the altruistic mother and the sexual degenerate to uncover the personal strength and the political presence of these women. Hall has argued that these novels reveal "a current of leftist feminist fiction that linked the personal to the political, reproduction to production, and attempted to make vivid to readers how the double oppression of working women marked their bodies and minds" ("Women Writers" 28). Because Vorse, Page, Lumpkin, and Dargan give their female characters a voice in these previously undeveloped issues, their novels also explore the potential that poor white women have to change themselves and their environment, potential that the altruistic mother image and the sexually degenerate image work to deny poor white female characters.

Moreover, the female authors set themselves apart from the male authors of the Depression era. As Schachner suggested, these female authors did challenge the "bourgeois man-made codes" of the time. Perhaps they defied social expectations and the dualistic stereotypes because they felt a connection between their struggle as female authors to gain a voice and the struggle of poor white women to gain personal independence both in their homes and in society. They may have also been more in tune with the women because they had worked beside them in factories, in unions, and in the Gastonia strike. Lumpkin and Dargan had also taught and cared for members of the lower class. Regardless of these authors' motivations, Vorse, Page, Lumpkin, and Dargan created a new kind of Depression-era "propaganda": "propaganda" in favor of the individuality and, therefore, the "progressive" renewal of southern poor white female identity in America.

CONCLUSION

DESPITE THE ATTEMPTS BY THE "Gastonia novelists," Vorse, Page, Lumpkin, and Dargan, to portray poor white southern women outside of the dualistic stereotypes of the altruistic mother and the sexual degenerate, these stereotypes created a persistent social perception of poor white southern women that plagued them well beyond the Depression era, thereby solidifying their status as the "Other" in American society. In the 1950s, a series of popular "backwoods" novels were released by "paperback publishers" to capitalize on the success of Caldwell's novels *Tobacco Road* and *God's Little Acre,* which were still incredibly popular in the 1940s and the 1950s (Crider 47).[1] The publishing companies even promoted "backwoods" novels so that potential readers would connect them with Caldwell's. By using titles for the novels such as *Cabin Road* (1951), *Uncle Good's Girls* (1952), *Back-Country Woman (A Time to Sow)* (1953), and *Girl Out Back* (1958), publishers were able not only to generate images of "the [s]outhern backwoods" but also to suggest, as evidenced by the references to women, that a version of Caldwell's Darling Jill might be found within the pages of the novel (59).[2] The covers of the novels further emphasized the sexual content that lurked within because most of them featured sexually posed, scantily clad "backwoods" women (47).[3] These types of titles and covers were even employed when the novels did not feature "backwoods" characters and sexually adventurous women (59).[4] Because of these promotional techniques, "backwoods" novels remained popular throughout the 1950s as publishers reprinted them several times throughout the decade.

In the 1960s, although "backwoods" novels lost their appeal and the nation's attention was turned towards the struggles of the Civil Rights movement, the dualistic stereotypes of southern poor white women did not disappear. Despite its initial poor selling in 1941 when it was first published, Agee and Evans's *Let Us Now Praise Famous Men* gained in popularity during the Civil Rights movement (Hershey xxxvi). According to John Hershey, *Let Us Now Praise Famous Men* appealed to "America's social consciousness" in the 1960s because "bright young people who, like James Agee, had the privilege of attending good schools and colleges [. . .] were delicately turned to Agee's irony and idealism and guilt" (xxxvi). Although both "[w]hite and black" activists in the 1960s may have been "motivated" by Agee's humility in their fight for racial equality (xxxvii–xxxviii), they were also still inundated with the stereotypes represented by the supposedly sexually promiscuous Emma and altruistic mother Annie Mae. Even the 1960 classic, Harper Lee's *To Kill a Mockingbird,* promotes these stereotypes. Mayella Ewell, the poor white female character who accuses an innocent black man, Tom, of rape, is another example of the sexually overt and dangerous poor white woman. Not only is she the one who tries to seduce Tom, but her lies lead to the death of Tom and to the death of her father, who is killed trying to get revenge on Tom's lawyer, Atticus (194, 235, 266). Because of Mayella's sexual desires, she creates so much destruction that she is really the danger to society, not Tom. Although *Let Us Now Praise Famous Men* and *To Kill a Mockingbird* may be best known for how they positively affected the Civil Rights movement, these works did so by employing some of the same stereotypes that confined poor white southern women in the 1930s.

By the late twentieth century, however, poor white southern literature began to change as lower-class men and women were given the chance to tell their own stories, but in telling their own stories, they still had to contend with the stereotypes that had characterized them in literature since the nineteenth century. In the literature written by poor white men, the male authors must not only contend with society's expectations of them as shiftless and violent, but they must also contend with their own assumptions about their lower-class female counterparts, whom they too seem to associate with the dualistic stereotypes. As a result, authors such as Rick Bragg, Dennis Covington, and Harry Crews face the challenges of reconciling their own poor white histories with their present class status and of overcoming their own prejudices against the women in their lives. Ironically, coming to terms with their pasts seems much easier than seeing the women outside of the stereotypes. Although Rick Bragg in *All Over But the Shoutin'* (1997) centers his autobiography on his devotion to his mother, he never fully realizes her as a woman outside of her role as his mother. Dennis Covington falls prey to the overtly sexual stereotype of poor white women when, in his autobiography about his spiritual journey in the Holiness religion, *Salvation on Sand Mountain* (1995), he equates sexual ecstasy with spiritual ecstasy, thereby diminishing his relationship with his spiritual guide, a Holiness woman named Aline McGlocklin (78–79, 192–93). Harry Crews, on the other hand, seems intent on reconciling poor white stereotypes with the actual realities that affect how members of the lower class act. Interestingly, in his novel *Car* (1979), he includes a poor white female prostitute; however, unlike the sexual degenerates of Depression-era literature, Crews's prostitute is given a chance to explain her choice of professions, revealing that social pressures, not genetic problems, have led her to this lifestyle (367, 436). Unlike Crews, who like the female "Gastonia novelists" sees beyond the stereotypes to uncover the realities of the women's lives, Bragg and Covington reveal that, despite all of their efforts to the contrary, they are still holding onto dualistic stereotypes of poor white women. These authors' efforts to understand their class history and their fellow members of the lower class, even if failed, still reveal a progression within the poor white class to get beyond the stereotypes that have historically defined them.

The work of late-twentieth-century southern female authors, from all classes, seems to hearken back to the female-oriented "modern southern literature" of the 1920s and the female-authored Gastonia novels of the 1930s. Lee Smith, Kaye Gibbons, Janisse Ray, and Dorothy Allison all use their portrayals of poor white women, whether fictional or autobiographical, to uncover the ways in which the dualistic stereotypes have confined these women both in literature and in real life. They actually highlight the negative effects of these stereotypes by focusing on mother/daughter relationships, similar to those found in the Gastonia novels by Page and Lumpkin, in which the daughter must learn from the mistakes of their mothers and must fight against the social constraints that their mothers have allowed to dictate their lives. Smith explores this dynamic in *Saving Grace* (1995) as it relates to the sexual and religious identities of Grace and her mother, Fannie. In *Ellen Foster* (1987), Gibbons focuses on a poor white girl who must raise herself after her mother dies trying to hold onto her relationship with her abusive husband. Ray has written two autobiographical works about her childhood and her attempts to reclaim her past, *Ecology of a Cracker Childhood* (1999) and *Wild Card Quilt: Taking a Chance on Home* (2003). Although Ray does not spend a great deal of time discussing her mother in either work, her decision to choose a life opposite that of her seemingly altruistic mother resonates throughout both books. Allison's *Bastard Out of Carolina* (1992) is perhaps the most violently drawn depiction of what harm these stereotypes can cause in a poor white woman's life. Bone's mother, Anney, is so torn between her desire to be a good mother to her children and society's condemnation of her as a sexual degenerate that she actually forsakes her children for a man who sexually abuses her daughter Bone, seemingly because Anney does not believe that she can be a good mother (308–9). Each of these authors explores the confining nature of the dualistic stereotypes in the mothers and then shows how the daughters must gradually begin to see themselves as being beyond the confines of the altruistic mother and sexual degenerate stereotypes that they know do not allow the space to define their lives fully.

As evidenced by the numerous works from the 1950s to the late twentieth century that either employ these stereotypes or try to give poor white women the chance to get beyond them, the dualistic stereotypes promoted in Depression-era literature had a profound and lasting effect on how southern poor white women were viewed in American society. With the recent work of southern male and female authors challenging these stereotypes, however, poor white women may finally get the opportunity to be recognized as much more than simply these stock labels. The "progressive" poor white female characters that once dominated poor white literature in the 1920s and that the female Gastonia novelists tried to revive in the 1930s are once again becoming "dynamic" as southern authors begin to develop them as characters outside of the altruistic mother and sexual degenerate stereotypes in an effort to help the real women the characters represent reclaim that individuality that has been stripped from them.

Notes

Introduction

1. For more information about the topic of common feminine stereotypes, see *The Cinderella Test: Would You Really Want the Shoe to Fit?* by Vera Sonja Maass. Maass discusses the effects of the "opposing images of the Madonna and whore," various "physiological" theorists, and mainstream media on the evolution of female sexuality from the nineteenth century to the early twenty-first century (85–107).

2. Susan Currell argues that the change in eugenic "focus" combining "the popular interest in sterilization" with "self-improvement, mass leisure, and the family" helped "eugenic ideals [become] broadly compatible with wider social ideals of the New Deal and the Popular Front" (5).

3. Byrd, a prominent Virginia landowner, wrote *Histories of the Dividing Line* about his 1728 expedition to determine the boundary between Virginia and North Carolina (Adams ix–x).

4. Two of the most popular Old Southwest humor characters, Sut Lovingood and Simon Suggs, are marked by their uncivilized character traits. Sut Lovingood is actually proud of his "impiety, cowardice," and drunkenness (Cohen and Dillingham 194), and Simon Suggs spends his life living as "merrily and comfortably as possible at the expense of others" because shiftlessness is a way of life to him (Hooper 257). Simon Suggs's "ethical" system can be summed up in his favorite line: "IT IS GOOD TO BE SHIFTY IN A NEW COUNTRY" (257).

5. For more information about the role of female characters in Old Southwest stories, refer to William E. Lenz's article "The Function of Women in Old Southwestern Humor: Rereading *Big Bear* and *Quarter Race* Collections."

6. Murfree came from a "distinguished" family which had "[t]owns in North Carolina and Tennessee" named after it. Although she grew up on a plantation in Murfreesboro, Tennessee, and attended private schools, she spent her summers in the mountains, where she learned about mountain culture, which she found both "charming" and "uncultivated" (Satterwhite 61). She wrote *In the Tennessee Mountains* under the pseudonym Charles Egbert Craddock.

Chapter 1

1. Discussions about eugenics have often been focused on how eugenics affected races and nationalities separate from the American white upper class; however, Kline notes that to think of eugenicists' racial improvement as excluding other whites is to compartmentalize the term "race." According to Kline, "American eugenicists often made references to 'improving the race' without specifying whether they meant the human race, the Anglo-Saxon race, or some other type of racial differentiation" (5). The eugenics movement is often considered all-"inclusive" because the main goal was to achieve a superior "race" above all (5).

Although I focus on how the American eugenics movement affected southern poor white women, books such as Edwin Black's *War Against the Weak: Eugenics and America's Campaign to Create a Master Race,* Christina Codgell's *Eugenic Design: Streamlining America in the 1930s,* Daylanne K. English's *Unnatural Selections: Eugenics in American Modernism and the Harlem Renaissance,* and Wendy Kline's *Building a Better Race: Gender, Sexuality, and Eugenics from the Turn of the Century to the Baby Boom* explore how eugenics affected other races and nationalities in America.

2. American eugenicists worried that other races and nationalities would mix with the "white Protestant majority" and create a new weak race in America (Kevles 46–47).

3. Eugenicists regarded "germ-plasm" as a "force of heredity [. . .] impermeable to environmental influence" (Kevles 70).

4. Gregor Mendel's pea plant experiments in the 1860s first started genetic theory; however, these experiments did not gain prominence until after Mendel's death in 1884 (Black 26). When twentieth-century eugenicists discovered Mendel's work, his "laws of heredity" became a focal point in the eugenics movement, but they knew his experiments could only partially explain human genetics (Black 26–27). Francis Galton introduced "the family-study" method of determining the genetic makeup of individuals in his 1869 book *Hereditary Genius.* He studied upper-class British families (Rafter, Intro. to *White Trash* 1; English 6). He also coined the term "eugenics" in 1883 (English 3; Kline 13).

5. The term "feeble-minded" referred to all people "who today would be categorized as mentally handicapped" (Noll, *Feeble-Minded* 2). This term began to be phased out by the 1920s and replaced by the term "mental defective"; however, feebleminded was still used until the 1940s (2). In the "1929–1935 U.S. government census report on institutional populations," the U.S. Census Bureau used the term "mental defective" instead of "feeble-minded" because the bureau felt that the two terms meant the same thing (160).

6. Twentieth-century eugenicists used Mendel's "laws" when discussing "[h]eight, hair color, eye color, and other physical attributes" (Black 27); hence the eugenicists' use of the term "Mendelizing human characters" to describe physical "inferior" traits.

7. Although North Carolina, South Carolina, Alabama, and Georgia had instituted child labor laws by 1913 prohibiting "children under twelve" from working and "restricting" work hours of children "below fourteen," many of the laws were "ignored" (Hall et al. 58). Because of the inadequacy of "state legislation," President Woodrow Wilson established "the Keating-Owen Child Labor bill" in 1916, but the Supreme Court struck the law down citing that "the law violated the rights of the worker" (59–60). Despite the resistance to

child labor regulations, child labor was eventually phased out in the textile mills because the "changes in the industry [. . .] required more strength and skill" and because of "the growing supply of adult workers" (60). In fact, in the Carolina mills, children only made up about "6 percent" of the workforce by World War I (60).

8. In a 1929 article for *Eugenics: A Journal of Race Betterment,* Thomas Nixon Carver explained why "normal" men were attracted to "feeble-minded" women. According to Carver, a eugenically sound man is "likely to select as a wife, not the capable, but the fluffy type" (5). Instead of desiring a "helpmate," he wants "a wife as a luxury" who will "advertis[e] his own success" (5). Carver's article is written from a "socialist geneticist" standpoint, so the women would not necessarily have a physical disfigurement marking them as "inferior."

9. Diane B. Paul notes that, in the 1920s, Sanger's writings and the writings of other authors that appeared in *Birth Control Review* followed "standard eugenic themes" (*Controlling* 95).

10. Despite the reasoning that these institutions helped their patients, Noll states that a "complex interplay between [. . .] humanitarian impulses and the need for social control" led many in charge of these institutions such as "social workers, physicians, [. . .] philanthropists[, . . .] legislators and governors" to view these facilities as "protection for society from retarded people, and not the reverse, as their major priority" (Noll, *Feeble-Minded* 4–5).

11. Havelock Ellis wrote in 1931 that sterilization was just another form of "birth control" (*More Essays* 204). English notes that sterilizations, although performed on all races deemed "inferior," were "generally" performed on "rural—and generally white—lower-class Americans" (15). Leef Smith further states that most sterilizations were performed on lower-class southerners (B1). The large number of sterilizations performed on so-called "white" men and women further suggests that eugenicists worried just as much about class designation as they did about racial classification.

12. Rafter also notes that "shorter family studies that appeared in journals and pamphlets are today difficult—in some cases, nearly impossible—to find" (Intro. to *White Trash* 3).

13. The "myth" partly emerged because the family studies made eugenic concerns seem universal. Studies were conducted on families in other countries and on northern and southern rural American families. For example, "The Tribe of Ishmael: A Study in Social Degradation" focuses on an "inferior" family that reaches from the northern to the southern United States.

14. The family name "Kallikak" is taken from the Greek words "*kallos*" and "*kakos*" (Kline 25). "[*K*]*allos*" means "good," and "*kakos*" means "bad" (25).

15. Florence H. Danielson and Charles B. Davenport, the authors of *The Hill Folk,* used "at least nine families" that could supposedly be traced back to the same origin; however, no evidence supports this supposition (Rafter, Intro. to *White Trash* 18).

16. While I see Dugdale's study as gender specific in whom it blames for the "Jukes" demise, Rafter argues that this negative treatment of females only "appears in embryonic form" in Dugdale's study (Rafter, Preface to Davenport, "Hereditary Crime" 66).

17. Davenport's "Hereditary Crime," focused on the Zero family, is a summary of a 1905 study conducted by Jörger, "director of the Insane Asylum of Waldhaus-Chur in Switzerland" (Davenport 68). His study was originally published in German in *Archiv für*

Rassen-und Gesellschafts-Biologie as "Die Familie Zero" (68). Rafter notes that this study is the "only" one "of a European tribe published in the U.S." (Rafter, Preface to Davenport, "Hereditary Crime" 66).

18. Twelve editions of Goddard's *The Kallikak Family* appeared between 1912 and 1939. During the 1920s and 1930s, it could be found "in scholarly books and journals, college and even high school textbooks, serious and popular magazines" (Paul, *Controlling Human* 50).

19. A "granddaughter" of Martin Kallkak Jr. told the details of Martin's birth (Goddard 17).

20. Kite worked as "a field worker at the Vineland, N.J., Training School for Backward and Feeble-Minded Children" with Goddard (Preface to Kite, "Two Brothers" 74). She assisted Goddard in his research on the Kallikaks and actually wrote chapter 4 of *The Kallikak Family* (74).

21. Although I only discuss Dugdale's *"The Jukes,"* Gertrude Davenport's "Hereditary Crime," Goddard's *The Kallikak Family,* Kite's "Two Brothers," and Estabrook's and McDougle's *Mongrel Virginians* in detail in this section, other family studies included in Rafter's collection also present "inferior" women as the breeders of a "defective" generation. Danielson and Davenport's "The Hill Folk" focuses on the "uncontrolled sexual instincts" of the women in the "family" and on the high pregnancy rate of the women (89, 128). Oscar C. McCulloch in "The Tribe of Ishmael: A Study in Social Degradation" says that he has only seen one "honorable man" escape from the horror of this family's degeneration (54). Then, he continues his study by saying that the women turn to "prostitution" and then have their own "illegitimate" children (54). Kite's "The 'Pineys,'" a popular family study in its time, and Mary Storer Kostir's *The Family of Sam Sixty* are full of stories of female promiscuity, wife swapping, adultery, and illegitimate children (Rafter, Preface to Kite, "Two Brothers" 74).

22. Although Dugdale suggests that environmental issues could possibly create negative characteristics in a family, he obviously did not include female sexuality in this set of characteristics because, as he mentions earlier in his study, "harlotry" can be passed from woman to woman "regardless of the [. . .] environment" (19, 26).

23. Ironically, Goddard's *The Kallikak Family* had already provided an example of an "inferior" person able to "pass for normal." Deborah Kallikak, the feebleminded woman who spurred Goddard's family study, did not appear physically "inferior" (2).

24. Eugenicists claimed that Carrie's mother Emma had supposedly led a "normal" life until her husband died, but when Carrie turned three, court officials sent her mother, Emma, to the Colony of Epileptics and Feeble-Minded because she was convicted of "prostitution," a common charge that did not actually mean that a woman was "selling her body" (Black 108–9). At seventeen, Carrie joined her mother at the colony because she had become pregnant (108–9). Despite Carrie's appeal that her boyfriend had raped her and that her high marks in school proved her intellectual ability, the doctors at the colony still held her there (109).

25. Although H. J. Muller did not publish *Out of the Night* until 1935, Paul cites that Muller finished this work in 1925 (Paul, "Eugenics" 17).

26. One branch of the Bunglers consisted of two men, one wife, and numerous children, a polygamous family unit (332). Ira also suggested that the children of these types of

families do not have adequate parental guidance about familial and sexual societal expectations; therefore, they simply follow the example of their parents (204, 209).

27. Ira does not mention in "The Bunglers" his attempt to help the Bunglers escape from poverty.

28. Previously, some Soviet Marxists had stated their adherence to Lamarckism, but while Lamarckism on the surface suggests that improvement in environment will create "hereditary improvement," some geneticists argued that Lamarckism also supported the idea that, because of "generations of oppression, malnutrition, ignorance, and disease," lower-class proletarians had become over time genetically "inferior" and, therefore, unable to lift themselves up in society (Joravsky, *Lysenko* 263).

29. The advocates of "socialist eugenics" wanted to combat the negative social perception of the lower class that was worsened by "'bourgeois'" eugenics. For example, "'bourgeois'" eugenicists felt that the birth control movement needed to be stopped. N. V. Kol'tsov, a prominent Soviet geneticist, expressed in 1924 his concern that, with access to birth control, people who should have children would not have them and those in the lower class who should not have children would continue having them (Joravsky, *Lysenko* 260). This line of thinking disturbed many Bolshevik leaders because it promoted the idea that the lower class housed most of the genetically "inferior" in society (260).

30. The Bolshevik Party was created by Lenin, and the party argued that "the standpoint of the working class is taken clearly and consistently only by the party of the working class—Lenin's Bolshevik's" (Joravsky, *Soviet* 26).

31. Serebrovskii even related this "Plan" to animal breeding. Interestingly, he seemed to separate procreation from sexual pleasure because, although women would still be allowed to choose with whom they had sex, they were not allowed to choose with whom they would have children (Joravsky, *Lysenko* 266).

32. The CPUSA's association with eugenics and its promotion of "anti-fascism" reflects one of the many contradictions that emerges when looking at the party's association with eugenic ideology. The Germans, the very fascists the party worked against, were most known for the use of "negative eugenics."

33. One issue in 1940 was almost completely dedicated to speeches given in Moscow at the 1939 Conference on Genetics and Selection.

34. The CPUSA's exclusion of women from the workforce does not follow Friedrich Engels's views. In "The Origin of the Family, Private Property, and the State," Engels encourages women to join "public" service so that they can "take part in public industry and earn [their] living independently," thereby keeping them from being solely dependent upon their husbands (744). He argues that, if women work outside of the home, then marriage will not be based upon "capitalist production" but upon "mutual affection" (750).

35. The CPUSA's stance on "monogamous marriage" is ironic considering Karl Marx's and Engels's views. In *The Communist Manifesto,* Marx and Engels call for the "[a]bolition of the family" arguing that, in "bourgeoisie [*sic*] famil[ies,]" women are "mere instruments of production" (71–72). Engels explains this idea further in "The Origin of the Family, Private Property, and the State" when he notes that, in a "[b]ourgeois marriage," men expected

women to be monogamous even though the men were not. According to Engels, marriage in a class-based society is based upon money and class relations, thereby reducing it to "the crassest prostitution" (737–38, 742–43).

36. Paul notes that the fall of eugenics in America began when the Eugenics Record Office closed in 1939, but it was not until "the late 1940s, [that] eugenics—whether reform or mainline—had fallen out of fashion with the public" (*Controlling* 120).

Chapter 2

1. Walter B. Rideout has pointed out that, although proletarian literature has gained a great deal of critical attention since it first became prominent in the 1930s, this type of literature was not actually popular with the American public. Apparently, even the "American proletariat" did not read most of these novels, and some who had read them did not really care for them (235–36). For that very reason, understanding the popularity of *As I Lay Dying, Tobacco Road, God's Little Acre,* and *The Grapes of Wrath* becomes increasingly important.

2. Most of the New Deal policies put into place to help poor white southerners did not actually provide very much assistance (Flynt 80–86). The FSA seems to have been an exception, though, because this agency obviously offered productive assistance to tenant families as evidenced by how many it helped (84–85).

3. Many of the men and women sterilized were told that they had had their appendices removed or that the doctors had performed "procedures to improve their health" (Smith B1).

4. *As I Lay Dying* was not near as popular as *Tobacco Road, God's Little Acre,* and *The Grapes of Wrath;* however, it is important because of its significant critical response and because of the increased public interest it gained throughout the 1930s into the 1960s. In 1946, it was reprinted as a single volume with *The Sound and the Fury* (Cox xxii). Almost twenty years later, in 1965, *As I Lay Dying* was adapted for television by John McGiffert (Meriwether 163).

5. In *The Art of Faulkner's Novels,* Peter Swiggart argues, "Usually the important characters in a Faulkner novel struggle against an environment to which, as the action develops, they are seen to be symbolically related. In this way the actions of stylized figures become vehicles for the revelation of serious themes. But in *As I Lay Dying,* even though the materials for thematic synthesis are present, Faulkner deliberately refrains from exploiting them. He goes to the opposite extreme and carefully eliminates from the epic venture every vestige of moral and social significance" (57–58). Although Swiggart does not consider *As I Lay Dying* a social critique, he does argue that it is a "modern psychological novel" because of Faulkner's use of "interior monologue" (61). Swiggart neglects, however, to notice that the "interior monologue[s]" are the source of Faulkner's social critique as Addie Bundren and her children struggle through their individual narratives to rectify their familial burdens with social expectations.

6. Wainwright notes that Faulkner read Hippolyte Taine's *History of English Literature* (1863–67), Ludwig Lewisohn's *A Modern Book of Criticism* (1919), and Willard Huntington

Wright's *The Creative Will: Studies in the Philosophy and the Syntax of Aesthetics* (1916). All of these books included some sort of Darwinian ideology (Wainwright 25, 27, 28).

7. One of the characters in *Mosquitoes* references Ellis's role in redefining feminine sexuality and, as a result, feminine identity. He calls what Ellis has created with his new ideas a "park of dark and rotten trees" (251). Faulkner actually seems to have applied Ellis's theories to his female characters in *Mosquitoes.* The novel is full of sexually open women who experiment both with heterosexual and homosexual relationships.

8. For more information on this topic, see pages 18–19 in chapter 1. Ellis discussed his views on "[moulding] the human race" in *Little Essays* 177, *More Essays* 185, and *Studies* 4: 611.

9. Caldwell despised the film version of *Tobacco Road* because he thought it was too sentimental and that it did not follow the novel closely enough (Miller 285–86). Despite negative reviews from Caldwell and from film critics, the movie earned "over eleven million dollars" (285–86). When *God's Little Acre* was released as a film in 1957, it became just as nationally popular as *Tobacco Road* (366).

10. Jeeter trades Pearl to Lov for seven dollars, some quilts, and almost a gallon of "cylinder oil" (Caldwell, *Tobacco* 25)

11. *Tobacco Road* became popular only after the release of *God's Little Acre.* When *Tobacco Road* was re-released, it sold "one million" copies in a year (Miller 335).

12. In "Re-examining the Political Left: Erskine Caldwell and the Doctrine of Eugenics," Holmes argues that Caldwell's novels and his associations with the leftist movement "[put] into serious question the ideological goals of the political left" (257). The leftist and eugenic images in Caldwell's work, however, do seem reconciled when examined through the rhetoric of "socialist geneticists."

13. Caldwell was not awarded any money from the Guggenheim Foundation (Miller 148).

14. Early in the novel, the Waldens feast on "two large Senator Watson watermelons" (Caldwell, *God's* 28), and after catching Dave, the albino, they celebrate with a "hearty supper of grits and sweet potatoes, hot biscuits and fried ham" (82).

15. Although Ty Ty applauds Darling Jill for her sexuality, Ty Ty tells Shaw, who spends most of his time chasing women in town, that his sexual behavior is going to get him into "trouble" (Caldwell, *God's* 3). Ty Ty's double standard about sex reflects eugenicists' notions that poor white women are either non-sexual altruistic mothers or sexually driven women. Ty Ty never expects any other behavior from Darling Jill or from Griselda.

16. The idea for the documentary picture-book was originally Bristol's idea (Howarth 77). By the time Bristol had chosen the pictures for the book, Steinbeck had decided to write the story as a novel (77). Howarth suggests that Steinbeck backed out of the collaborative project because of his "arrogance" (78). Bristol has apparently said that Steinbeck "'was secretive [. . .] and wanted to feel that anything he did was his, and nobody else had any influence on it'" (qtd. in Howarth 78).

17. Hearle discusses the work of eugenicists Smuts and Huntington in his article, "These Are American People: The Spectre of Eugenics in *Their Blood Is Strong* and *The Grapes of Wrath*" (249–52). Huntington was actually president of the American Eugenics Society during part of the 1930s (Kline 130).

18. Hearle focuses his discussion on Steinbeck's use of the phrase "new race" to describe the poor whites (*Their Blood* 3; Hearle 246–59). He sees this as proof either of Steinbeck's belief in a racial hierarchy dominated by whites or of the novelist's lack of understanding of the eugenic language he used (Hearle 247, 248–49). Steinbeck does not, however, portray foreign workers as "inferior." In fact, he chastises elite whites for treating them as "scrap" (*Their Blood* 26). He assumes that they treated the foreign workers poorly because the foreigners could be threatened with deportation and were from incredibly poor backgrounds (2–3). Since the new American lower-class white workers do not fear deportation and do not always come from poor backgrounds, according to Steinbeck, then the privileged whites cannot justify treating them like "scrap" (3).

19. Louis Kronenberger in a 1939 review for *Nation* said that "[t]he picturesqueness of the Joads" at times seems "false" and leaves the reader "dissatisfied" (140–41). Harry Schofield found the book unbelievable because of Steinbeck's depiction of the lower class as "the good, the wise, the salt of the earth" (151). Philip Rahv called Steinbeck's characters "idealized portraits," which he counts as one of the "faults" of the novel (152).

20. In this chapter, I have used the Viking Critical Revised Edition of *The Grapes of Wrath* edited by Peter Lisca and Kevin Hearle. All references to the novel will be indicated by *Grapes*.

21. Howard Levant refers to the general, expository sections as "interchapters" used to "'locate' and generalize the narrative chapters, somewhat like stage directions" (108).

22. In *Parallel Expeditions: Charles Darwin and the Art of John Steinbeck,* Brian Railsback examines how Steinbeck illustrates Darwin's survival theories through the Joads because, according to Railsback, the Joads, along with other members of the lower class, survive because they are able to compete with upper-class people who spend their energy defending themselves (134–35). Donald Pizer emphasizes how the lower class gains power because of their commitment to "group identity," also known as the "phalanx" (67–68).

23. Steinbeck was greatly influenced by the philosophical and biological ideas of Ed Ricketts, co-author of *The Sea of Cortez* (Astro 13–14; Owens 17), and evidence suggests that Ricketts was knowledgeable of the Russian "socialist geneticist" movement in the 1930s. In "About Ed Ricketts," Steinbeck's eulogy for his friend, the novelist noted that Ricketts followed the work of Russian scientists after the Bolshevik Revolution. Ricketts apparently "thought that there might be something new in Russia, some human progression that might be like a mutation in the nature of the species" ("About Ed" xliv). With this research, Ricketts supposedly concluded that members of the lower class "may be the ones who will deliver our species from the enemies within and without which attack it" (xxxiii).

24. Sylvia Jenkins Cook argues that Steinbeck explores how a group affects man's behavior. Furthermore, she links this idea with communistic principles ("Steinbeck" 84–85). Parini notes, however, that, even though Steinbeck "sympathized deeply with the plight of the workers and admired the idealism that lay, in theory, behind communism," he never became a communist (151, 359). Gladstein argues that the final scene is Steinbeck's way of emphasizing how women must save men from their own "disheartened and defeated" state ("The Indestructible" 84).

Chapter 3

1. Stott defines "social documentary" as a work that "shows man at grips with conditions neither permanent nor necessary, conditions of a certain time and place" and that "encourages social improvement" (20, 21).

2. Eight months before *You Have Seen Their Faces* came out in 1937, Roosevelt had already put together a committee to study the lives of sharecroppers and tenant farmers. This "special Committee on Farm Tenancy" had written a report on their findings before the public even saw Caldwell and Bourke-White's book (Stott 218).

3. Originally, the FSA began as the Resettlement Administration (hereafter abbreviated RA) (Stryker 7). The RA attempted "to address rural poverty by setting up experimental communal reforms, by establishing green-belt model communities for unemployed workers, and by building housing for migrants" (Denning 80). Stryker and his group were "to document" those people to whom the RA intended to give assistance (Lesy, Intro. to *Long* 9).

4. Although the FSA only has five of the photographs on file, a sixth photograph appeared in a 1970 article in *American West* written by Lange's husband, Paul Taylor (Curtis 49; Taylor 43).

5. Apparently, Lange took the pictures to the *News* to be published before she took them to Stryker in the FSA office. Stryker did not appreciate this move by Lange, and Curtis argues that, because of Lange's independence, Stryker took her "off the payroll little more than six months" after she took the "Migrant Mother" photographs (15).

6. Curtis notes that leaving the father out of FSA photographs was not an uncommon practice by the photographers. Russell Lee, another FSA photographer, took a set of photographs titled *Christmas Dinner in Iowa.* The photograph published from this selection reveals a group of children eating alone at a supper table. Lee took another photograph with their father at the head of the table eating with them; however, this photograph was not published until Curtis included it in his 1989 collection, *Mind's Eye, Mind's Truth: FSA Photography Reconsidered* (51).

7. In 1935, the FWP was started with the intention of giving "white-collar" workers a chance to work for the government. The "proposal" for the project "called for the preparation for a guidebook of the United States, reports of WPA progress, an encyclopedia of government functions, and a limited number of special studies by qualified individual writers" (Penkower 27).

8. Roosevelt called the South "the nation's No. 1 economic problem" on July 4, 1938, in Washington, D.C., at the Conference on the Economic Conditions of the South (Leuchtenburg 103). A stolen copy of the speech was printed the next day in the *New York Times* (104).

9. Although *These Are Our Lives* includes stories about poor white and poor black southerners, I have chosen to focus on the stories about poor white families. The majority of the stories about poor whites are completely centered on family, making their lives seem important only because they are parents or children. I do, however, note that, in "Plow

Beams for Pills," Dr. Cain makes no distinction between poor white women and poor black women since he thinks all poor women need to be issued some form of birth control (Harris 273–74).

10. Although Stott says that Couch had "more than 400" interviews to choose from, Jerrold Hirsch and Tom E. Terrill put the number of interviews at over a thousand (xi).

11. The families' real names are the Tingles (Ricketts), the Fields (Woods), and the Burroughs (Gudger) (Hershey xvi–xvii). Interestingly, just as authors of eugenic family studies often used degrading pseudonyms to describe families, Agee also seems to do this. The term "rickets" is defined as "bone-softening disease of children," and its adjective form, "rickety" is defined as "insecure" or "shaky" (*Oxford* 687). Along with the obvious definition of "wood," the word is also used to describe people thought of as "insane" or "mad" (*Webster's* 2630). Although the name "Gudger" has no specific meaning, its prefix "gud" refers to the word "good" (*Webster's* 1008). The definitions associated with these names just reinforce the negative ways he presents the Ricketts and the Woods family and the positive way he presents the Gudger family.

In 1989, Dale Maharidge and Michael Williamson followed up *Let Us Now Praise Famous Men* with *And Their Children After Them,* an account of how these families handled the popularity of Agee and Evans's book and of the adult lives of the three tenant families' children. Maharidge and Williamson found that most of the members of the three families took offense to how Agee and Evans presented them. Most of those interviewed, usually the children of the three families, took this new opportunity to rewrite Agee and Evans's interpretations of their lives and their future possibilities.

12. While Agee's discussion of the crucifixion of poor white babies may be seen as Lamarckian because of the focus on learned behavior the baby could acquire from his already "beaten" parents, I argue that Agee's references to the genetic traits passed through the "blood" and the "sperm" seem just as important to the child's future as what s/he learns from her/his parents after birth.

13. Although generally this term is connected to the crucifixion of Jesus, hence the connection to "holiness," to be "crucified" is also defined as to be "defeat[ed] thoroughly" and to be "torment[ed]" (*Oxford* 175). This definition seems connected to the physical devastation that results from a crucifixion. I argue that, while Agee's use of the term may be connected to the "holiness" of the parents, his other language suggests that these parents, like their children, must endure physical "defeat" also.

14. This directly contradicts Agee's previous statement that Annie Mae's son Squinchy looks as if "children" have dressed him. Agee's conflicting views of Annie Mae are discussed later in this chapter.

15. Evans's photograph of Squinchy is the only negative portrayal of the Gudger family because his eyes are half-closed and his mouth is partially open, making his face appear somewhat awkward. This photograph, however, does correspond with Agee's comments about Squinchy in the text because Agee refers to Squinchy as having "the comic and foolish look of a dog."

16. *Let Us Now Praise Famous Men* did not become popular until the 1960s during the Civil Rights movement (Hershey xxxvi).

Chapter 4

1. I have put "scientific" in quotation marks because, according to Nicole Hahn Rafter, eugenic family studies were not usually based upon sufficient data and, at times, were just fictional (Intro. to *White Trash* 2, 18, 26). For more details, see chapter 1.

2. Myra Page wrote *Gathering Storm* under the pen name Dorothy Myra Page. Although her real name was Dorothy Page, she altered it because she did not want to upset her parents or affect her career as a sociologist with her controversial topics. She later adopted the name Myra Page as her pen name (Baker 109). Olive Tilford Dargan wrote *Call Home the Heart* and *A Stone Came Rolling,* the sequel to *Call Home the Heart,* under the pen name Fielding Burke. To avoid confusion, I refer to the authors as Myra Page and Olive Tilford Dargan.

3. Lisa Schreibersdorf defines a "documentary novel" as a novel based upon a factual event, even though the events of the novel are not always factual (306).

4. The complete lyrics for Wiggins's "Mill Mother's Lament" appear in *Like a Family: The Making of a Southern Cotton Mill World* (Hall et al. 226–27).

5. One article on Appalachian music appeared in the *Journal of American Folklore* in 1889 (Whisnant 54, 111). In 1913, C. Alphonso Smith, a folklorist at the University of Virginia, suggested that the U.S. commissioner of education, P. P. Claxton, encourage the public to begin collecting these ballads (54). Olive Dame Campbell and Cecil Sharp published their own collection of ballads, *English Folk Songs of the Southern Appalachians,* in 1916 (117). Other collections include Loraine Wyman and Howard Brockway's *Lonesome Tunes* (1916) and Josephine McGill's *Folk Songs of the Kentucky Mountains* (1917) (Whisnant 118).

6. As stated in chapter 1, Gold, in his 1928 article, "Go Left, Young Writers," described the proletarian author only in masculine terms, conveying the message that male work was more important than female work (188–89).

7. Vorse actually finished *Strike!* before the Gastonia strike ended (Urgo 68). For this reason, Dee Garrison has noted that, although most of the novel follows the events she witnessed while in Gastonia, the end of *Strike!,* with the martyrdom of Fred Beal and other men who faced imprisonment because of Aderholdt's death, actually reflects how a strike in Marion, North Carolina, ended (Intro. to *Strike!* xiv–xv).

8. Although Vorse is connected with communism because of *Strike!,* she never joined the Communist Party because she did not fully agree with its principles and because she was disturbed by the party's "infighting" (Garrison, Intro. to *Strike!* xviii).

9. Since Vorse worked as a journalist, her style of writing seemed more journalistic than creative. Many of the events of the novel are not explained well, and most of the characters do not have much depth. One reviewer argued that her style of writing in the novel was "too near journalism" (Brickell 198). Another reviewer for *The New York Times Book Review* complained that Vorse's journalistic writing style took away from the "powerful dramatic material" associated with the real strike ("The Gastonia" 6). Although the novel often jumps from event to event without much exposition, she does highlight the lives of the female workers and how the women affect their surroundings. They are the only characters that Vorse spends a great deal of time describing.

10. Vorse was actually near the truck that Wiggins was riding in when Wiggins was killed by a sniper (Garrison, Intro. to *Strike!* xiv).

11. Shope was the father of Wiggins's fifth child; however, this fact is usually not mentioned when Wiggins's life is discussed (Garrison, Intro. to *Strike!* xiv).

12. Lewis wrote this review of *Strike!* for Hoover because he did not agree with a speech that Hoover had recently given in the Carolinas. Hoover said, in his speech, that, since America offers a free education to everyone, only the ones who adapt to this "free" learning system can survive in America. Since *Strike!* highlights how not all people are "trained" by America's educational system because of their environments, Lewis argued that Hoover should read this novel to get an accurate picture of those people who have not been "trained" to adapt (Lewis 474).

13. Page is the only author of the four who was not personally present for at least part of the Gastonia strike.

14. Her dissertation was originally titled "Some Behavior Patterns of Southern Textile Workers" (Baker 92). While it did consist mostly of "'statistics,'" she wanted, in *Southern Cotton Mills and Labor,* to focus on the mill workers "'sympathetically,'" and she intended to accomplish this goal by "'avoid[ing] academic language'" (qtd. in Baker 92, 98).

15. She titled the novel *Gathering Storm* because she "'thought that socialism would continue to grow'" as racial unity strengthened (qtd. in Baker 111). In fact, Page places a great deal of emphasis on race relations in this novel. Ironically, despite her use of Wiggins in the novel, Marge's brother, Tom, is the character who contributes to the racial unity of the union and the CPUSA. While living in the North, he befriends two southern black men, Fred and George. Fred eventually goes to the Soviet Union to attend school (Page, *Gathering* 238), and near the end of the novel, Tom and George return to the South to help Marge form a union after her family has died (261–62). Fred returns from the Soviet Union to meet up with Tom and Marge at a communist convention in Cleveland. He intends to return to the South with them to continue fighting for working-class rights (368).

16. For further explanation of how birth control was used as a tool for the "negative eugenic" campaign, see chapter 1, page 20, in this study.

17. For more information about Ellis's view of lower-class abortion, refer to chapter 1, page 19.

18. Unlike Vorse, Page actually was a member of the CPUSA. She joined the party in 1925 and wrote articles for leftist journals such as *The Daily Worker, New Masses,* and *Working Woman.* By 1953, she was no longer a member of the party, but she "remained a strong advocate for socialism, civil rights, environmental protection, and world peace" (Baker xviii).

19. Grace Lumpkin's sister, Katharine Du Pre Lumpkin, wrote *The Making of a Southerner,* published in 1946.

20. Wendy Kline, as noted in chapter 1, refers to the dualistic images of poor white women as the "mother of tomorrow" and the "moron" girl (3, 29).

21. Although never a member of the CPUSA, Dargan reveals her affiliation with the communist cause in her works, specifically *Call Home the Heart* and *A Stone Came Rolling* (Shannon 433).

22. In *A Stone Came Rolling,* Dargan includes a scene in which Derry Unthank and Ishma Waycaster discuss the writings of Julian Huxley (320).

23. Dargan's decision to move the setting of the novel from the mountains to the mill towns was reviewers' main criticism. Reviewers for *The Saturday Review of Literature* and *Booklist* felt that the mill town section hurt the novel (Loveman 684; *Booklist* 349). In contrast, reviewers for *Christian Century* and *The New Republic* actually noted that using the two settings makes the novel stronger in context than if Ishma had just stayed in once place (*Christian* 710–11; *New* 27).

24. Dargan reveals in *A Stone Came Rolling* that Ishma's name means "waste" (Dargan 381); however, she gives no indication from which language this definition of Ishma's name is derived.

25. Although Ishma has saved fourteen dollars that she hopes will be enough to help her escape the mountains, she must give the money to her family when Jim injures himself so severely that he cannot work at all (Dargan, *Call* 24, 60).

26. Although Dargan wanted the section of the novel with Butch and Gaffie Wells to reveal the negative effects of racism, Dargan actually uses racist language to describe Gaffie. Dargan describes Gaffie as "very fat and very black" with "an odor that an unwashed collie would have disowned" (383). Because of this description, Dargan's message of racial unity gets overshadowed (Elfenbein 194–95).

27. Urgo argues that Page uses only stock poor white characters in her novel because the "women inevitably become pregnant as men move from abusive sex mania to depleted obsolescence" (75). He also argues that the women in *To Make My Bread* only have power because they "can inspire men to greatness" (73). Hapke states that all four novelists, even Dargan, focus on creating "an ideologically acceptable Depression Era female militant, in the South, or elsewhere," a typical altruistic mother figure focused on her children's future rather than on her own rights as a laborer (170). Cook refers to *Gathering Storm* as "tendentious, arbitrary, and fallacious in its handling of southern problems" (*From Tobacco* 98). Like Urgo, Cook considers *Call Home the Heart* "the best" novel written about Gastonia, despite her criticism of the ending (98).

Conclusion

1. Penguin Books reprinted *Tobacco Road* in 1947 "in a 25¢ mass-market paperback edition," and it became a "huge paperback success" (Crider 47).

2. Bill Crider in "Sons of *Tobacco Road:* 'Backwoods' Novels" notes that many of the publishing houses actually changed the authors' original titles to reflect this "backwoods" theme (47, 54).

3. Crider includes several photographs of these sexually lurid "backwoods" covers in his article.

4. For example, although *Girl Out Back* written by Charles Williams is a murder mystery about an upper-class man who finds a large amount of stolen money and who kills to keep it, the title, the cover, and the blurb on the back of the book suggest that a lower-class, sexually enticing woman is actually the main protagonist. Ironically, Jewell, the lower-class female character heavily promoted, is a minor character in the novel.

Bibliography

Abels, Cyrilly. "*To Make My Bread.*" *Bookman* 75.7 (1932): 739–40.

Adams, Percy G. Introduction to the Dover Edition. *Histories of the Dividing Line betwixt Virginia and North Carolina.* By William Byrd II. New York: Dover Publications, Inc., 1987. v–xxii.

Agee, James, and Walker Evans. *Let Us Now Praise Famous Men.* 1941. Boston: Houghton Mifflin Co., 1988.

Alaimo, Stacy. "'Skin Dreaming': The Bodily Transgressions of Fielding Burke, Octavia Butler, and Linda Hogan." *Ecofeminist Literary Criticism: Theory, Interpretation, Pedagogy.* Ed. Greta Gaard and Patrick D. Murphy. Urbana: U of Illinois P, 1998. 123–38.

Allison, Dorothy. *Bastard Out of Carolina.* New York: Plume, 1993.

Anderson, Sherwood. *Beyond Desire.* 1932. New York: Liveright, 1961.

Astro, Richard. *John Steinbeck and Edward F. Ricketts: The Shaping of a Novelist.* Minneapolis: U of Minnesota P, 1973.

Baker, Christina Looper. *In a Generous Spirit: A First-Person Biography of Myra Page.* Chicago: U of Illinois P, 1996.

Beach, Joseph Warren. *American Fiction: 1920–1940.* New York: Macmillan, 1941.

Bein, Alfred. *Let Freedom Ring: A Play in Three Acts.* New York: Samuel French, Ltd., 1936.

Bendel-Simso, Mary Michele. "The Politics of Reproduction: Demystifying Female Gender in Southern Literature." Diss. State University of New York at Binghamton, 1992.

Benson, Jackson J. *Looking for Steinbeck's Ghost.* Norman: U of Oklahoma P, 1988.

Black, Edwin. *War Against the Weak: Eugenics and America's Campaign to Create a Master Race.* New York: Four Walls Eight Windows, 2003.

Bloom, Harold, ed. *Modern Critical Interpretations: John Steinbeck's The Grapes of Wrath.* New York: Chelsea House Publishers, 1988.

Blotner, Joseph. *Faulkner: A Biography.* New York: Random House, 1984.

"Books and Book Folk." Portland *Evening Express* (15 April 1939): 6.

Bragg, Rick. *All Over But the Shoutin.'* New York: Vintage Books, 1997.

Brickell, Hershel. "Gastonia's Tragedy." *The Saturday Review of Literature* 7.12 (1930): 198.

Burke, Fielding [Olive Tilford Dargan]. *Call Home the Heart.* 1932. New York: Feminist P, 1983.

———. *A Stone Came Rolling.* New York: Longmans, Green and Co., 1935.

Burns, Mattie Ann. "The Development of Women Characters in the Works of William Faulkner." Dissertation. Auburn University, 1974.

Byerly, Victoria. *Hard Times Cotton Mill Girls: Personal Histories of Womanhood and Poverty in the South.* Ithaca, NY: ILR P, 1986.

Byrd, William. *Histories of the Dividing Line betwixt Virginia and North Carolina.* 1929. New York: Dover Publications, Inc., 1987.

Caldwell, Erskine. "Georgia Land Barons Oust Dying Girl and Her Father." MacDonald, ed. 102–5.

———. "Georgia Poverty-Swept, Says Caldwell." MacDonald, ed. 97–100.

———. *God's Little Acre.* 1933. Athens: U of Georgia P, 1995.

———. Interview with Erskine Caldwell. *Conversations with Erskine Caldwell.* Ed. Edwin T. Arnold. Jackson: UP of Mississippi, 1988. 265–96.

———. Letter to John Simon Guggenheim Memorial Foundation. 21 July 1931. In *Erskine Caldwell: Selected Letters, 1929–1955.* Ed. Robert L. McDonald. Jefferson: McFarland, 1999. 63–65.

———. *Some American People.* New York: Robert M. McBride and Co., 1935.

———. "Starving Babies Suckled by Dog in Georgia Cabin." MacDonald, ed. 105–7.

———. *Tobacco Road.* 1932. Athens: U of Georgia P, 1995.

———. "U.S. Aid Forces Oust Georgia Share Croppers." MacDonald, ed. 100–102.

———, and Margaret Bourke-White. *You Have Seen Their Faces.* New York: Modern Age Books, Inc., 1937.

Caldwell, I. S. "The Bunglers: A Narrative-Study in Five Parts." *Eugenics: A Journal of Race Betterment* 3.6 (1930): 203–10; 3.7 (1930): 247–51; 3.8 (1930): 293–99; 3.9 (1930): 332–36; 3.10 (1930): 377–83.

"*Call Home the Heart.*" Review. *Booklist* 28.8 (1932): 349.

"*Call Home the Heart.*" Review. *The Christian Century* (1 June 1932): 710–11.

"*Call Home the Heart.*" Review. *The New Republic* (18 May 1932): 27.

Cantwell, Robert. "Effective Propaganda." *The Nation* (19 October 1932): 372–73.

Carlson, Elof Axel. *Genes, Radiation, and Society: The Life and Work of H. J. Muller.* Ithaca, NY: Cornell UP, 1981.

Carver, Thomas Nixon. "The Economic Test of Fitness." *Eugenics: A Journal of Race Betterment* 2.7 (1929): 3–7.

Casey, Janet Galligani. "Agrarian Landscapes, the Depression, and Women's Progressive Fiction." *The Novel and the American Left: Critical Essays on Depres-*

sion-Era Fiction. Ed. Janet Galligani Casey. Iowa City: U of Iowa P, 2004. 96–117.

Clarke, Deborah. *Robbing the Mother: Women in Faulkner.* Jackson, UP of Mississippi, 1994.

Cogdell, Christina. *Eugenic Design: Streamlining America in the 1930s.* Philadelphia: U of Pennsylvania P, 2004.

Cohen, Hennig, and William B. Dillingham, eds. *Humor of the Old Southwest.* 3rd ed. Athens: U of Georgia P, 1994.

———. Introduction. Cohen and Dillingham, eds. xv–xl.

Coiner, Constance. "Literature and Resistance: The Intersection of Feminism and the Communist Left in Meridel Le Sueur and Tillie Olsen." *Left Politics and the Literary Profession.* Ed. Lennard J. Davis and M. Bella Mirabella. New York: Columbia UP, 1990. 162–85.

Conroy, Jack. "Passion and Pellagra." MacDonald, ed. 17–18.

Cook, Sylvia Jenkins. "Critical Afterword." *Call Home the Heart.* By Fielding Burke [Olive Tilford Dargan]. New York: Feminist P, 1983. 447–62.

———. *Erskine Caldwell and the Fiction of Poverty: The Flesh and the Spirit.* Baton Rouge: Louisiana State UP, 1991.

———. "'Erskine Caldwell's Nonfiction." MacDonald, ed. 375–92.

———. *From Tobacco Road to Route 66: The Southern Poor White in Fiction.* Chapel Hill: U of North Carolina P, 1976.

———. "Steinbeck, the People, and the Party." *Literature at the Barricades: The American Writer in the 1930s.* Ed. Ralph F. Bogardus and Fred Hobson. University: U of Alabama P, 1982. 82–95.

Cosgrove, Peter. "Snapshots of the Absolute: Mediamachia in *Let Us Now Praise Famous Men.*" *American Literature* 67.2 (1995): 329–57.

Couch, W. T. "Instructions to Writers." Couch, ed. 417–20.

———. "Landlord and Tenant." MacDonald, ed. 56–59.

———. Preface. Couch, ed. ix–xx.

———, ed. *These Are Our Lives: As Told by the People and Written by Members of the Federal Writers' Project of the Works Progress Administration in North Carolina, Tennessee, and Georgia.* Chapel Hill: U of North Carolina P, 1939.

Coughlan, Robert. *The Private World of William Faulkner.* New York: Cooper Square Publishers, Inc. 1972.

Covington, Dennis. *Salvation on Sand Mountain: Snake Handling and Redemption in Southern Appalachia.* New York: Penguin Books, 1995.

Cowley, Malcolm. "American Tragedy." *New Republic* 98 (3 May 1939): 382–83.

———. *Portable Faulkner.* Revised Ed. New York: Penguin Books, 1967.

Cox, Dianne L. Introduction. *William Faulkner's As I Lay Dying: A Critical Casebook.* New York: Garland Publishing, Inc., 1985.

Crews, Harry. *Car. Classic Crews: A Harry Crews Reader.* New York: Simon and Schuster, 1993. 323–436.

Crider, Bill. "Sons of *Tobacco Road:* 'Backwoods' Novels." *Journal of Popular Culture* 16.3 (1982): 47–59.

Cuddy, Lois A. and Claire M. Roche, eds. *Evolution and Eugenics in American Literature and Culture, 1880–1940.* Lewisburg: Bucknell UP, 2003.

Currell, Susan. Introduction. Currell and Cogdell, eds. 1–14.

Currell, Susan, and Christina Cogdell, eds. *Popular Eugenics: National Efficiency and American Mass Culture in the 1930s.* Athens: Ohio UP, 2006.

Curtis, James. *Mind's Eye, Mind's Truth: FSA Photography Reconsidered.* Philadelphia: Temple UP, 1989.

Daniels, Jonathan. "Farm and Mill." McDonald, ed. 29–31.

Danielson, Florence H., and Charles B. Davenport. "The Hill Folk: Report on a Rural Community of Hereditary Defectives." Rafter, ed. 85–163.

[Dargan, Olive Tilford.] *Call Home the Heart.* By Fielding Burke. 1932. New York: Feminist P, 1983.

Davenport, Basil. "In the Mire." *The Saturday Review of Literature* 7.12 (1930): 362.

Davenport, Gertrude C. "Hereditary Crime." Rafter, ed. 67–73.

Davidson, Donald. "Erskine Caldwell's Picture Book." MacDonald, ed. 59–67.

Dawson, Margaret Cheney. "People of the Mountains." *New York Herald Tribune Books* (21 February 1932): 5.

Denning, Michael. *The Cultural Front: The Laboring of American Culture in the Twentieth Century.* New York: Verso, 1997.

Dixler, Elsa Jane. "The Woman Question: Women and the American Communist Party, 1929–1941." Diss. Yale U, 1974.

Duck, Leigh Anne. *The Nation's Region: Southern Modernism, Segregation, and U.S. Nationalism.* Athens: U of Georgia P, 2006.

Dugdale, R. L. *"The Jukes": A Study in Crime, Pauperism, Disease, and Heredity.* 3rd ed. New York: G. P. Putnam's Sons, 1877.

Dunnagan, Claude V. "Get Out and Hoe." Couch, ed. 30–37.

East, Edward. M. *Heredity and Human Affairs.* 1927. New York: Charles Scribner's Sons, 1935.

———. "Hidden Feeblemindedness." *The Journal of Heredity* 8 (1917): 215–17.

Elfenbein, Anna Shannon. "A Forgotten Revolutionary Voice: 'Woman's Place' and Race in Olive Dargan's *Call Home the Heart.*" *The Female Tradition in Southern Literature.* Ed. Carol S. Manning. Chicago: U of Illinois P, 1993. 193–208.

Ellis, Havelock. *Little Essays of Love and Virtue.* New York: George H. Doran Co., 1922.

———. *More Essays of Love and Virtue.* Garden City, NY: Doubleday, Doran & Co., Inc., 1931.

———. *Studies in the Psychology of Sex.* Vol. 1. 1901. New York: Random House, 1936.

———. *Studies in the Psychology of Sex.* Vol. 4: *Sex in Relation to Society.* 1906. New York: Random House, 1936.

Engels, Friedrich. "The Origin of Family, Private Property, and the State." *The Marx-Engels Reader.* Ed. Robert C. Tucker. 2nd ed. New York: W. W. Norton and Co., Inc. 1978. 734–59.

English, Daylanne K. *Unnatural Selections: Eugenics in American Modernism and the Harlem Renaissance.* Chapel Hill: U of North Carolina P, 2004.

"Erskine Caldwell." MacDonald, ed. 119–31.

Estabrook, Arthur H. "The Country Slums." *Eugenics: A Journal of Race Betterment* 2.7 (1929): 8–12.

———, and Ivan E. McDougle. *Mongrel Virginians: The Win Tribe.* Baltimore: Williams and Wilkins Co., 1926.

Fadiman, Clifton. "Highway 66—A Tale of Five Cities." *New Yorker* 15 (15 April 1939): 81–83.

———. "Morbidity in Fiction." *The Nation* 131 (1930): 500–501.

Faulkner, William. "Address Upon Receiving the Nobel Prize for Literature." *The Portable Faulkner.* Rev. ed. Ed. Malcolm Cowley. New York: Penguin Books, 1967. 723–24.

———. *As I Lay Dying.* 1930. New York: Vintage International, 1990.

———. *Mosquitoes.* 1927. New York: Liveright, 1997.

———. *The Sound and the Fury.* 1929. New York: Vintage International, 1990.

Fender, Stephen. "Poor Whites and the Federal Writers' Project: The Rhetoric of Eugenics in the Southern Life Histories." Currell and Cogdell, eds. 140–63.

Flynt, J. Wayne. *Dixie's Forgotten People: The South's Poor Whites.* Bloomington: Indiana UP, 1980.

Foley, Barbara. *Radical Representations: Politics and Form in U.S. Proletarian Fiction, 1929–1941.* Durham: Duke UP, 1993.

Fontenrose, Joseph. "*The Grapes of Wrath.*" Heavilin, ed. 71–86.

Galton, Francis. *Hereditary Genius: An Inquiry into Its Laws and Consequences.* 1869. New York: D. Appleton and Co., 1881.

Garrison, Dee. Introduction. *Strike!* Mary Heaton Vorse. Urbana: U of Illinois P, 1991. vii–xxi.

———. *Mary Heaton Vorse: The Life of an American Insurgent.* Philadelphia: Temple UP, 1989.

———, ed. *Rebel Pen: The Writings of Mary Heaton Vorse.* New York: Monthly Review P, 1985.

"The Gastonia Mills." *The New York Times Book Review* (2 November 1930): 6.

"*Gathering Storm.*" *The New Republic* (19 April 1933): 290.

"*Gathering Storm.*" *The Times Literary Supplement* (24 November 1932): 905.

Gibbons, Kaye. *Ellen Foster.* 1987. New York: Vintage Books, 1990.

Gladstein, Mimi Reisel. "*The Grapes of Wrath:* Steinbeck and the Eternal Immigrant." *John Steinbeck: The Years of Greatness, 1936–1939.* Ed. Tetsumaro Hayashi. Tuscaloosa: U of Alabama P, 1993. 132–44.

———. "The Indestructible Women: Ma Joad and Rose of Sharon." Bloom, ed. 115–27.

Glasgow, Ellen. *Barren Ground.* 1925. New York: Hill and Wang, 1977.

Goddard, Henry Herbert. *The Kallikak Family: A Study in the Heredity of Feeble-Mindedness.* 1912. New York: Macmillan Co., 1923.

Gold, Mike. "Go Left, Young Writers!" *Mike Gold: A Literary Anthology.* Ed. Michael Folsom. New York: International Publishers, 1972. 186–89.

Gray, James. "New Realist Depicts South's Poor Whites' Pitiable Existence." MacDonald, ed. 13–15.

Grosskurth, Phyllis. *Havelock Ellis: A Biography.* New York: Alfred A. Knopf, 1980.

Hagood, Margaret Jarman. *Mothers of the South: Portraiture of the White Tenant Farm Woman.* 1939. New York: W. W. Norton and Co., Inc., 1977.

Hagood, Taylor. *Faulkner's Imperialism: Space, Place, and the Materiality of Myth.* Baton Rouge: Louisiana UP, 2008.

Haldane, J. B. S. "A Dialectical Account of Evolution." *Science and Society* 1.4 (1937): 473–86.

Hall, Jacquelyn Dowd. "Women Writers, the 'Southern Front,' and the Dialectical Imagination." *Journal of Southern History* 69.1 (2003): 3–38.

———, et al. *Like a Family: The Making of a Southern Cotton Mill World.* 1987. Chapel Hill: U of North Carolina P, 2000.

Hapke, Laura. *Daughters of the Great Depression: Women, Work, and Fiction in the American 1930s.* Athens: U of Georgia P, 1995.

Harris, Bernice Kelly. "Plow Beams for Pills." Couch, ed. 263–77.

———. "Some Sort o' How." Couch, ed. 37–44.

Hearle, Kevin. "These Are American People: The Spectre of Eugenics in *Their Blood Is Strong* and *The Grapes of Wrath.*" *Beyond Boundaries: Rereading John Steinbeck.* Ed. Susan Shillinglaw and Kevin Hearle. Tuscaloosa: U of Alabama P, 2002. 243–54.

Heavilin, Barbara A., ed. *The Critical Response to John Steinbeck's Grapes of Wrath.* Westport: Greenwood P, 2000.

Hershey, John. "Introduction: Agee." *Let Us Now Praise Famous Men.* By James Agee and Walker Evans. 1941. Boston: Houghton Mifflin Co., 1988. v–xl.

Hicks, Granville. "Steinbeck's Powerful New Novel." *New Masses* 31 (2 May 1939): 22–24.

Hicks, Mary A., and Willis S. Harrison. "You're Gonna Have Lace Curtains." Couch, ed. 3–17.

Hirsch, Jerrold. *Portrait of America: A Cultural History of the Federal Writers' Project.* Chapel Hill: U of North Carolina P, 2003.

Hirsch, Jerrold, and Tom E. Terrill. Introduction. *Such as Us: Southern Voices of the Thirties.* Ed. Terrill and Hirsch. Chapel Hill: U of North Carolina P, 1978. xi–xxvi.

Hoffman, Frederick J. *William Faulkner.* 2nd ed. Boston: Twayne Publishers, 1966.

Holmes, Sarah C. "Re-examining the Political Left: Erskine Caldwell and the Doctrine of Eugenics." Cuddy and Roche, eds. 240–58.

Hooper, Johnson Jones. "Simon Plays the 'Snatch' Game." Cohen and Dillingham, eds. 255–61.

Hoover, Herbert. *The New Day: Campaign Speeches of Herbert Hoover 1928.* 1928. Stanford U: Stanford UP, 1929.

Howarth, William. "The Mother of Literature: Journalism and *The Grapes of Wrath.*" Wyatt, ed. 71–99.

Howe, Irving. *William Faulkner: A Critical Study.* 2nd ed. New York: Vintage Books, 1962.

Humphries, Ray R., and James R. Aswell. ". . . And Costs." Couch, ed. 305–17.

Hutchins, Grace. *Women Who Work.* New York: International Publishers, 1934.

"Investigation Is Made to Determine Basis Caldwell Had for All His Writings." MacDonald, ed. 117–19.

Jehlen, Myra. *Class and Character in Faulkner's South.* New York: Columbia UP, 1976.

Jennings, H. S. *The Biological Basis of Human Nature.* New York: W. W. Norton and Co., Inc., 1930.

Joravsky, David. *The Lysenko Affair.* Cambridge: Harvard UP, 1970.

———. *Soviet Marxism and Natural Science, 1917–1932.* New York: Columbia UP, 1961.

Karl, Frederick R. *William Faulkner: American Writer.* New York: Weidenfeld & Nicholson, 1989.

Kartiganer, Donald M. *The Fragile Thread: The Meaning of Form in Faulkner's Novels.* Amherst: U of Massachusetts P, 1979.

Keely, Karen A. "Poverty, Sterilization, and Eugenics in Erskine Caldwell's *Tobacco Road.*" *Journal of American Studies* 36.1 (2002): 23–42.

Kelley, Edith Summers. *Weeds.* 1923. Old Westbury, NY: Feminist P, 1982.

Kellicott, William E. *The Social Direction of Human Evolution: An Outline of the Science of Eugenics.* New York: D. Appleton and Co., 1923.

Kevles, Daniel J. *In the Name of Eugenics: Genetics and the Uses of Human Heredity.* New York: Knopf, 1985.

King, Richard H. *A Southern Renaissance: The Cultural Awakening of the American South, 1930–1955.* New York: Oxford UP, 1980.

Kite, Elizabeth S. "The 'Pineys.'" Rafter, ed. 165–84.

———. "Two Brothers." Rafter, ed. 76–80.

Kline, Wendy. *Building a Better Race: Gender, Sexuality, and Eugenics from the Turn of the Century to the Baby Boom.* Berkeley: U of California P, 2001.

Kostir, Mary Storer. *The Family of Sam Sixty.* Rafter, ed. 186–209.

Kronenberger, Louis. "Hungry Caravan." White, ed. 140–41.

Lange, Dorothea. "The Assignment I'll Never Forget." *Popular Photography* 46.2 (1960): 42, 126.

———. "Draggin'-Around People." *Survey Graphic* 25.9 (1936): 524.

———. *Photographs of a Lifetime.* Oakland: Aperture, Inc., 1982.

Larson, Edward J. *Sex, Race, and Science: Eugenics in the Deep South.* 1995. Baltimore: Johns Hopkins UP, 1996.

Laughlin, Harry Hamilton. *The Legal Status of Eugenical Sterilization: History and Analysis of Litigation Under the Virginia Sterilization Statute, Which Led to a Decision of the Supreme Court of the United States Upholding the Statute.* Chicago: Fred J. Ringley Co., 1930.

Lee, Harper. *To Kill a Mockingbird.* 1960. New York: Warner Books, 1982.

Lenz, William E. "The Function of Women in Old Southwestern Humor: Rereading Porter's *Big Bear* and *Quarter Race* Collections." *The Humor of the Old South.* Ed. M. Thomas Inge and Edward J. Piacentino. Lexington: U of Kentucky P, 2001. 36–51.

Lesy, Michael. "Assigned Readings." Lesy, ed. 114–20.

———. Introduction. Lesy, ed. 9–11.

———, ed. *Long Time Coming: A Photographic Portrait of America, 1935–1942.* New York: W. W. Norton and Co., 2002.

Leuchtenburg, William E. *The White House Looks South: Franklin D. Roosevelt, Harry S. Truman, and Lyndon B. Johnson.* Baton Rouge: Louisiana State UP, 2005.

Levant, Howard. "The Fully Matured Art: *The Grapes of Wrath.*" Bloom, ed. 17–44.

Levine, Lawrence W. "The Historian and the Icon: Photography and the History of the American People in the 1930s and 1940s." *Documenting America, 1935–1943.* Ed. Carl Fleischhauer and Beverly W. Brannan. Berkeley: U of California P, 1988. 15–42.

Lewis, Sinclair. "A Novel for Mr. Hoover." *The Nation* (29 October 1930): 474.

Loveman, Amy. "Books of the Spring II." *The Saturday Review of Literature* 8.40 (1932): 684–85.

Ludmerer, Kenneth M. *Genetics and American Society: A Historical Appraisal.* Baltimore: Johns Hopkins UP, 1972.

Lumpkin, Grace. *To Make My Bread.* 1932. Chicago: U of Illinois P, 1995.

Maass, Vera Sonja. *The Cinderella Test: Would You Really Want the Shoe to Fit? Subtle Ways Women Are Seduced and Socialized into Servitude and Stereotypes.* Santa Barbara, CA: Praeger, 2009.

MacDonald, Scott, ed. *Critical Essays on Erskine Caldwell.* Boston: G. K. Hall and Co., 1981.

Maharidge, Dale and Michael Williamson. *And Their Children After Them.* New York: Pantheon Books, 1989.

Mangione, Jerre. *The Dream and the Deal: The Federal Writers' Project, 1935–1943.* Boston: Little, Brown, and Co., 1972.

Manning, Carol S. "Southern Women Writers and the Beginning of the Renaissance." *The History of Southern Women's Literature.* Ed. Carolyn Perry and Mary Louise Weaks. Baton Rouge: Louisiana State UP, 2002. 242–50.

Mantooth, Wes. *"You Factory Folks Who Sing This Rhyme Will Surely Understand": Culture, Ideology, and Action in Gastonia Novels of Myra Page, Grace Lumpkin, and Olive Dargan.* New York: Routledge, 2006.

Marx, Karl and Friedrich Engels. *The Communist Manifesto.* 1848. New York: Signet Classic, 1998.

Maslin, Marshall. "Bookworm Sees a New Steinbeck." *San Francisco Call-Bulletin* (15 April 1939): 3.

Matthews, T. Pat. "I Saved My Money." Couch, ed. 91–100.

McClure, Robert E. "Books Worth Reading." *Santa Monica Evening Outlook* (28 April 1939): 8.

McCulloch, Oscar C. "The Tribe of Ishmael: A Study in Social Degradation." Rafter, ed. 48–54.

McDonald, Robert L., ed., *The Critical Response to Erskine Caldwell.* Westport: Greenwood P, 1997.

McKay, Nellie Y. "'Happy[?]-Wife-and-Motherdom': The Portrayal of Ma Joad in John Steinbeck's *The Grapes of Wrath.*" Wyatt, ed. 47–69.

Meriwether, James B. *The Literary Career of William Faulkner: A Biographical Study.* Princeton, NJ: Princeton U Library, 1961.

Miller, Dan B. *Erskine Caldwell: The Journey from Tobacco Road.* New York: Alfred A. Knopf, Inc., 1995.

Millgate, Michael. *The Achievement of William Faulkner.* New York: Random House, 1966.

Minter, David. *William Faulkner: His Life and Work.* Baltimore: Johns Hopkins UP, 1980.

Mixon, Wayne. *The People's Writer: Erskine Caldwell and the South.* Charlottesville: UP of Virginia, 1995.

Moore, Ida. "Outline for Life Histories." Couch, ed. 420–21.

Moore, James Tice. "Review of *Mothers of the South: Portraiture of the White Tenant Farm Woman.*" *Mississippi Quarterly* 51.2 (1998): 385–89.

Morrison, Toni. *Playing in the Dark: Whiteness and the Literary Imagination.* New York: Vintage Books, 1993.

Muller, H. J. *Out of the Night: A Biologist's View of the Future.* New York: Vanguard P, 1935.

Murfree, Mary Noailles (Charles Egbert Craddock). *In the Tennessee Mountains.* 1884. Ridgewood: Gregg P, 1968.

Newman, Dean, and James R. Aswell. "Lived Too Long." Couch, ed. 77–91.

Nies, Betty. "Conservative Arguments Against Eugenics in the Depression Era South." Currell and Cogdell, eds. 44–69.

Noll, Steven. "'A Far Greater Menace': Feebleminded Females in the South, 1900–1940." *Hidden Histories of Women in the New South.* Ed. Virginia Bernhard, et al. Columbia: U of Missouri P, 1994. 31–51.

———. *Feeble-Minded in Our Midst: Institutions for the Mentally Retarded in the South, 1900–1940.* Chapel Hill: U of North Carolina P, 1995.

Nordan, Louis. Foreword. *Tobacco Road.* Athens: U of Georgia P, 1995. v–ix.

"A Novel of the Southern Mills." *New York Times Book Review.* (25 September 1932): 7.

Odem, Mary E. *Delinquent Daughters: Protecting and Policing Adolescent Female Sexuality in the United States, 1885–1920.* Chapel Hill: U of North Carolina P, 1995.

Olin, Margaret. "'It Is Not Going to Be Easy to Look into Their Eyes': Privilege and Perception in *Let Us Now Praise Famous Men.*" *Art History* 14.1 (1991): 92–115.

Owens, Louis. *John Steinbeck's Re-Vision of America.* Athens: U of Georgia P, 1985.

The Oxford Desk Dictionary and Thesaurus. Ed. Frank R. Abate et al. New York: Berkley Books, 1997.

Page, Dorothy Myra (Myra Page). *Gathering Storm: A Story of the Black Belt.* New York: International Publishers, 1932.

Page, Myra. *Southern Cotton Mills and Labor.* New York: Workers Library Publishers, 1929.

Page, Sally R. *Faulkner's Women: Characterization and Meaning.* Deland: Everett/Edwards, inc., 1972.

Parini, Jay. *John Steinbeck: A Biography.* New York: Henry Holt and Co., 1995.

Paul, Diane B. *Controlling Human Heredity: 1865 to the Present.* Atlantic Highlands, NJ: Humanities P, 1995.

———. "Eugenics and the Left." Shaner, ed. 11–35.

———. "Genes and Contagious Disease: The Rise and Fall of a Metaphor." Shaner, ed. 157–71.

———. Introduction. Shaner, ed. 1–10.

———and Hamish G. Spencer. "Did Eugenics Rest on an Elementary Mistake?" Shaner, ed. 117–32.

Penkower, Monty Noam. *The Federal Writers' Project: A Study in Government Patronage of the Arts.* Chicago: U of Illinois P, 1977.

Pizer, Donald. "The Enduring Power of the Joads." Bloom, ed. 83–98.

Rabinowitz, Paula. *Labor and Desire: Women's Revolutionary Fiction in Depression America.* Chapel Hill: U of North Carolina P, 1991.

———. *They Must Be Represented: The Politics of Documentary.* New York: Verso, 1994.

Rafter, Nicole Hahn. *Creating Born Criminals.* Chicago: U of Illinois P, 1997.

———. Preface to "Hereditary Pauperism as Illustrated in the 'Juke' Family." Rafter, ed. 33–35.

———, ed. *White Trash: The Eugenic Family Studies 1877–1919.* Boston: Northeastern UP, 1988.

Rahv, Philip. "A Variety of Fiction." White, ed. 152.

Railsback, Brian E. *Parallel Expeditions: Charles Darwin and the Art of John Steinbeck.* Moscow: U of Idaho P.

———. "The Darwinian *Grapes of Wrath.*" Heavilin, ed. 221–31.

Ray, Janisse. *Ecology of a Cracker Childhood.* Minneapolis: Milkweed Editions, 1999.

———. *Wild Card Quilt: Taking a Chance on Home.* Minneapolis: Milkweed Editions, 2003.

Rideout, Walter B. *The Radical Novel in the United States 1900–1954: Some Interrelations of Literature and Society.* Cambridge: Harvard UP, 1956.

Roberts, Diane. *Faulkner and Southern Womanhood.* Athens: U of Georgia P, 1994.

Roberts, Elizabeth Madox. *The Time of Man.* New York: Grosset and Dunlap, 1927.

Robinson, Paul. *The Modernization of Sex: Havelock Ellis, Alfred Kinsey, William Masters, and Virginia Johnson.* New York: Harper & Row, Publishers, 1976.

Roche, Claire M. "Reproducing the Working Class: Tillie Olsen, Margaret Sanger, and American Eugenics." Cuddy and Roche, eds. 259–75.

Rollins, William. *The Shadow Before.* New York: Robert M. McBride, Co., 1934.

Rosenfelt, Deborah. "From the Thirties: Tillie Olsen and the Radical Tradition." *Feminist Studies* 7.3 (1981): 371–406.

Satterwhite, Emily. "Reading Craddock, Reading Murfree: Local Color, Authenticity, and Geographics of Reception." *American Literature: A Journal of Literary History* 78.1 (2006): 59–88.

Schachner, E. A. "Revolutionary Literature in the United States Today." *The Windsor Quarterly* 2 (1934): 27–64.

Schofield, Harry. "Today's Book." White ed. 150–51.

Schreibersdorf, Lisa. "Radical Mothers: Maternal Testimony and Metaphor in Four Novels of the Gastonia Strike." *JNT: Journal of Narrative Theory* 29.3 (1999): 303–22.

Schroeder, Patricia R. "The Comic World of *As I Lay Dying.*" *Faulkner and Humor: Faulkner and Yoknapatawpha, 1984.* Ed. Doreen Fowler and Ann J. Abadie. Jackson: UP of Mississippi, 1986. 34–46.

Scott, Anne Firor. Introduction. Margaret Jarman Hagood. iii–x.

Shaffer, Robert. "Women and the Communist Party, USA, 1930–1940." *Socialist Review* 9 (1979): 73–118.

Shaner, David Edward, ed. *The Politics of Heredity: Essays on Eugenics, Biomedicine, and the Nature-Nurture Debate.* Albany: State U of New York P, 1998.

Shannon, Anna W. "Biographical Afterword." *Call Home the Heart.* Fielding Burke. New York: Feminist P, 1983. 433–46.

Shloss, Carol. "The Privilege of Perception." *Virginia Quarterly Review* 56 (1988): 596–611.

Smith, J. Russell. *North America: Its People and the Resources, Development, and Prospects of the Continent as an Agricultural, Industrial, and Commercial Area.* New York: Harcourt, Brace, and Co., 1925.

Smith, Lee. *Saving Grace.* New York: Ballantine Books, 1996.

Smith, Leef. "Robbed of the Promise of Life—Victim of Virginia's Old Sterilization Law Says Amends Can't End Pain Over Loss." *Washington Post* (13 May 2002): B1.

Sowinska, Suzanne. Introduction. *To Make My Bread.* Grace Lumpkin. Chicago: U of Illinois P, 1995. vii–xliii.

Staub, Michael. "As Close As You Can Get: Torment, Speech, and Listening in *Let Us Now Praise Famous Men.*" *Mississippi Quarterly* 41.2 (1988): 147–60.

Steinbeck, John. "About Ed Ricketts." *The Log of the Sea of Cortez.* New York: Viking P, 1951. vii–lxvii.

———. *The Grapes of Wrath.* 1939. New York: Penguin Books, 1976.

———. Letter to Pascal Covici. January 16, 1939. *Steinbeck: A Life in Letters.* Ed. Elaine Steinbeck and Robert Wallsten. New York: Viking P, 1975. 166–67.

———. *Their Blood Is Strong.* San Francisco: Simon J. Lubin Society, 1938.

———and E. F. Ricketts. *The Log from the Sea of Cortez.* 1941. New York: Viking P, 1951.

Stott, William. *Documentary Expression and Thirties America.* 1973. Chicago: U of Chicago P, 1986.

Strode, Hudson. "Pictures of the South, Drunk on Cotton." McDonald, ed. 73–75.

Stryker, Roy Emerson. "The FSA Collection of Photographs." Stryker and Wood, eds. 7–9.

———, and Nancy Wood, eds., *In This Proud Land: America, 1935–1943, As Seen in the FSA Photographs.* 1973. Boston: New York Graphic Society, Ltd., 1975.

Swiggart, Peter. *The Art of Faulkner's Novels.* Austin: U of Texas P, 1962.

Taylor, Paul. "Migrant Mother: 1936." *American West* 7.3 (1970): 41–45.

"Title Page." *Science and Society* 1.1 (1936): i–ii.

Trilling, Lionel. "Greatness with One Fault in It." *Kenyon Review* 42.1 (1942): 99–102.

Urgo, Joseph R. "Proletarian Literature and Feminism: The Gastonia Novels and Feminine Protest." *The Minnesota Review* 24 (1985): 64–84.

Vorse, Mary Heaton. "Gastonia." Garrison, ed. 113–27.

———. "Grind My Bones." *The New Republic* (7 December 1932): 104–5.

———. "How Scottsboro Happened." Garrison, ed. 149–52.

———. *Strike!* 1930. Urbana: U of Illinois P, 1991.

———. "Why I Have Failed As a Mother." Garrison, ed. 342–45.

Wadlington, Warwick. *As I Lay Dying: Stories Out of Stories.* New York: Twayne Publishers, 1992.

Wagenknecht, Edward. "Chamber of Horrors—Southern Exposure." McDonald, ed. 159–61.

Wagner-Martin, Linda. "*Let Us Now Praise Famous Men*—and Women: Agee's Absorption in the Sexual." *James Agee: Reconsiderations.* Ed. Michael A. Lofaro. Knoxville: U of Tennessee P, 1992. 44–58.

Wainwright, Michael. *Darwin and Faulkner's Novels: Evolution and Southern Fiction.* New York: Palgrave Macmillan, 2008.

Watkins, J. Raiford. "Caldwell's Novel Is of Georgians." MacDonald, ed. 11–13.

Watson, Jay. "The Rhetoric of Exhaustion and the Exhaustion of Rhetoric: Erskine Caldwell in the Thirties." McDonald, ed. 285–97.

Webster's Third New International Dictionary of the English Language Unabridged. Ed. Philip Babcock et al. Springfield: Merriam-Webster, Inc., 1986.

Whisnant, David E. *All That Is Native and Fine: The Politics of Culture in an American Region.* Chapel Hill: U of North Carolina P, 1983.

White, Kenneth. "American Humor." MacDonald, ed. 18–19.

———. "Notes on Novels." *The New Republic* 65. 833 (1930): 26–27.

White, Ray Lewis, ed. "*The Grapes of Wrath* and the Critics of 1939." *Resources for American Literary Study* 13.2 (1983): 134–64.

Wiggam, Albert Edward. *The Fruit of the Family Tree.* Garden City, NY: Garden City Publishing Co., Inc., 1924.

Williams, Charles. *Girl Out Back.* New York: Dell Publishing Co., Inc., 1958.

Williams, David. *Faulkner's Women: The Myth and the Muse.* Montreal: McGill-Queen's UP, 1977.

Winn, Ralph B. "Dialectics: General Principles." *Science and Society* 2.4 (1938): 520–26.

Winsten, Archer. "Call Home the Heart." *Bookman* 75.3 (1932): 319–20.

"A Witch's Brew." *The New York Times Book Review* (19 October 1930): 6.

Wood, Nancy. "Portait of Stryker." Stryker and Wood, eds. 10–17.

Woodside, Moya. *Sterilization in North Carolina: A Sociological and Psychological Study.* Chapel Hill: U of North Carolina P, 1950.

Wyatt, David, ed. *New Essays on The Grapes of Wrath.* New York: Cambridge UP, 1990.

Yoe, Della, and Jennette Edwards. "Snappy Feeding." Couch, ed. 342–47.

———. "Till the River Rises." Couch, ed. 372–80.

Yukins, Elizabeth. "'Feeble-Minded' White Women and the Spectre of Proliferating Perversity in American Eugenics Narratives." Cuddy and Roche, eds. 164–86.

Index

abortion: in *As I Lay Dying,* 49, 57, 59, 61, 95–96; as a eugenic tool, 19, 20, 27, 44, 47, 49, 200n17; in *Gathering Storm,* 154–55; mentioned, 136; in *These Are Our Lives,* 113; in *Weeds,* 8. *See also* eugenics

adultery: in *As I Lay Dying,* 51, 55; in *Call Home the Heart,* 172; in eugenic family studies, 192n21; in *God's Little Acre,* 78; in *To Make My Bread,* 163; in *Tobacco Road,* 64. *See also* sexuality, poor white female

African Americans: as creators of "American" identity, 1–2; and eugenics, 15; as literary characters, 1–2; as "Other," 1, 2, 3, 8; separate from white society, 2; like southern poor whites, 3; as stereotypes, 1

Agee, James: difficulties in writing *Let Us Now Praise Famous Men,* 123–24; and *Fortune* magazine, 122–23; popularity in the 1960s, 185; sexual attraction to Emma in *Let Us Now Praise Famous Men,* 127–28; and the use of pseudonyms in *Let Us Now Praise Famous Men,* 198n11; and Walker Evans, 122–23. See also *Let Us Now Praise Famous Men* (Agee and Evans)

All Over But the Shoutin' (Bragg), 186

Allison, Dorothy, 186, 187. See also *Bastard Out of Carolina* (Allison)

American identity, definition of. *See* African Americans; Great Depression; "Other"; whiteness

And Their Children After Them (Maharidge and Williamson), 198n11

Anderson, Sherwood, 158, 180, 181, 182. See also *Beyond Desire* (Anderson)

artificial insemination, 32, 34. *See also* eugenics

As I Lay Dying (Faulkner), 10, 46, 47, 48–61, 93, 94, 97, 132, 154, 194n1, 194n4, 194n5. *See also* "hybridity," in *As I Lay Dying*

Back Country Woman, 184

"Backwoods" novels, 184, 201n2

Barren Ground (Glasgow), 7–8

Bastard Out of Carolina (Allison), 187

Beyond Desire (Anderson), 180–81, 182

birth control: in *Call Home the Heart,* 169, 172–73, 176, 178; and eugenic ideology, 27, 33, 49, 99, 133, 191n11, 193n29, 200n16; in *Gathering Storm,* 154, 155, 169; and Margaret Sanger, 20, 133, 191n9; in *Mothers of the South,* 121, 122, 198n9; in *These Are Our Lives,* 114, 116. *See also* eugenics

Bolshevik geneticists, 47. *See also* Soviet Union

Bourke-White, Margaret: and John Steinbeck, 80; method of photography used in *You Have Seen Their Faces,* 103–5, 106–7; and the New Deal, 99; and Roosevelt administration, 197n2. See also *You Have Seen Their Faces* (Caldwell, Erskine and Bourke-White)

Bragg, Rick, 185, 186. See also *All Over But the Shoutin'* (Bragg)
breastfeeding: in Erskine Caldwell's *New York Post* articles, 104; in *Gathering Storm,* 155, 157; in *The Grapes of Wrath,* 92; in *Let Us Now Praise Famous Men,* 128–29; in *Their Blood Is Strong,* 83; in *You Have Seen Their Faces,* 104
"Bunglers, The" (Cadlwell, Ira), 30–31, 63, 69, 82, 192–93nn26–27. See also *God's Little Acre* (Caldwell, Erskine); *Tobacco Road* (Caldwell, Erskine)
Byrd, William, II, 189n3. See also *Histories of the Dividing Line* (Byrd)

Cabin Road, 184
Caldwell, Erskine: and "The Bunglers," 63; and the CPUSA, 68, 69; and documentary work, 99, 100, 106; and eugenics, 63, 64; focus on poor white women, 48, 77–78; and "grotesque" images, 68; and the Guggenheim Foundation, 68–69, 195n13; and Malcolm Cowley 68; and Margaret Bourke-White, 99, 103; mentioned, 10, 11, 46; and Mike Gold, 68; and obscenity charge, 62; popularity of novels, 61–62; and "socialist geneticist" ideas, 47, 69, 195n12; son of Ira Caldwell, 30; sympathy towards poor white characters, 67–68, 78–79, 95–96; writings for *New York Post,* 100–1, 104, 105. See also *God's Little Acre* (Caldwell, Erskine); *Some American People* (Caldwell, Erskine); *Tobacco Road* (Caldwell, Erskine); *You Have Seen Their Faces* (Caldwell, Erskine and Bourke-White)
Caldwell, Ira: father of Erskine Caldwell, 61; focus on the South, 47; influence on Erskine Caldwell's *New York Post* articles, 100–1; influence on *God's Little Acre,* 69, 78; influence on *Tobacco Road,* 63, 67; writing of "The Bunglers," 30–31, 63. *See also* "Bunglers, The" (Caldwell, Ira)
Call Home the Heart (Dargan), 136, 139, 168, 169–79, 182, 199n2, 200n21, 201n27
Car (Crews), 186
Carrie Buck vs. Bell, 21, 28
Carver, Thomas Nixon, 30, 63, 191n8
child labor, 17, 134, 190–91n7
childbirth, 33, 162
Civil Rights Movement, 184, 185, 198n16
Communist Manifesto, The (Marx and Engels), 193n35
Communist Party of the United States (CPUSA): and Erskine Caldwell, 68; and eugenics, 15, 35–38, 42, 193n32; focus on the family, 14, 42; and *Gastonia Strike,* 138; in *Gathering Storm,* 200n15; and Grace Lumpkin, 159, 160; and Myra Page, 200n18; and *New Masses,* 38, 68, 94, 158, 160, 200n18; and Olive Tilford Dargan, 168, 200n21; and Popular Front, 36, 38, 42; and proletarian literature, 46, 141; and the Roosevelt administration, 13–15, 35; and *Science and Society,* 37–38, 81; and women, 14, 38–39, 41, 135, 188, 193nn34–35
Couch, W. T.: as defender of the South, 111; feud with Erskine Caldwell, 106–7, 111, 112; instructions for *These Are Our Lives,* 112, 198n10. See also *These Are Our Lives* (Couch)
Covington, Dennis, 185, 186. See also *Salvation on Sand Mountain* (Covington)
Crews, Harry, 185, 186. See also *Car* (Crews)

Dargan, Olive Tilford (Fielding Burke): challenging eugenic ideology, 11, 136, 137, 179–80, 182–83; connection to poverty, 168; as creator of new female "heroine," 178–79; and the Gastonia Mill Strike, 136; and Julian Huxley, 169; and Margaret Sanger, 168. *See also Call Home the*

Heart (Dargan); *Stone Came Rolling, A* (Dargan)
Darwin, Charles, 49, 88, 194–95n6, 196n22
Davenport, Gertrude C., 191–92n17, 192n21. *See also* "Hereditary Crime" (Davenport)
"documentary novel," 139, 199n3
Dugdale, Richard L., 16, 22, 23, 24, 26, 191n16, 192nn21–22. See also *"Jukes, The"* (Dugdale)

East, Edward M., 28
Ecology of a Cracker Childhood (Ray), 187
Ellen Foster (Gibbons), 186–87
Ellis, Havelock: and abortion, 19, 47, 57, 59, 155, 200n17; and birth control, 20; and female sexuality, 18–19; focus on the mother in the family, 19, 195n8; mentioned in Faulkner's *Mosquitoes*, 49, 195n7; and sterilization, 191n11
Engels, Friedrich, 32, 37, 38, 193–94nn34–35
environment: in *As I Lay Dying*, 47, 61, 95, 194n5; in "The Bunglers," 30–31, 193n28; in Erskine Caldwell's *New York Post* articles, 100–1, 102; in *God's Little Acre*, 69, 73, 77, 95; in *The Grapes of Wrath*, 88, 90, 96; and Herbert Hoover, 200n12; in *"The Jukes,"* 23, 26, 192n22; in *Let Us Now Praise Famous Men*, 125, 126; in *Mothers of the South*, 118–19, 122; nature vs. environment eugenic debate, 4, 14, 23, 27–29, 38, 81, 190n3; in *Out of the Night*, 33; in *The Sea of Cortez*, 81; in *Some American People*, 103; and Soviet "Marxist geneticists," 31–32, 193n28; in *Their Blood Is Strong*, 82, 83, 96; in *Tobacco Road*, 67, 68, 95. *See also* eugenics
Estabrook, Arthur H., 25–26, 30, 31, 47, 63, 65, 71, 192n21. See also *Mongrel Virginians* (Estabrook and McDougle)
eugenic family studies: and the Eugenics Record Office, 21, 191n12; focus on southern poor white women, 5, 14, 16–17, 24, 26, 47, 99; "Hereditary Crime," 24; *The Hill Folk*, 192n21; *"The Jukes,"* 16, 23; *The Kallikak Family*, 16, 24–25; *Mongrel Virginians*, 25–26, 30; as "myth," 22–23, 43, 191n13, 199n1; popularity of, 21–22, 191n12; "Tribe of Ishmael," 191n13, 192n21; "Two Brothers," 25; use of pseudonyms in, 22, 198n11; used as structure for Depression-era literature about poor whites, 10, 43–44, 47, 94–95, 99. *See also* eugenics
eugenics: and abortion, 19, 20, 27, 44, 47, 49, 200n17; and African Americans, 15; and birth control, 27, 33, 49, 99, 133, 191n11, 193n29, 200n16; and CPUSA, 35–38, 42; and documentary work, 98–100; focus on motherhood, 4, 5, 9, 12, 14–15, 19–21; and Francis Galton, 16, 190n4; and FSA, 110–11; and Gregor Mendel, 16, 190n4, 190n6; and immigrants, 15; and industrialism, 15–16; and "Mendelian traits," 16–17, 23, 27; and the "moron" woman, 19–20, 24, 40, 42, 43, 48, 64, 66, 161, 163, 200n20; and the "mother of tomorrow," 19–20, 24, 40, 42, 43, 48, 64, 66, 161, 163, 200n20; "negative eugenics," 20, 21, 23, 44, 133, 193; popularity of in United States, 14, 34–35; "positive eugenics," 19, 20, 33, 34, 35, 44, 110; and "race suicide," 19; and "recessive" genes, 27–28; and Roosevelt Administration, 42–43; and segregation, 21, 27, 44, 98; and "selective reproduction," 20; and "socialist geneticists," 28–30, 31, 37–38; and the South, 29–31, 47, 98–99; and the Soviet Union, 31–33; and sterilization, 21, 27, 44, 49, 189n2, 191n11; and working women, 17–18. *See also* abortion; birth control; environment; "Feeble-minded"; motherhood; sexuality, poor white female; sterilization

Eugenics: A Journal of Race Betterment, 30, 191n8
Eugenics Record Office (ERO), 21, 194n36
Evans, Walker: and the FSA, 122–23; method of photography in *Let Us Now Praise Famous Men,* 129–31, 198n15; sexual attraction to Emma in *Let Us Now Praise Famous Men,* 127–28. See also *Let Us Now Praise Famous Men* (Agee and Evans)

Farm Security Administration (FSA), 46, 80, 107, 109, 110, 111, 122, 131, 194n2, 197nn3–4, 197nn5–6
Faulkner, William: and Darwinian ideology, 49, 194–95n6; knowledge of eugenic ideology, 49; mention of Havelock Ellis in *Mosquitoes,* 49, 195n7; Nobel Prize acceptance speech, 61; writing of *As I Lay Dying,* 48–49. See also *As I Lay Dying* (Faulker); *Mosquitoes* (Faulker); *Sound and the Fury, The* (Faulker)
Federal Writers' Project (FWP), 111, 115, 132, 197n7
"Feeble-minded," 16, 18, 21, 24, 25, 122, 124, 174, 190n5, 191n8, 192n20, 192n24. *See also* eugenics

Galton, Francis, 16, 190n4. *See also* eugenics
Gastonia Mill Strike, 12, 137–39, 141, 142, 143, 150, 151, 159, 160, 180, 181, 182, 183, 199n7, 200n13. *See also* Wiggins, Ella May
"Gastonia Novels," 11, 133, 137, 180–83. See also *Call Home the Heart* (Dargan); *Gathering Storm* (Page); *Strike!* (Vorse); *To Make My Bread* (Lumpkin)
Gathering Storm (Page), 136, 139, 150, 151–59, 161, 162, 166, 169, 170, 177, 178, 181, 182, 199n2, 200n15, 201n27
Gibbons, Kaye, 186. See also *Ellen Foster* (Gibbons)
Girl Out Back, 184, 201n4
Glasgow, Ellen, 6, 7, 8, 46. See also *Barren Ground* (Glasgow)
Goddard, Henry H., 26, 192n20. See also *Kallikak Family, The* (Goddard)
God's Little Acre (Caldwell, Erskine), 10, 46, 47, 62, 68–80, 81, 86, 93, 97, 100, 132, 134, 135, 181, 184, 194n1, 194n4, 195n9, 195n11
Grapes of Wrath, The (Steinbeck), 10, 46, 47, 80–81, 84–94, 96, 97, 132, 134, 138, 155, 194n1, 194n4, 195n17, 196n20
Great Depression: as a consequence of human "degeneration," 3–4; and the definition of "American," 2; familial changes caused by, 2, 35; fears created by, 2; and the growth of CPUSA, 36; and increased focus on poor white women, 13, 43; and lost social boundaries, 2; and the New Deal, 42; and the South, 9. *See also* Roosevelt administration; South

Hagood, Margaret Jarman: connection to eugenics, 118–19, 122; and dissertation project, 116–17; focus on positive images of southern poor white women, 117–18, 134; view of the South, 117. See also *Mothers of the South* (Hagood)
Hardy-Weinberg theorem, 27, 28. *See also* eugenics
"Hereditary Crime" (Davenport), 24, 191–92n17
Hill Folk, The (Danielson and Davenport), 22–23, 191n15, 192n21
Histories of the Dividing Line (Byrd), 5, 189n3
Holmes, Oliver Wendell, 21, 28, 68, 195n12. *See also* Carrie Buck vs. Bell
Hoover, Herbert, 35, 149, 200n12
Hooverville camps, 87

Hutchins, Grace, 17, 39, 40–41, 135. See also *Women Who Work* (Hutchins)
Huxley, Aldous, 49
Huxley, Julian, 169, 200n22
"hybridity," in *As I Lay Dying,* 50, 52, 55, 59, 60, 61, 86

In the Tennessee Mountains (Murfree), 6

Jennings, H. S., 27–28, 29. *See also* eugenics
"Jukes, The" (Dugdale), 16, 22, 23, 26, 191n16, 192n21

Kallikak Family, The (Goddard), 16, 24–25, 42, 69, 163, 192nn18–19, 192n21, 192n23
Kelley, Edith Summers, 6, 7, 8, 46. See also *Weeds* (Kelley)
Kellicott, William, 16, 20, 64, 69. *See also* eugenics

Lamarckism, 193n28, 198n12
Lange, Dorothea: "The Assignment," 107–8; and FSA, 107, 197n5; and Paul Taylor, 197n4; *San Francisco News,* 108–9, 197n5; and Walker Evans, 131. *See also* "Migrant Mother" (Lange)
Laughlin, Harry Hamilton, 21, 29. *See also* sterilization
Let Us Now Praise Famous Men (Agee and Evans), 99, 123–32, 185, 198n11, 198n16
Loray Mill Strike. *See* Gastonia Mill Strike
Lumpkin, Grace: challenging stereotypes of southern poor white women, 11, 136–37, 141–42, 179, 180, 182–83, 184; and the CPUSA, 159, 160; and the Gastonia Mill Strike, 160; growing up in the South, 160, 200n19; writing of *To Make My Bread,* 139. See also *To Make My Bread* (Lumpkin)

Marx, Karl, 34, 38, 193n35. See also *Communist Manifesto, The* (Marx and Engels)
McDougle, Ivan E., 25–26, 31, 47, 65, 71, 192n21. See also *Mongrel Virginians* (Estabrook and McDougle)
Mencken, H. L., 62
Mendel, Gregor, 16, 190n4, 190n6. *See also* eugenics
"Mendelian traits": difference between physical traits and "mental" and "moral" traits, 16–17; in eugenic family studies, 23; in *God's Little Acre,* 70; as "recessive" genes, 27; in *Tobacco Road,* 64. *See also* eugenics
"Migrant Mother" (Lange), 80, 99, 107–11, 112, 131, 133, 197n5
"Mill Mother's Lament" (Wiggins), 140, 148, 149, 178, 199n4
mill work: children in, 190–91n7; mothers in, 41; as relief from poverty, 29; sexuality in, 40; and unions, 40–41; and women's wages, 39
miscegenation: in *God's Little Acre,* 71; in *Mongrel Virginians,* 25–26, 65; in *Tobacco Road,* 65
Mongrel Virginians (Estabrook and McDougle), 25–26, 30, 31, 65, 71, 192n21
Morrison, Toni, 1–3, 8. See also *Playing in the Dark* (Morrison)
Mosquitoes (Faulkner), 49, 195n7
motherhood: Ada in *Tobacco Road,* 63–64, 66; Addie in *As I Lay Dying,* 50–59; 60–61; in *Beyond Desire,* 180; in *Call Home the Heart,* 170–76; in the Carrie Buck vs. Bell case, 28; and CPUSA, 13–14, 36, 41–42; in early 1920s literature, 7–8; in Erskine Caldwell's *New York Post* articles, 101; in the eugenics movement, 4, 5, 9, 12, 14–15, 19–21; in *Gathering Storm,* 153–58; in *The Grapes of Wrath,* 89–93; in "Hereditary Crime," 24; as an iconic

motherhood *(continued)*
image, 36, 41, 43; in *The Kallikak Family,* 24–25; in *Let Us Now Praise Famous Men,* 125, 126–27, 128–30, 131, 133; in "Migrant Mother," 108–10, 133; and mill work, 41, 135–36; mothers as the "supreme" parent, 19, 44, 49; in *Mothers of the South,* 117–22; in *Out of the Night,* 34; and the Roosevelt administration, 13–14, 42; in *Some American People,* 102–3; in *Strike!,* 147–50; as symbols of America's future possibilities, 43; in *Their Blood Is Strong,* 83–84; in *These Are Our Lives,* 113, 115, 116; in *To Make My Bread,* 161–65, 164–68; in *You Have Seen Their Faces,* 104–5. *See also* eugenics; poor white women, southern
Mothers of the South (Hagood), 99, 116–22, 132, 134
Muller, H. J., 28, 29, 34. *See also* eugenics; *Out of the Night* (Muller)
Murfree, Mary Noailles, 6. See also *In the Tennessee Mountains* (Murfree)

New Deal: and the CPUSA, 4, 14, 37; and documentary work, 10, 98–99; and eugenics, 4, 14, 42–43, 189n2; and family stability, 42–43, 189n2; and FSA, 107, 194n2; and "Migrant Mother," 109; and the South, 46, 98–99, 194n2; and *These Are Our Lives,* 111. *See also* Roosevelt administration
Nineteenth Amendment, 7

Old Southwest Humor Stories, 5–6, 8, 189nn4–5
"Other": African Americans as, 1, 2; poor white women as, 2–3, 9, 10, 11, 12, 184; southern poor whites as, 11, 16; used to define "American," 1. See also *Playing in the Dark* (Morrison)
Out of the Night (Muller), 29, 33–34, 36, 38, 192n25

Page, Myra (Dorothy Myra Page): author of "propaganda," 159; challenging stereotypes of southern poor white women, 11, 136, 161, 167, 179, 180, 182–83, 184, 201n27; and the CPUSA, 200n18; dissertation on southern textile workers, 151, 166; and the Gastonia Mill Strike, 200n13; knowledge of poor white life, 150–51; and race relations, 200n15; use of pen name, 199n2. See also *Gathering Storm* (Page)
Playing in the Dark (Morrison), 1–3, 8
poor white men, southern: Anse in *As I Lay Dying,* 50, 51, 55, 56, 58, 59, 61; in *Call Home the Heart,* 170–71; and eugenics, 4, 17, 18; in *Gathering Storm,* 153, 154; George Gudger in *Let Us Now Praise Famous Men,* 127–28, 129, 131; in *The Grapes of Wrath,* 86, 91, 92–93; in *Histories of the Dividing Line,* 5, 6; Jeeter in *Tobacco Road,* 63, 64, 66, 67, 69, 195n10; in Old Southwest Humor Stories, 5–6; in *Strike!,* 143; in *These Are Our Lives,* 113–14; in *To Make My Bread,* 161–62, 163–64, 167; Walden men in *God's Little Acre,* 70, 71–72, 77–79, 93; Will in *God's Little Acre,* 71–77, 78, 93; in *You Have Seen Their Faces,* 104
poor white women, southern: and abortion, 27, 47, 49; and birth control, 20–21, 27, 49, 99, 133; in early 1920s literature, 7–8; as a focus of eugenics, 3–4, 19–21; as laborers, 13, 17–18, 39–41; as "moron" woman, 19–20, 24, 40, 42, 43; in nineteenth-century literature, 5–7; as "Other," 2–3, 9; segregation of, 21, 27, 47; sterilization of, 21, 27, 47, 49, 191n11; as a symbol

of the Great Depression, 8–9. *See also* eugenics; motherhood; sexuality, poor white female; stereotypes
poor whites, southern: and agriculture, 45; in the Appalachian Mountains, 30, 140–41, 199n5; during the Great Depression, 46–47; and the eugenics movement, 15, 16, 17, 47; and industrialism, 15; as "Other," 2, 11, 16; as subjects of eugenic family studies, 16, 25–26; as victims of poverty stereotypes of, 88. *See also* poor white men, southern; poor white women, southern
Popular Front, 36, 37, 38–39, 41–43, 189n2. *See also* Communist Party of the United States
Progressive Movement, 13
prostitution: in *Car,* 186; in the Carrie Buck vs. Bell case, 192n24; in *"The Jukes,"* 23; as marriage according to Friedrich Engels, 194n35; in *These Are Our Lives,* 115–16; in *Tobacco Road,* 65; in *To Make My Bread,* 163, 166; in "The Tribe of Ishmael," 192n21

"race suicide," 19. *See also* eugenics
Ray, Janisse, 186, 187. See also *Ecology of a Cracker Childhood* (Ray); *Wild Card Quilt* (Ray)
Roberts, Elizabeth Madox, 6, 7, 8, 46. See also *Time of Man, The* (Roberts)
Rollins, William, 180. See also *Shadow Before, The* (Rollins)
Roosevelt administration: and CPUSA, 13–15, 35, 37, 42; and eugenicists, 14–15, 35, 42–43; and motherhood, 14–15, 42, 111; and New Deal, 10, 14–15, 35, 37, 42, 46, 111; worries about the South, 111, 117, 197n2, 197n8. *See also* New Deal
Rural Rehabilitation Division, 46
Salvation on Sand Mountain (Covington), 186
San Francisco News, 80, 109. *See also* Lange, Dorothea; Steinbeck, John
Sanger, Margaret, 20, 133, 154, 168–69, 191n9. *See also* birth control
Saving Grace (Smith), 186
Sea of Cortez, The (Steinbeck and Ricketts), 81, 88, 196n23
segregation, 21, 27, 44, 98. *See also* eugenics
sexuality, poor white female: in *As I Lay Dying,* 49, 57; in *Beyond Desire,* 182; in *Call Home the Heart,* 169; and eugenic ideology, 9, 13, 18–19, 20, 25, 192n22, 195n7; in *Gathering Storm,* 152, 158; in *God's Little Acre,* 69, 71, 73, 74–79, 195n15; in *Grapes of Wrath,* 85, 91–92; in *Let Us Now Praise Famous Men,* 126–28, 132; mentioned, 99, 136, 137, 189n11; as a product of labor, 13, 18, 40; in *The Shadow Before,* 181; in *Strike!,* 149, 150; in *These Are Our Lives,* 115, 116, 121; in *To Make My Bread,* 164, 167; in *Tobacco Road,* 65, 66. *See also* eugenics
Shadow Before, The (Rollins), 180, 181, 182
Smith, Lee, 186. See also *Saving Grace* (Smith)
"social documentary," 97, 98, 197n1
"socialist geneticists": and *As I Lay Dying,* 47; and "The Bunglers," 30–31; definition of, 28–30, 31; focus on women, 37–38; and *God's Little Acre,* 47, 69, 195n12; and *The Grapes of Wrath,* 47, 88–89; and *Mothers of the South,* 118–19. *See also* eugenics
sociologists, 10, 21, 26, 98, 106, 107, 133
Some American People (Caldwell, Erskine), 102–3
Sound and the Fury, The (Faulkner), 49
South: and agriculture, 45, 118; as a eugenic focus, 29–31, 47, 98–99; as a national

South *(continued)*
problem, 111, 117; and sharecropping, 29, 45, 99, 106; and the "southern belle," 6; and tenant farming, 29, 45, 99; and "white supremacy," 9–10, 11, 83. *See also* poor white men, southern; poor white women, southern; poor whites, southern
Soviet Union: and the Bolshevik Revolution, 32; and "bourgeois" eugenics, 32, 33, 88, 193n29; and "Five Year Plan," 32, 34; and Friedrich Engels, 32, 33, 88, 193n29; and Karl Kautsky, 32; and "Marxist geneticists," 31–32; and "socialist geneticists," 31; and Stalin, 33
Steinbeck, John: and awards, 80; and communism, 196n24; and Darwin, 196n22; and FSA, 80; and Horace Bristol, 80, 195n16; knowledge of eugenics, 81, 96, 196n18; and *San Francisco News,* 80, 81; and *The Sea of Cortez,* 81, 88, 196n23; and "socialist geneticists," 47, 196n23; working alongside migrant workers, 80. See also *Grapes of Wrath, The* (Steinbeck); *Sea of Cortez, The* (Steinbeck and Ricketts); *Their Blood Is Strong* (Steinbeck)
stereotypes: of African Americans, 1; mentioned, 110; of southern poor white women, 4, 5, 9, 10, 11, 12, 96, 133, 134, 135, 136, 137, 143, 149, 150, 158, 159, 161, 167, 169, 179, 180, 181, 182, 183, 184, 185, 186, 187; of southern poor whites, 88; of women, 3, 143, 189n1
sterilization: in *Augusta Chronicle* articles about Erskine Caldwell, 102, 103; in "The Bunglers," 30; in documentary work, 98, 133; as a eugenic solution, 21, 27, 44, 49, 189n2, 191n11; in *God's Little Acre,* 79–80; laws, 29, 35, 43; in *Let Us Now Praise Famous Men,* 131; on southerners, 47; in *These Are Our Lives,* 116; in *You Have Seen Their Faces,* 106, 107. *See also* eugenics
Stone Came Rolling, A (Dargan), 176–77, 178, 199n2, 200nn21–22, 201n24
Strike! (Vorse), 133, 137, 139, 142, 143–50, 152, 159, 166, 167, 169, 178, 181, 182, 199nn7–8, 19n10, 200nn11–12
Stryker, Roy, 107, 110, 197n3, 197n5

Their Blood Is Strong (Steinbeck), 80–84, 86, 87, 88, 90, 92, 153, 195n17
These Are Our Lives (Couch), 106, 111–16, 132, 133, 154, 197n9
Thompson, Florence, 108. *See also* "Migrant Mother" (Lange)
Time of Man, The (Roberts), 7, 8
To Kill a Mockingbird (Lee), 185
To Make My Bread (Lumpkin), 136, 139, 159–68, 170, 177, 181, 182, 201n27
Tobacco Road (Caldwell, Erskine), 10, 46, 47, 62–68, 70, 72 78, 79, 81, 93, 97, 100, 112, 132, 138, 184, 194n1, 194n4, 195n9, 195n11, 200nn1–2
"traditional" family values, 4, 6, 7, 13, 17, 18, 30, 41, 78, 121
"Tribe of Ishmael," 22, 191n13, 192n21
"Two Brothers," 24, 25, 192nn20–21. *See also* *Kallikak Family, The* (Goddard)

Uncle Good's Girls, 184
U.S. Census Bureau, 190n5

Vorse, Mary Heaton: challenging stereotypes of southern poor white women, 136–37, 139, 141–42, 160, 179, 180, 182–83, 184; and communism, 199n8; critique of *To Make My Bread,* 159; and the Gastonia Mill Strike, 199n7, 199n10; as a journalist, 142–43, 199n9; struggles with motherhood, 142–43. See also *Strike!* (Vorse)

Weeds (Kelley), 7, 8
whiteness: defined by "Other," 1, 2; as definition of "American," 1; and Great Depression, 15; as "parasitical," 1; related to African Americans, 1; stripped from poor white women, 3, 9
Wiggam, Albert Edward, 19–20, 44
Wiggins, Ella May: and ballad singing, 139; in *Call Home the Heart,* 139, 177, 178; in *Gathering Storm,* 139, 156–57; and "Mill Mother's Lament," 140–41, 199n4; in *Strike!,* 139, 147–50, 179; in *To Make My Bread,* 139, 164–68; and union work, 139–40. *See also* Gastonia Mill Strike; "Mill Mother's Lament" (Wiggins)
Wild Card Quilt (Ray), 187
Wilson, Woodrow, 190–91n7
Women Who Work (Hutchins), 17, 39, 40–41, 135
Works Progress Administration (WPA), 111, 197n7
World War I, 17, 39, 138, 191n7

You Have Seen Their Faces (Caldwell, Erskine and Bourke-White), 80, 103–7, 112, 120, 122, 132, 133, 197n2